"Every woman in search of her true, brav
read this book. One story in particular m
nerability of its writer, facing every womar
positive in her experience. We should all be
—Julie Chaiken, CEO, Chaiken Clothing

"Read this book and you'll understand why women will change the
world. *Nothing But the Truth So Help Me God* is an inspiring testament
to the power, resilience, and courage of womankind. This book is a poignant and persuasive plea to modern women to band together and share
our stories. There we'll gain a collective strength, courage, and wisdom
and redefine what it means to be a strong woman in American society.
—Ivory Madison, founder, Redroom

"This book brought to my mind a more contemporary revelation of the
notion that sisterhood is indeed powerful but it also brings to light the
notion we get from Germaine Greer that women can indeed be a distinctive tribe and must open their hearts to their own stories for themselves and the others in their tribe. But there is much here, too, for men
who love and care about women. The stories are compelling and the
tale tellers speak with voices that are honest, elevating and valorous."
—Michael Krasny, author, professor, and host of KQED's Forum on
NPR, San Francisco

"I felt I was living each story as I read it. This book is a much-needed
celebration of our depth as women. The stories in *Nothing But the Truth
So Help Me God* remind us that we can lift each other up so high if we
just remember how special each woman is and how much we can learn
from each other."
—Sheryl O'Loughlin, executive director, Center for Entrepreneurial
Studies, Stanford University

"A heartfelt, personal, and inspirational ode to women and friendship."
—Lonnie Barbach, Ph.D., clinical psychologist and bestselling author

"*Nothing But the Truth So Help Me God* combines the support of a self-
help book, the wit of a skilled essayist, and the frankness of a best

friend in one fantastic book. These essays, which span topics from BFFs to abortion, are a must-read for any woman age 12–122, and will remind you that, whatever you're going through, you're not alone."
—Katie J.M. Baker, staff writer, *Jezebel*

"Living life with eyes wide open is not something we are taught to do in today's world. These stories remind me that underneath the facade of perfection we strive for, we are all women: vulnerable, strong, sad, scared, empathetic, and insightful—banded together we will all have a better more fulfilling experience."
—Kimberly Ellis, executive director, Emerge California

"What a beautiful and varied look at the power of female connection. When times are dark and women seek the strength to face illness, infertility, addiction, depression, divorce, and a host of life's other miseries—the caring words of a friend can become a life raft, buoying us until the skies clear. For anyone who has offered or received such comfort, this series of tales will ring true and remind you what a treasure sisterhood truly is. Buy one copy for yourself and one for every friend on your speed dial."
—Kat Gordon, founder and creative director, Maternal Instinct

"*Nothing But the Truth So Help Me God* celebrates the woman we dare not speak of: the REAL one. These stories remind us that the more we strive for perfection the more we lose what is perfect about us. This book proves the real woman is so much more interesting and astounding than anything we could make up or air brush."
—Christina Harbridge, author, artist, and founder of Allegory Inc.

"I recently was at a party for my one of my best friends, a card was given that said 'when we were little, it was all about our girlfriends, then it became all about the boyfriends, now, it's all about the girlfriends again.' *Nothing But the Truth So Help Me God* is all about that; women speaking the truth to other women. We are connected. It's a fantastic book that reminds us about that in a multitude of ways."
—Tiffany Shlain, filmmaker & founder, The Webby Awards

Nothing But the
Truth
So Help Me God

Nothing But the
Truth
So Help Me God

51 Women Reveal the Power of Positive Female Connection

Author
A Band of Wives, LLC

Editors
Christine Bronstein and Carol Pott

Assistant editors: Mickey Nelson and Eve Batey

Nothing But The Truth, LLC   *   San Francisco

Nothing But The Truth, LLC
1010 Sir Francis Drake Blvd. #102
Kentfield, CA   94904
NOTHING BUT THE TRUTH™ and the NOTHING BUT THE TRUTH Cover Design are trademarks of Nothing But The Truth, LLC.

For information about book purchases please contact A Band of Wives, or visit the *Nothing But the Truth So Help Me God* website at NothingButtheTruth.com
Also available in ebook.

Library of Congress Control Number: 2012950512

A Band of Wives.
Nothing But the Truth So Help Me God: 51 Women Reveal the Power of Positive Female Connection.
Compiled by A Band of Wives, LLC.
Christine Bronstein and Carol Pott, Editors. Mickey Nelson and Eve Batey, Assistant Editors.

ISBN 978-0-9883754-1-3
ISBN 978-0-9883754-0-6 (ebook)

Printed in the United States of America.
Cover design by theBookDesigners, Fairfax, CA
First edition

Share Your Story

Please flex your voice and share your own story about positive female connection on our website, nothingbutthetruth.com.

You can also connect immediately with the authors and artists from this book (and thousands of other supportive women) by joining A Band of Wives, the private social network for all women—married, single, and everything in between—at abandofwives.com.

If you are interested in becoming a published author or artist, or if you are already a published author or artist and have a story or artwork you would like to share, we are collecting essays and art for our next book about life's transitions. You can learn more about submissions for the upcoming anthology on either of our websites.

We would love to hear from you!

Contents

Acknowledgments   / *xiii*
Introduction   / *xv*

Section One: Self-Love
Overwhelmed, Overworked, and Over It!   *Christine Arylo*   / 1
100 Pounds Lighter   *Laura Fenamore*   / 11
Femininely Divine   *Leila Radan*   / 17
Healing   *Lissa Rankin*   / 22

Section Two: Overcoming Obstacles
No One Should Ever Have To Write This   *Mickey Nelson*   / 35
Joy Along the Rough Road   *Joy M. Nordenstrom*   / 41
Warriors   *Amie Penwell*   / 47
My Abortion Brought Us Together   *Aspen Baker*   / 52
Far From Shore   *Margaret Kathrein*   / 58
Friends, Strangers, Sisters, and Saviors   *Medea Isphording Bern*   / 66
Taking Turns   *Janine Kovac*   / 72
Common Sense   *Susan Blankenbaker Noyes*   / 80

Section Three: Modern Motherhood
My Mother's Chutney   *Joyce Maynard*   / 89
My Many Mothers   *Cristina Robinson*   / 93
The Book List   *Marie McHale Drake*   / 98
I Don't Need Ovaries to be Fertile   *Rebecca Nelson Lubin*   / 106
Labor of Love   *Andrea Drugay*   / 111
A Girl's Best Friend Is Another Girl   *Eileen Chao*   / 120

Section Four: BFF and BFF-Less

Sister Soul Mates   *Christine Bronstein*   / 127
Changing Friendship   *Shasta Nelson*   / 131
BFF-Less   *Mimi Towle*   / 138
Lessons from the Playground   *Kimberly Danek Pinkson*   / 142
Ode to Women   *Lenore Perry*   / 147
Friend Collector   *Ana Hays*   / 150

Section Five: Finding Yourself

A Breasted Development   *Carol Pott*   / 157
Looking Through a New Lens   *Lone Morch*   / 168
Safe Sisterhood and the Good Girl   *Kim Shannon*   / 176
One Good Reader   *Chieko Murasugi*   / 181

Section Six: Mischief Makers

Vexing the Ex   *Judy Zimola*   / 189
Jesse's Girl   *Violet Blue*   / 196
Ex Communication   *Hyla Molander*   / 202

Section Seven: Race and Culture

Maggie   *Yvonne Latty*   / 211
Women's Day   *Diane Tober*   / 216
Friendship Amidst the Ruins   *Liesl Gerntholtz*   / 224
Manti   *Jen Siraganian*   / 228
Anatomy of a Story   *Sarah Ladipo Manyika*   / 230

Section Eight: Mother Earth

The Lions and Me   *Deborah Santana*   / 241
Mother's Voices   *Dominique Browning*   / 246
Wrap-Around Porch   *Tracy Chiles McGhee*   / 249
Help a Sister Out!   *Jessica Buchleitner*   / 251
A Journey for Good   *Joanie Wynn*   / 256

Artwork

Exposed   *Lone Morch*   / xiv
Pool   *Victoria Loren Miller*   / 9
Deaf, Dumb & Blind   *Nancy Calef*   / 21
Pool Girl   *Vicki Nelson*   / 32
Rescue   *Susan Schneider*   / 104
Conjoined Twins   *Colleen Joyce*   / 118
Untitled   *Dana King*   / 166
Boudoir   *Lone Morch*   / 175
Mischief   *Kristin Gerbert*   / 194
#queensofrockingtheboat   *Tamara Holland*   / 201
Ancients   *Caitlin McCaffrey*   / 244
A Moment in the Louvre   *Monica Michelle*   / 266

Acknowledgments

We want to extend an extra special thanks to our children, who sat patiently through repeated meetings, dealt with endless hours of our typing furiously on our computers, iPads, and phones, and put up with cancelled vacations and activities during the production of this book; and to Chris' husband, Phil Bronstein, because without his constant reassurances and support, this book would never have come to fruition.

Thank you to Mickey Nelson (who we poached from Phil) for swooping in, saving our butts, and making us laugh. DM forever! Thank you, to each and every one of our brave contributors and to every member of A Band of Wives, for supporting our mission. To Eve Batey for being able to so stunningly and effortlessly do everything from editing Chris (not easy) to building our website. Thank you Alicia Dunams, for keeping us on schedule and connecting us with so many wonderful resources.

Thanks also to Alan Hebel and the team at *the*BookDesigners for our awesome cover. We also have to acknowledge our many Jennifer angels: Jennifer Stewart and Jennifer Stivers—without you we would be titleless; and Jennifer Omner for laying it all out so beautifully. And to the formidable Judy Alexander for covering all 51 of our asses—legally, that is.

A special thanks to the handful of doubters who didn't believe that positive stories about women could sell books and thus steeled our resolve to publish this book.

—Christine Bronstein and Carol Pott

Exposed, photograph by Lone Morch

Introduction

Christine Bronstein

In the summer of 2009, I finally had something I had never believed was even possible: a relatively normal family. But my tears would not stop. Even as I held my newborn baby girl, our two sons swarming around with jealous interest, I couldn't stop crying. Help arrived swiftly, as my friends—those with and without children—swooped in, assuring my worried husband that my postpartum depression would pass as soon as my antidepressants kicked in, making me laugh even at my lowest moments, while busying my boys with all kinds of distractions.

My friend, Christina Flach, stared in awe of my tears. "I didn't even know you had tear ducts!" she joked.

Inspired by the feelings of isolation that postpartum depression brings and the community that surrounded me in my time of need, I realized I wanted to create a vehicle for women to connect and find support in a private place. My husband and I spoke endlessly about how and why this would be an important tool for women. He even wrote an article about it for the *San Francisco Chronicle*.

During this time, I began researching women's issues and was surprised to find that my daughter would not be given the same opportunities in this world as my sons. I found that the statistics for women in the upper echelons of power today are as dismal as the statistics for female lawyers and doctors were in the 1950s and 1960s.

I was also baffled by the obvious lack of women in my husband's field of journalism. Since my research showed that 85 percent of all public opinion is generated by men, I wondered—where were all of the women's voices? What will be the impact to our society when women no longer feel that their voices matter? I couldn't stop thinking about these questions.

Around this same time, Christina Flach started calling all of us in her inner circle of women her "wives" because we had been through so many marriages, divorces, births, and deaths together. The word "friend" no longer seemed to capture the depth of our relationships.

So, when I stood in a grocery line reading a magazine article about Ning's social networking software, I felt that the universe was banging me on the head; God's message sounded something like: "Enough thinking and talking, Christine! How many signs do you need me to give you?" It was like that bumper sticker that says "I wish somebody would do something about that. Oh right, I am somebody."

I knew I was somebody and that I could do something about those dismal statistics.

Thus was born the online social network A Band of Wives (ABOW), a private place for all women to connect and flex their voices.

I now believe that if every woman connected with and supported the women in her own backyard, the world would change dramatically. But too often, we women feel isolated in our ever more hectic lives.

Gathering with women and taking care of each other is in our DNA as a gender and it has been shown, in many recent scientific studies, to be the most important thing we can do for our health. Sometimes it is too intimidating, or we are too overwhelmed to know how to do it, but when we decide to do it, to just make it happen, we are damn good at it.

ABOW is a safe place for women to connect both on and offline and the stories that have come up through the connections women have made on the site have been life changing for them . . . and for me. Through ABOW, I found my voice.

The stories were so profound and such a critical tool for moving beyond feelings of isolation and disconnection that I wanted to create a way for these women to be heard on a larger scale. I felt the world needed something that could illustrate the power of positive female connections. I started collecting essays and art from members of ABOW to create an anthology that would balance out the negative images of women that we're bombarded with every day. Immediately I knew it could only be Nothing But the Truth. You will not find any hyper-positive, Photoshopped postings here. (Although some names and places have been changed at the demand of our lawyers.)

The raw and real essays made me laugh, feel anger at injustice, and even cry—something I now do very rarely thanks to my Zoloft. They reminded me to appreciate the women in my life, both past and present. These essays are truly stories from the hearts of these women, brave tales of love, death, sexuality, cancer, self-love, motherhood, and many more topics. They are told with breathtaking honesty through the often-disregarded lens of positive female connection.

Some of the women included in this anthology are professional writers, but most are women of all ages and from all walks of life, who know that sharing their story is important. We are all revealing our inner voices, flipping our dresses up for you, showing that we women can be brave, vulnerable, sexy, kind, interesting, entertaining, and most of all, supportive.

We know that women change each other's lives just by being there for one another and sharing these stories allows us to be more courageous, more authentic, and more loving to ourselves and others.

It is only by supporting one another and by knowing that each of our voices matter that women will, one by one, break through the new, higher, but just as solid glass ceilings.

Please enjoy these stories and contribute your own by joining us and sharing your story of female connection. You can comment on this book and post your own story on our Nothing But the Truth website. You can join A Band of Wives and connect with all the writers and artists in the book, contribute to our blog, or just share your story personally with a friend. Just keep the movement going and use your voice for positive change in your community!

Section One

Self-Love

Overwhelmed, Overworked, and Over It!

Christine Arylo

Start a company, support your family, save the world, all while looking no older than 25. And by the way, don't break a sweat while doing it . . . after all, other women seem to be keeping it together, what's wrong with you?

That's the mind chatter that's been stamped into our brains as twenty-first century super women who look like we have it all together when we are really gritting our teeth and trying to smile the stress away. Behind the facade of perfection is the reality that almost every woman feels completely overwhelmed and overworked, without a clue how to manage life differently. Although few of us would ever admit just how stretched and full of self-doubt we are, the truth is that most of us are overworked, overwhelmed, and over it!

Why do we all keep this secret from each other? Why not just blow the whistle, start a super-woman revolution, and stop the madness that has become our unsustainable lives once and for all? We are smart, powerful, liberated women. "Hear us roar," right? Yet, we remain silent.

We're too afraid to roar. We've convinced ourselves that we are the only woman who feels like she is failing, falling behind, and not measuring up. With inner critics—who are more like inner mean girls—comparing us to other women like it's sport, we've conditioned ourselves into thinking that everyone else has mastered the balancing act and has time to spare for changing the world, taking care of herself, and taking care of her loved ones. How often has your mind ranted with thoughts like *She has it figured out, what's wrong with me? I should be able to balance all of this better.*

We've become ashamed to roar. We stay silent on the outside because our inner mean girls are roaring with sabotaging and abusive words that we don't want anyone (including ourselves) to hear. Plagued by society's unrealistic definition of success, we've become riddled with feelings of inferiority that we do not know how to express or acknowledge—deep-seated and often subconscious beliefs that we are not being enough, having enough, or doing enough. Rather than speaking up and roaring, "Living this way is unsustainable, this has to change!" and gathering our tribe of women to make the necessary individual and collective shifts, we become insular. The feeling that we are alone in this dilemma then causes us to push even further past our limits as we strive for a reality that is simply unattainable for the mortal woman. The cycle is crazy (and crazy making)!

Even though not a single one of us has ever gone to bed with our to-do list complete, we begin every day anew, psyching ourselves into thinking that this will be the day we get it all done. As long as we keep doing our yoga poses and drinking those green drinks, we delude ourselves into believing that we are healthy and happy. In truth, our spirits are dying, our emotions are all over the place, and our bodies are exhausted. The time has come, however, when we can neither look past the signs of our overexertion nor hold onto the empty hope that our efforts will one day lead to a Mecca of happiness, success, and inner peace. Living this way, silent and complacent, will never lead to the paradise we seek and deserve.

So, what do we do? Equally as important, who do we need to become in order to make changes that stick, so we can create a healthy reality not just for ourselves, but also for our daughters, who are growing up small in our superwoman shadows?

It's important to realize that this insanity of our lives is not totally our fault. We didn't start off as achievement junkies, productivity addicts, and obsessive perfectionists. We were conditioned, not born this way. As a generation of women, we have more opportunities, self-confidence, and independence today than in any generation before.

Many women and men fought hard for us to have those advantages, and we don't want to give them back. While it would be nice if we could just rest on the laurels of all that was done in the past to improve women's lives, there is now a five-alarm fire bell ringing that we as women need to respond to. The fight is not over.

I am not talking about fighting for the women in Africa and other war-torn developing countries. While that is essential, of course, the war I am talking about is happening right in our backyards, inside our own hearts, and the hearts of our daughters, mothers, sisters, friends, and wives!

Women in the Western and developed world born after the 1960s were born with more freedoms than any generation before them. Today, many of us have more choices than our mothers and grandmothers combined. With those choices have also come mountains of stress and self-criticism, without the pay-off of more happiness—a fact backed up by the *What Women Want Now: State of the American Woman* study conducted by the Rockefeller Foundation and *Time Magazine* in 2009, which compared the level of women's happiness in the 1970s to that of women today. The results were revealing. Despite having more opportunities and equality, women aren't happier. In fact, we have more work and less happiness. What a raw deal!

Women have been liberated in many ways, but in the process, we've become trapped in a new jail cell, with a nameplate bearing the motto we all live by—and unknowingly teach our daughters:

I feel empowered to do, be, and have anything, but I feel pressured to do, be, and have everything.

Where did we get this message that we have to do, be, and have it all in order to measure up?

Where did we get the notion that the superwoman was the model for what it means to be a successful, happy woman? And why do we allow it to drive us so?

I had the great pleasure of asking Gloria Steinem, feminism and self-esteem advocate and founder of *Ms. Magazine*, "Where did this memo of having to do, be, and have it all come from?" Her answer was enlightening, as I knew it would be.

Gloria told me that the message of the feminist movement was never that women had to do, be, and have it all. That is society's message—the trade-off that is offered to women. Society said women could be free to get the education, career, and lifestyle of their choice, but they would still be expected to do all the domestic tasks traditionally assigned to women: raise the children, take care of the family, manage the household, hold the community together, look pretty and sexy for their lover, etc. It is a never-ending list that I don't have to repeat here for you because you live it. Now I understand why my stressed-out sisters and I only got half the message.

What was the real, complete message of the feminist movement that had been intended for us? Quite plainly, Gloria explained that women don't have to be and do it all. Instead, we should feel empowered to make choices that allow us to both achieve and receive, to both give to others and to ourselves, and to both love ourselves and others. Had that memo actually reached us, I suspect it would have looked something like this:

Dear Twenty-First Century Woman,

Yes, you can do, be, and have anything! You can't do, be, and have everything at the same time. You must make choices, which means you can't have it all right now, so you can stop trying so hard to get it all right now. Phew! What a relief!

You want to be empowered? Then make choices that make you happy, not choices that make you crazy. Tell the world, "No, I can't do, be, and 'have it all' the way society has defined 'it all,' but I will make choices. I will say no to some things and yes to others, without apology or guilt. I will make choices based on what brings me joy, peace, and love, because that is what truly makes me feel happy and successful. I will follow my heart and my conscience instead of some imposed, external standard. I won't rely on someone else's measure to tell me when I have done enough or accumulated enough. Instead, I will know without a doubt that I alone am enough."

This memo and the ability to live by it evaded me for 36 years, until I found myself completely taken over by what I now call The Superwoman Sob. I was in a bathroom in Dallas, Texas, at the end of a six-month promotional book tour for my first book. I was in tears, alone, and sobbing in utter exhaustion, with no end in sight. I had poured my heart into *Choosing Me Before We,* a book to help women love themselves first in romantic relationships. I traveled around the country, from city to city, doing whatever I could to get the word out. I even worked three jobs to make ends meet. The expense of a cross-country book tour also caused me great stress about my finances. I had been striving and driving to do what a successful woman does, but I found myself alone, missing my home and life, and looking out for a finish line that seemed like it would never come. My body was exhausted, my spirit bankrupt. I had become a bank that only allowed withdrawals and didn't accept deposits!

I gave into The Superwoman Sob and it was a turning point for me. I experienced a sheer "this is my life" moment, thinking, *this is unsustainable, and I can't do it any longer.* I had a choice: tell the truth and make a change, or buck up and carry on. I am not sure if God was in that bathroom with me or not, but after the tears subsided, I felt like a fog had lifted and I was able to see my life and myself more clearly. I could finally see the truth. I knew that I was the only one who could lift me out of the hell that was the superwoman's pace.

What I saw on the surface wasn't pretty, but the truth underneath was freeing. While I looked successful on the outside, there was something inside of me that wasn't *feeling* successful. I had promised to love myself, but I had turned my body into a slave. I considered myself a spiritual person, but I had put more faith into fear than trust. I had proven that I could juggle three jobs, a household, a marriage, my finances, and my friends, but I was doing it at the cost of my health and wellness. In that moment, I decided I no longer wanted to live this unsustainable lifestyle and I began my own superwoman revolution.

I came home and changed my life. I set down my superwoman mantle and began the journey toward learning how to live differently. I didn't begin by taking yoga or coming up with a new scheduling system—I knew changing things on the outside wasn't going to work. I needed to go deep inside myself to find the source of the misguided messages I'd been sending myself that caused me to judge myself so harshly.

What I found inside of me is inside all of us. That made me want to roar on behalf of all the women on the planet.

Jean Kilbourne has studied the impact of media on women and girls for more than two decades and created the documentary *Killing Us Softly* to showcase her findings. In her research, she found that the underlying concept of most advertising, imagery, and messaging in our mainstream media is "You are not enough." Kilbourne identified that only seven percent of all media that we consume goes through our conscious mind, and the rest goes straight into our subconscious mind. That means that 93 percent of the mainstream messaging we have consumed since we were old enough to watch TV or read a magazine has been programming us to believe that we need to do, be, and have more before we will ever be considered enough.

As a result of this subconscious brainwashing, we unknowingly tie our sense of self-worth to an external value system fueled by materialism and consumption. In our material culture, an unrealistic model that always leaves us feeling insufficient in comparison has defined our self-worth. Confident on the outside, we obsessively compare ourselves against perfection on the inside. Our brains are flooded with external images of success, so we have become accustomed to constantly evaluating our standing as compared to those images. Our very language is set up to understand through comparison: better and best, more and less. It's no wonder we are always trying to understand who we are and where we fit.

As soon as you compare yourself to someone else, real or Photoshopped, you lose. If you compare yourself to unrealistic external expectations or to an idealized form of yourself, you are setting yourself up for failure. Even if you compare yourself to something less than yourself in a way that makes you feel superior, you still lose, because artificially boosting your confidence teaches the wrong lessons and reinforces a disconnection from what we need most: compassion with ourselves and the company of other women.

Women are harder on themselves than any other demographic. Even those who appear the most confident on the outside are likely to be hypercritical of their own flaws. When we succumb to this sort of self-disrespect, we fail in the most important job we have—to love ourselves. That is a message I'd like to see in the mainstream media: "The most important job you have is to love yourself well, for when you do that, everything else falls into place. The better you love yourself, the better you can love everyone else. If all you do is show up, love yourself and others well, then you have done enough."

We do have the power to adjust this superwoman standard. I asked Gloria Steinem what I should tell women as I wrote and spoke about setting down the mantle of the superwoman. I asked her, "If we aren't trying to be superwomen, what kind of women should we be?" Her answer? "Mad women!"

This answer made me smile. I heard truth in it. Based on what I'd experienced myself and seen in the hearts of women, what I understood it to mean is that being a mad woman is not about being an angry banshee, but is instead about being mad, bold, and having enough conviction to take a stand for yourself and for women and girls everywhere.

It is our job to take a stand and roar that we will not live this way anymore. Every night before we go to bed, it's our duty to love ourselves by saying, *Honey, put down that to-do list and that list of judgments* tied to unrealistic expectations. Instead, use these compassionate, accepting questions and give yourself a sense of purpose and meaning:

- *Did I serve myself well today?*
- *Did I serve others well today?*
- *Did I love myself today?*
- *Did I love others today?*

Remind yourself: *Honey, you are doing the best that you can.* If you can't tell yourself that, call up a friend and ask her to tell you. Give yourself the gift of knowing and feeling that you have indeed done enough, and that you indeed are enough.

Join me and the rest of your superwoman sisters for this superwoman revolution. Stand shoulder to shoulder with every person who has ever roared for the rights of women and girls, take a bold stand and say, "We no longer accept this unsustainable life. There is a different way."

You are woman. Let us hear you roar! We'll be roaring right next to you.

Christine Arylo

Christine Arylo, MBA, writer, coach, and speaker, is an inspirational catalyst dedicated to teaching women how to stop running themselves ragged, putting themselves last, and believing they must "have it all." Her opinions on the challenges this generation of super girls and super women face have been featured on CBS, ABC, FOX, E!, the *Huffington Post*, radio shows, conferences and stages worldwide. Christine is the internationally published author of the books *Choosing ME Before WE* and *Madly in Love With ME, the Daring Adventure to Becoming Your Own Best Friend*. She is also the founder of the International Day of Self Love, February 13th. Get your free Self-Love Kit at ChooseSelfLove.com or visit her at ChristineArylo.com

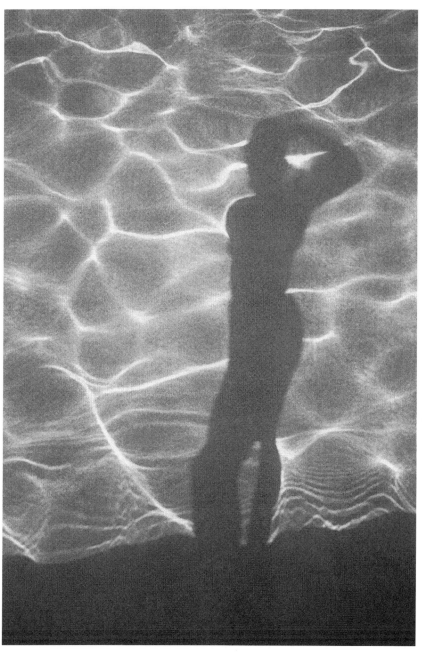

Pool, photograph by Victoria Loren Miller

Victoria Loren Miller

Victoria Loren Miller views the world through an abstract expressionist lens—and a camera lens. Born in San Francisco, California, Victoria's immersion in art began in her family's gallery. Inspired by twentieth century American greats like Stella and Rauschenberg, and local luminaries Nathan Oliveira and Wayne Thiebaud, she has produced a body of work that exposes the drama and beauty of reflections, motion, and the mystery of the interaction between light and color. Victoria earned her degree in design from UCLA and is a creative director and designer for global brands. Her work has earned industry accolades and is included in the Smithsonian's Permanent Collection.

100 Pounds Lighter

Laura Fenamore

How it all began for me . . .

I was a compulsive eater out of my mother's womb. The youngest of eight children in an abusive home in Long Island, New York, I was born feeling that the world was not safe for me. I used food to feel safe and I could not stop eating. I obsessed about food regularly; when I was not eating, I was thinking about it. I overate every day and hated myself for it, yet I could not stop.

I started drinking heavily at age 13 and was a wild child until young adulthood. From seventh grade until age 24, I smoked two packs of cigarettes a day, and by age 24, I was suicidal. I was a fat, depressed drunk who hated herself. My self-hatred took me on a path that made me feel hopeless and defective on a daily basis.

Then I was gifted with a moment of clarity when I had the choice to either give up or go on. I owe that moment to a strong, courageous, and generous woman. It was her willingness to share her own struggles that led me to take action for myself. She and three other beautiful women offered me the hope and inspiration I needed to change the course of my life.

By early adolescence, I was an alcoholic and a regular drug user and I was having promiscuous sex. Drinking and driving every day led to a couple of car accidents and I knew I was in really bad shape; if I stayed in New York, I was going to die young.

So I moved to California, a place I thought would cure me overnight. After a drunken, binge-eating plane ride, California turned out to be as difficult as New York, because beaches and sunshine couldn't remedy my deep-seated self-hatred. Six months in, I called my sister, Madeleine, and said, "I'm coming back to New York."

She said, "Laura, I know you want to come back, but I don't think you should. I think you should stay, grow up, and stop being a baby. How can you give up so easily? You'll be okay." It was tough love, and I resented her words, but I stayed. I not only survived, but eventually I thrived. I made my way into college, despite being told repeatedly that I was dumb and a complete failure. Now my sister was telling me that she believed in me! Hearing her say that she believed I was strong enough really hit home. Even as I continued to abuse my body, I felt her presence and heard her voice telling me I would be OK.

Self-hatred is no fun, and it controlled my life for a long time. I hated myself and couldn't see a way out of my pain, fat or thin. I was in college enjoying school for the first time, but still not loving my body or myself. I desperately turned to bulimia and laxatives to control my weight. One day, a miracle happened. I heard a voice say, "If you put all that negative energy into loving yourself, then you can be free of your pain." Even though I did not know what it really meant, I knew on some level that my self-pity was starting to melt away. This personal epiphany coincided with my meeting Simone.

I was working at a liquor store—pretty much the worst job for an alcoholic. It was at this job that I met Simone, a gorgeous woman inside and out. Days after meeting me, she said she was in love with me. This made no sense. I was a big, fat, smoking drunk. But she said, "I see your light. I see who you really are."

Before I met her, I knew that I liked girls more than boys and yet I had nowhere to go with that information. It just made my feeling different stand out even more. Throughout my childhood, homosexuality was not discussed; however, the one time it did come up, it was referred to as the "ultimate sin," so that was the message I heard in my head. Even after I moved to San Francisco, I continued to feel uncomfortable talking about my sexuality. I dreaded coming out, even though when I did, people accepted me graciously. Being a lesbian was a huge part of my pain, but to hear that this amazing woman loved me, including the body I was ashamed of, transformed my being gay into a wonderful thing.

Another huge gift Simone gave me was Overeaters Anonymous (OA). Right up front, Simone told me she attended Alcoholics Anonymous (AA) meetings. She said one day, "I think you might want to acknowledge that you have a problem with food and with alcohol." I listened to her. Even though I understood I had some serious addictions, I had hidden that truth very well. It was huge for me that someone could clearly see my faults and still love me.

I instantly became determined to get well; knowing that I was loved and supported for the first time gave me the strength to face myself. What I also understood from Simone was that there was no way I could heal without the power of community. In the fall of 1987, I went to my first meeting of OA, because I knew my primary addiction was food. What I remember most about that meeting was the love I felt from the moment I walked in the door. We humans have an amazing capacity to heal, transform, and become our best selves, all the while loving, holding, and supporting one another through the darkness and into the light.

I felt no pressure in OA to do it right, and I began to see and feel glimmers of hope and peace. It was about willingness; if I was sitting in that room, they said, then that was the first step. A particular inspiration was a woman who had lost over 100 pounds. It had taken eight years before she was willing to change anything for herself. Knowing that I could attend meetings without being forced to change felt liberating. I believe we are all longing for love, community, and sisterhood; no one has to overcome anything alone. We need each other to thrive and prosper and I see this as strength, not as weakness. Simone had given me this amazing gift.

In OA meetings, I started to talk about my addiction, yet on my way home I would run to the grocery store. I would binge my brains out thinking, *Well, I'm not ready and I am doing the best I can right now.* That went on for months. And still, I hung on to the belief that something might change. I kept going to meetings until one day, I heard four words that transformed my life.

Although I had taken the important step of joining OA, I really was not ready to take my life back and turn things around. Though I continued to go to meetings, my pain was obedient to my addiction and I still felt defective. I had begun to wake up and see my pain more clearly, yet I was still living in my old world of self-abuse. Part of me was seeking something better and the other part was desperate. One wanted to live and the other did not.

My latest New Year's resolution to heal had died and, once again, I was using food and alcohol every day. There was an OA conference and, as disappointed as I was in myself, I knew I needed to go. My intuition got me in the door. The very first speaker, a normal-sized woman, had a story similar to mine—a lifetime of yo-yo diets and self-hate. She talked about feeling desperate and determined at the same time, of living her life in two parts: the one who knew there was more and the one who felt defeated. I can remember so much about her and yet I cannot recall her name. She talked about all of her excuses, stories, lies, and self-betrayals. She, like me, had wanted out of the quicksand, but could never find anything to pull herself out. One day in a meeting, she heard a woman share her story about her own attempts and failures and the four words that changed her life.

"If not now, when?"

As soon as she said this, I burst into tears and experienced a release in my body, an earthquake in my cells. Everything changed and just then, I got it. *If not now, when? What was I waiting for?*

As I cried, I thought, *how long am I going to play this game of dieting, cheating, and lying to myself? How long will I feel so ashamed of myself? How much longer will I allow myself to hope for death and fantasize about taking my life?*

If not now, when?

Until I heard this, I had been sitting alone in a conference room full of people, feeling fat, isolated, stupid, useless, and helpless. The words took me home to the person I was; home to the infant born innocent, who was told she was fat, ugly, and dumb and should never have been born in the first place; home to the person who was not defective, but who was capable of healing and changing her story; home to what was possible; home to believing that I could stop hating myself, learn to love myself, and release the weight for good. It all flooded me as I sat there, weeping in pain and joy. I knew then that the part of me that wanted to die was right: some things would have to die in order for me to live. The seeker in me would have to embrace change fully and live in courage, no matter how hard it would get. This was my life and I needed to choose to take my power back.

I danced my way through the rest of the day's conference, feeling myself slowly crossing over from shame into glory.

My understanding of how to help my body finally outweighed my inclination to harm myself, and over the course of the next year, I released 100 pounds. I did it by eating healthily with lots of support. I was thin for the first time and I thought everything would fall into place after that. Boy, was I wrong.

A few years later, I was working for a gym. I wanted so much to reach out to those experiencing the same pain that I had for years, and yet a voice inside me said I was not yet worthy. On the outside, I was thin; seemingly, I had it all together and I looked it. But on the inside, I was a vacant shell. I still did not love who I was. How could I teach self-love if I didn't love myself?

The solution turned out to be two-fold, one mental and one physical. The first was turning 40. Coming into this new decade in my life was a serious wake up call and a tangible, numeric reminder of "if not now, when?" It felt like a rebirth, a new chance to let go of my self-loathing.

The second step was getting to know my body in the deepest way possible. I met Barbara Stamm Dose, certified SHEN therapist. The basic tenant of SHEN Therapy is that our emotions and our bodies are inextricably tied together. Barbara guided me to a connection with my body I had never known. Through this, I was able to forgive myself for how I had treated my body and forgive my body for how it made me feel. In this forgiveness, I found boundless love for myself and this amazing vessel I live in. Everything came together. I loved myself fully and I was finally ready to share what I had learned.

We should never underestimate the incredible power of sharing and reaching out to others. My interest was and still is in stopping the obesity epidemic, the one I nearly succumbed to, by changing how we women see our bodies. It's my intention to wake up women from their denial so that they can look at their reflection in the mirror or the number on the scale with acceptance and not hesitation. I want to share the truth that saved my life—self-love is the ultimate healer.

Sisterhood is powerful. Community is powerful. I found these life lessons and let them into my life before it was too late—thank God for that. Madeleine, Simone, the woman from OA, and Barbara are woven inextricably into the tapestry of my life. Each of them gave me a lesson in how to be honest, happy, and healthy. I honor them all every day by passing along the wisdom and love they gave to me to all women who struggle to love what they see in the mirror.

Laura Fenamore

Weight release and body image expert Laura Fenamore is on a mission, guiding women around the world to love life. Laura's Body Image Mastery curriculum is celebrated by hundreds of women who have released weight, reclaimed self-esteem, and let go of the belief that nothing will work for them. Author of *Weightless: 7 Tools to Love Your Body (and Release Weight For Good)*, Laura battled addictions, obesity, and eating disorders. Laura released 100 pounds in 1988 for good and she now guides women globally to live more joyous, balanced lives.

Femininely Divine

Leila Radan

I am not in love with my breasts. I am in LOVE with my breasts. There is a difference. My breasts are small, tiny even, but I affectionately call them my pimples. They don't have enough oomph for cleavage, but they are mine. Because of their size, perkiness, and character, and despite the wear and tear they've suffered over years of life, aging, and the nurturing of two children, they deserve some damn respect! However, that respect wasn't always there; how could it have been when I didn't acknowledge my self-worth, let alone the value of my breasts? Respect was a hard-fought change that was delivered lovingly into my life during a brief moment of sisterly connection that rocked me to my core and gave my once foggy appendages a solid presence and voice.

Yes, that respect wasn't always there. My breasts existed as mere protrusions on my lanky teenage frame, shameful in their small size, pathetic in their lack of cleavage, and perfect as the scapegoats for the growing self-loathing that consumed the woeful me of yore. I perceived my breasts to be the physical manifestations of my caregiver's criticism and by nursing their toxic voice they silenced my voice and became the antithesis of the desired and seemingly unattainable feminine divine. They lacked purpose and a calling and they set me aside from womankind, forever branded "not good enough," with the added insult of insufficiency attached to the small Bs that they were—all while I dreamt of the bigger Cs they could and (I misguidedly thought) should have been.

During my sexual awakening, my man ravenously declared that more than a mouthful was a waste and temporarily validated my neglected breasts while I lay in bed with him, naked and vulnerable. As we satisfied our appetites, he breathed new life into my breasts through his desire and his hunger. When exposed while in his arms or subject to his touch, my breasts were adequate . . . visible even. But they were his, not mine.

During motherhood my breasts became nurturers to my children. They were a food source that lived up to their utilitarian and biological role and were ever so practical . . . but still, they were not mine.

Yes, my own respect for my breasts had yet to blossom. So, when not fulfilling their sexual obligations or nurturing offspring, my breasts were hidden away and dutifully forgotten in nude, nondescript, and practical bras. *What was the point of lingerie to begin with?* I wondered. After all, a useless adornment that would be ripped off to, well . . . satisfy my man could never, and would never be my chosen method of self-expression! Why should I invest in mere adornments that did nothing to satisfy me and seemed only to further stifle my expressive self and smother my voice? WHY?

Oh, how life held an answer for me! One night, when at an event with my wives—sisters who nurture my being in its entirety, see through my multiple masks, and love me by recognizing my state of perfect imperfection—I was literally and figuratively stripped down with a casual tenderness that unsettled me. Our founding wife, Christine, embodying everything my caregiver wasn't, held my blind trust and my heart, and gently, lovingly, dragged a highly-resistant me into the lingerie-filled den of my fellow wives Mary and Gina, who, in no time, had their way with me. They immediately removed the nude-plain-for-lorn-unsupportive and worn-only-to-hide-my-ferocious-nipple-pro-trusions shackle of a bra from my neglected, invisible breasts, and all of this through my polite, masked-by-a-smile resistance. My defiant actions certainly belied that I was silently screaming *I don't need fancy bras! What is the point? They will never see the light of day and will hide under my clothes with my useless breasts. So let me be . . . LET ME GO!*

Christine just laughed and walked away. Mary and Gina, amused by my ignorance, were analytical as they poked and prodded me in a manner I had never been poked and prodded before—without any judgment.

I was astonished. Mary and Gina measured me, analyzed my cup size, and delighted in my itty-bitty, forlorn ladies with their Madonna/ whore complex. They dressed them up in mouth-watering lacy bits and, lo and behold, they gave me a never-before-experienced thing called a silhouette. A silhouette on my itty-bitty frame and with my itty-bitty breasts! I was aghast and amazed and, as I checked out my breasts, I mouthed *How YOU doin'?* at those charmingly fancy and uplifted (and oh how uplifted they were!) powerful forces that they'd become. I touched them. It was like touching them for the first time, these fresh, virgin breasts! Oh, how I touched them! I wanted my wives to touch them and I wanted the world to touch them because they were glorious. GLORIOUS! These breasts, my newly discovered breasts were magnificent and needed, wanted, had to scream for the entire world to hear, "WE ARE BREASTS! HEAR US ROAR!"

Years spent dressing my exterior through orgasmic acts of impulse buying that expressed my undying love for fashion and my Oh-MAMA-GIMME-GIMME-GIMME-'cause-I-must-I-want-I-can't-do-without-YEEEAH need to have shoes, hats, bags, skirts, dresses, purses, tops and bottoms, and this and that . . . none of that had even come close to delivering the supreme high that this simple act of fashion at its most foundational had given me—awakening to my breasts to their full glory. You heard it. I said "My breasts! MY BREASTS!"

Was this awakening all due to my breasts finally being measured and outfitted properly? As I stood in front of the mirror, my gaze fell beyond my reflection onto Mary and Gina who grinned profusely, elated at my reaction, all while Christine gathered a plethora of exquisite lacey bras to gift me in celebration of my awakening. Time stood still. Mary, Gina, and Christine were frozen in time as my awakening extended its reach beyond my breasts and straight to my heart, their matter-of-fact manner and easy, no-strings-attached love moving me to my very core. This was an initiation, a silent and instinctive rite of passage that saw my tribe filling a void I was unaware existed until that moment. My breasts were mine. *Mine!* And they were delivered to me through the power of a new vision of the feminine divine embodied in my wives!

Yes, they were finally mine! They had a voice. They were no longer shameful protrusions, pathetic scapegoats of self-loathing, or physical manifestations of mothering gone wrong. They needed, wanted, had to be proudly and unabashedly displayed in their full, kitted out, sexy glory, parading around for the entire world to behold! They had purpose, a calling, and were tailor-made just for me. They emerged from their foggy nude-bra-shackled past into a glorious here and now, ready to roar a proud ROAR!

So go on, world! Look at me as I sashay down my own private runway, head held high, back arched, and chest out oh so proudly. Heed my call to be seen! Hear my powerful ROAR as I strip down to my lacy foundations, unashamed and unapologetic! Look at me, and realize that my voice has absolutely nothing to do with you and absolutely everything to do with me. Feel my passion for my perky, newly uplifted, sexy, delightful, deserving, kinky, beautiful, practical, nurturing breasts, now the physical manifestation of an initiation spurred on by my tribe of wives and delivered gracefully to the no-longer neglectful arms of . . . me!

World, watch out! Behold the feminine divine in action! Behold . . . me.

Leila Radan

Leila Radan, an off-the-wall, off-the-cuff, hyper hyphenated, ranting-and-raving-writer-a-go-go, is described best by an avid reader and loyal fan as "Lewis Black on crack." Whether fueled by injustice-based rage or ecstasy-generating pleasure, the short circuitry in her brain is bound to elicit a dizzying stream of consciousness slam guaranteed to be as unforgettable, quirky, eccentric, explosive, unabashed, unashamed, and absolutely unapologetic as Leila herself. Leila is also the Chief Community Wife for A Band of Wives, a private online social network for all women.

Deaf, Dumb & Blind, painting by Nancy Calef

Nancy Calef

Nancy Calef creates "Peoplescapes," oil, sculpture, and applied objects on canvas that address cultural, political, and spiritual issues facing society. People juxtaposed in recognizable places and situations weave together a narrative about contemporary life, rich with details, symbolism, and humor. Born in Bronx, New York, Nancy majored in art at the College of New Rochelle at the age of 15, lived in Europe and Thailand, and traveled throughout the United States, Mexico, Central America, Southeast Asia, India and Nepal, all to serve and develop her uniquely expressive style. She resides in San Francisco, California and New York.

Healing

Lissa Rankin

The world is deeply in need of healing. Civil wars are breaking out in countries across the globe, children are starving, and global warming is turning natural disasters into catastrophes, destroying habitats, and killing our animal species. The global economic crisis is destroying lives and breaking apart countries. Rainforests are disappearing. Soldiers are killing civilians and bragging about it. Women around the world are oppressed, abused, silenced, and killed if they dare to step into their power.

And it's not just the world out there that's in need of healing. Things are tough right here in our own country. Our teachers and priests are molesting our youth. Serial killers are attacking our women. Families are disintegrating. Unemployment is skyrocketing. Women feel so pressured to be perfect, to be Superwomen, to keep it all together and to live up to society's expectations for us, that we've lost touch with each other, ourselves, and our capacity to be forces of healing in the world.

The Dalai Lama said "The world will be saved by the Western woman," and we all applauded and Tweeted and Facebooked the quote. We smiled and nodded knowingly, because as women, we're aware, deep down, that we are gifted peacemakers, unifiers, collaborators, and healers. We love deeply, prioritize the mending of fences, and understand that, regardless of what separates us, we are ultimately all part of a greater whole. As a collective, women tend to abhor violence, feel compassion for strangers, and open our hearts easily. And as Western women, we have freedom, financial resources, mobility, education, and other unprecedented liberties that make us ideally suited to heal the world.

This is all true, and frankly, I agree with the Dalai Lama about the capacity of the Western woman. But as an OB/GYN physician, I know intimately that women can't heal the world if we don't first heal each other and ourselves. It's like the rule of oxygen masks on airplanes. We can't truly love, heal, and care for others until we nurture ourselves.

Just to be clear, when I talk about health and healing, I'm talking about more than you might think. Sure, good nutrition, daily exercise, eight hours of sleep, and taking your vitamins are a wonderful foundation for living a healthy life, but I'd argue they're the least important part of being a wholly healthy, healed woman.

Although healthy bodies will certainly support us in our globe-changing efforts, you'll need more than that to live a vital life. I'm talking about healing any toxic relationships, hostile work life, thwarted creativity, spiritual disconnection, unfulfilled sexual hunger, unhealthy financial baggage, harmful environmental issues in your home, and any unhealthy thoughts, beliefs, and emotions. Not until we realize that we are mirrors of our interpersonal, spiritual, professional, sexual, creative, financial, environmental, mental, and emotional health will we truly heal. Only then can we step up to the plate and make big strides toward saving the world.

This kind of self-healing isn't for the faint of heart! You really can't do it alone. This is where your sisters come in.

When you're arm in arm with the feminine superheroes in your life who will blow pixie dust beneath your mighty wings as you blast off to the stratosphere, you can do anything. And when each of us rises to this level of empowerment, joy, wisdom, authenticity, and self-actualization, watch out world, here we come!

This kind of healing may feel completely out of your reach right now, and if you feel that way, please know you're not alone. You may even feel a wee bit bruised right now, because when you were little, you may not have known that life could be quite as hard as it's been. Maybe you dreamed of fairy castles and a happy ever after with your soul mate, becoming a parent and raising empowered children. Or maybe you fantasized about having a powerful career, achieving financial freedom, expressing yourself creatively, and changing the world. Or if you're like me, you dreamed about doing all of that and more.

And then life happened. Maybe you got thwacked with cancer, you struggle with endometriosis, or you're battling obesity. Maybe you lost a loved one, your husband left you for his secretary, your kid wound up on crack, or you got downsized at work after giving the company the best years of your life. Maybe you failed to achieve that dream, you declared bankruptcy, or you never did meet that guy and missed your window to become a mother. Maybe you were molested, raped, betrayed, or abandoned.

Maybe you're still angry that life just hasn't worked out the way you planned.

Maybe you went to school, got that job, and hunkered down in your cubicle, only to discover that your heart isn't in what you spend all day doing. Or maybe you gave up the job to raise your kids while your partner pursued professional dreams, and now the kids need you less and you wonder what your life is supposed to be about. Maybe you schlepped the kids to soccer practice for a decade and traded in your independence for the house with the white picket fence and the parent-teacher conferences.

But now what? Prozac?

You can numb your way through your day with busyness, but it's harder when you startle awake at 4:00 a.m. Unable to get back to sleep, you wrestle with the dark night of your soul, when the veil is thinner and the messages from your body bellow louder. Without the distractions of daytime, it's harder to escape the truth that your body is trying to communicate with you. You're forced to face your demons: fear, anxiety, stress, regret, resentment, and sadness.

You can't help wondering, *what if this is it?* You wonder why you're even here. Why has God forsaken you? Weren't you put on this earth for a reason? What is it? Will anyone ever really know the real you? Who is the real you, anyway? Who is that person you dreamed of being before you started wearing masks so you could fit in, so you could pretend to be like all the other moms, stockbrokers, students, lawyers, church-goers, and doctor's wives? What lights your fire? What turns you on? What big dreams do you harbor? What would you do if you knew you could not fail?

Maybe you honestly don't know that person anymore. You buried her back when you were younger, after you realized that the dreams you had when you were 15 were probably just pipe dreams, and you should just suck it up and feel grateful for what you have.

After taking another pill, you finally drop off into a fitful sleep, and two hours later, you push the replay button and start the whole thing over again.

You might think you're the only one who's drowning right now, like you're slogging through life underwater. But trust me, darling, you are not alone. More and more people are suffering from a growing, nameless, mojo-sapping epidemic for which the medical community has no diagnosis to name it, no pill to cure it, no vaccine to prevent it, and no surgery to cut it out. This insidious epidemic causes millions to suffer from fatigue, decreased energy, anxiety, depression, poor sleep, decreased libido, weight gain, and a whole host of physical conditions.

But that's not all. This epidemic goes much deeper, leaving people feeling discouraged, disappointed, depressed, and dissociated. It causes creative blocks, romantic challenges, professional disillusionment, and spiritual disconnection. It leads to career angst, bankruptcy, divorce, and broken family ties. Those afflicted feel lost at sea, as if something is missing from their lives—but they can't quite put their finger on it.

Many suffering from this epidemic show up at the doctor's office, feeling as if something must be physically wrong. They may indeed wind up diagnosed with an illness, but all too often, after experimenting with boatloads of lab tests, drugs, supplements, doctors, and alternative health care providers, these people fail to improve.

Even more commonly, the doctor orders a whole battery of tests that come back normal, pronounces the patient well, or chalks the whole thing up to depression and hands over a pill. Still, the patient doesn't feel well. She's lost her spark. It's been years since she's felt vital—if she ever did feel vital.

If you think you might be suffering from this epidemic, you are not alone. There are hundreds and thousands—dare I say millions— just like you. We are your neighbors, your colleagues, the people in the pews next to you, the athletes at your gym, and the other mothers in the schoolyard. We are everywhere. And our healing process begins with finding each other.

Six years ago, I was one of those women. I was your typical physician: burned out, stressed out, exhausted, and angry at the world. By the time I was 33 years old, I was twice divorced, taking three pills for high blood pressure, gaining weight, and about to get surgery for pre-cancerous changes on my cervix. On top of that, I was so desperate to be loved and accepted and so terrified of rejection that I covered up my true self with a complicated series of masks. I didn't even know who I was anymore. I had my doctor mask, where I donned the white coat, stood up on a pedestal, acted aloof and professional, and talked down to others because, after 12 years of education, surely I knew more than they did.

In addition to being a doctor, I'm also a professional artist, so I wore another mask to play the expected role of the dark, brooding, mysterious, and starving artist.

As if my professional masks weren't constrictive enough, I also had a new husband, and after having failed twice, I was terrified of being abandoned, so I wore the dutiful wife mask as I put beautiful dinners on the table and made sure I always wore sexy lingerie. Then I got pregnant, and all of a sudden, there was a whole new mask I was supposed to wear—the perfect-mommy mask. People expect you to cut your hair short, ditch the miniskirts, stop cussing, master baby talk, become a birthday party event planner, and learn to bake the perfect cupcake. But I just don't have that mommy gene.

I'd strap on various identities depending on the situation, so that, like a chameleon, I'd fit in reasonably well wherever I went. But in the process, I lost myself. I never felt vital. My *joie de vivre* disappeared and my health declined. I lost touch with my life's purpose and I felt really alone.

Then my perfect storm hit. In January of 2006, I gave birth to my daughter by C-section, my dog died, my healthy young brother wound up with liver failure as a side effect of a common antibiotic, and my beloved father died from a brain tumor—all within two weeks. Eight months later, just when I was starting to breathe, my stay-at-home-Daddy husband cut two fingers off his left hand with a table saw.

Just like that, I officially lost my mojo.

Losing my much-too-young physician father inspired me to ask myself, "If I knew I had only three months to live, would I be living like I'm living now?" The answer was a resounding "HELL NO!"

This realization made me hit my wall. Something deep within me knew in that moment that it was time to start my self-healing journey, but I was terrified because I knew that would mean big change. I'd had an inkling that I needed to make some changes in my life, but I was so paralyzed by my fear of change that I didn't take action until my perfect storm. After that, the pain of staying put exceeded my fear of the unknown, so I knew it was time to take a leap of faith. But this was no easy task.

First I had to face my fear—as in fear with a capital "F." So I marched right over to fear and told him to go to hell. Fear looked me in the eye and we stood there for quite some time, each daring the other to make a move. Fear told me that I was crazy to even consider what I was considering—after all, I'd lose everything I had worked so hard to achieve, I'd regret making such a bold step, and I should just be grateful for what I had and stop wanting so much more.

Fear threw daggers at me and when I failed to turn and run, fear got vicious and started spewing evil nothings at me, telling me I would never amount to anything, that I didn't deserve the life I desired, that

I wasn't smart enough, pretty enough, young enough, fill-in-the-blank enough to heal and thrive if I switched directions.

Before my perfect storm, I saw fear as a great and powerful wizard who would guide my way, help me survive, and protect me from myself. But my perfect storm pulled back the curtain, and suddenly, I saw fear for who he was—a pathetic, slimy, powerless figment of my primordial lizard brain who, instead of protecting me, was actually holding me back. For years, I had believed fear, thinking that fear would keep me safe, but in truth, fear had locked me in a dungeon where love couldn't get in, I couldn't heal, and my dreams couldn't possibly come true.

The bolder I got, the more wicked and panicked fear became. Fear started making up all kinds of lies to rein me back in. And fear was a crafty little devil. Fear attacked me when I was sleeping and vulnerable, lashing out at me in dreams. Fear possessed the people I love and came at me in the voices of my family members, my best friends, and my business colleagues. Fear didn't back down. So I learned to see fear for who he was—a powerless ghost who couldn't actually hurt me unless I believed he was real or gave him power.

I learned to make peace with fear. I called him The Gremlin. I imagined him looking something like Shrek: big, ogre-like, and seemingly scary, but ultimately a big softie. And whenever I noticed The Gremlin—in my mind, in my dreams, in the voices of those I love—I chided him and said, "Pipe down, Gremlin!" I'd pat him on the head and feed him peanuts.

The Gremlin didn't like this one bit. He jumped up and down. He screamed louder. He spewed lies. But after a while, The Gremlin realized I was averting my eyes and had inserted earplugs. The Gremlin was still prattling on, but I wasn't listening anymore. By taking back my own power, rather than handing it over to him, I was able to feel fear—and do what I wanted anyway. So I did.

I wrote my own prescription for how I needed to heal and reclaim my vitality, in my own individual way. For me, the prescription included stripping off my masks, promising to be unapologetically me, and letting the chips fall where they may. It meant quitting my lucrative, stable job, selling my house, liquidating my retirement account to buy my freedom, and moving to the country. For two years, I wrote, painted, hiked, did yoga, drank green juice, meditated, bonded with my husband and baby daughter, and licked my wounds.

I mourned the loss of my father and my dog, read loads of self-help books, saw an integrative medicine doctor, went on retreats, took personal growth workshops, explored my sexuality, and started blogging about my commitment to getting my mojo back.

As I navigated my healing journey, my blood pressure went down, I lost weight, my Pap smear returned to normal, and my creative energy came back in leaps and bounds. In addition to getting my body healthy again, I developed more intimate relationships with my family and friends, discovered my erotic creature, and reconnected with the divine. As extra credit, my healing process led me to discover my true calling. As Tama Kieves says, "It takes an intermission to find your mission." I realized that I felt called to unite the feminine, to feminize the broken, outdated, patriarchal model of medicine, to lead a self-healing revolution to change the face of health care, to teach these principles, and to guide women through the process of crafting their own self-healing prescriptions.

Certainly, many factors contributed to my healing process. But what was the secret sauce that made it all possible?

Women.

Women being who they really are, letting their freak flags fly, showing up without masks in all their beautiful vulnerability, celebrating their perfect imperfections, and lifting each other up.

When I started my blog in 2009, it was just me and the Internet, but within three months, it was a whole community of women committed to helping each other heal, connect, and thrive. At the time, I had just moved to the San Francisco Bay Area and hardly knew anyone, but weeks later, I had a tribe, and they had each other. The healing power of the feminine regularly moved me to tears.

Women were showing up to tell their stories, witness each other's wounds, celebrate their triumphs, support each other professionally, and find sisterhood. The community attracts women who fall into two categories: those in need of healing and those committed to helping others heal. But of course, we all take turns. Some days, I am the wounded. Others, I am the healer. Everyone else also takes turns swapping roles, for we are all healers, and we are all in need of healing. We give what we have, take what we need, and use it as rocket fuel to heal the world.

With women around the globe helping me heal so I could pay it forward and return the favor to others, a global web of feminine power began to generate. It was right around this time that I met Christine Bronstein, who had just started A Band of Wives.

Way too often, when women discover they share similar goals and visions, they polarize, turn catty, and lapse into a fear-based mentality, as if there's not enough room for all of us to shine our bright, sparkly lights. But Chris and I hit it off right away and we committed to doing anything we could to lift each other up. After talking, we realized that we are all in service to the same goal and that there's way more power in collaboration than in competition. When we join forces, we amplify our feminine power, and everybody wins.

This is the awesome power of women in community. When we support each other, love each other, and lift each other up, we not only heal each other, but we also heal our loneliness, we grow our businesses, we spread our visions, and we make a difference, even if only in our small way. When we're juiced up, full of mojo, overflowing with vitality, kicking fear to the curb, following our dreams, nurturing our bodies, tending our spirits, and linking arms with our sisters, we can do anything.

Can Western women save the world?

You betcha, sister! But we can't do it alone. We need each other to heal ourselves, so we can create as only women can do, love with open hearts, unite with collective spirit, and seek peace as the world leaders we all can be.

Are you on board to save the world? You can count on me to hold your hand, sister. Look left. Look right. We're all around you, love. And together, we can all heal.

Lissa Rankin

Lissa Rankin, MD is an integrative medicine physician, author, speaker, artist, and founder of the online wellness community OwningPink.com. In her research of what really makes people healthy and what predisposes them to illness, she discovered scientific fact that proves patients have immense self-healing powers. She is now leading a health care revolution to help patients heal themselves. She will be sharing her scientific findings in her upcoming book *Mind Over Medicine: Scientific Proof You Can Heal Yourself*. When not spreading the word, she paints, writes, does yoga, and hikes in Marin County, California with her husband and daughter.

Pool Girl, painting by Vicki Nelson

Vicki Nelson

Vicki Nelson has lived in Marin County, California for 33 years, but was born and raised in San Francisco. She always knew she wanted to be an artist—there was no other way to be truly herself. Vicki attended California College of Art and studied for her MFA in Modern Art History at San Francisco State University. Vicki put her education on hold to get married and raise three children, leaving her paintbrush aside until her children were grown, then she promptly converted a room in her home into a studio. Vicki is drawn to painting people in suburban settings with unusual angles; she loves to capture the private moments of seemingly ordinary subjects—that is when she can expose the extraordinary.

Section Two

Overcoming Obstacles

No One Should Ever Have To Write This

Mickey Nelson

I read this at the memorial service for my sister, Lauren Marie Nelson, August 20, 1982–September 29, 2010

Lauren, I wish we had driven here together today. We would have approved of each other's outfits at home first, blow dried our hair next to one another in our bathroom, reminded each other to grab a Diet Coke to split for the car ride, and blasted one of your famous mix CDs the whole way here.

But we didn't drive here together today. You, my dear sister, took a very different route.

When I was 11 and Lauren was 13, we coined the term "SSS." Secret Sister Stuff. Our mission statement was "I won't tell if you won't tell." Soon, the rest of my family caught on. From then on, when my mom, Lauren, and I would have an inside joke or funny experience together, my mom would shriek with excitement, "Oh! It's SSSM!"— Secret Sister Stuff with Mom! My brother was also determined to be included in our acronym. "This is so SSSB," he'd say. Everyone wanted to be a part of our hilarious, girly world, but to this day, SSS consists only of its two founding members.

Of course I was completely lost at the thought of writing this. Even for a writer, I had one paralyzing case of writer's block. Only this time, it wasn't because I couldn't think of something to say, it was because I didn't want to think of something to say. I don't want to be saying any of this.

I don't want to live a life without my sister. I don't want to accept that she won't get to have children, be married, or travel the world. I don't want to accept that I can't squeeze her again, be doubled over in fits of laughter together again, or bury my head in her chest and cry to her again. I don't want to give up all the things that having her present in my daily life added to my identity, my security, and my happiness—my world.

Then I realize that these are all selfish thoughts. It's not Lauren I need to worry about. She is at ultimate peace in infinite joyfulness. Knowing her, she is probably planning an exquisite ball for all the angels to attend as we speak. She is now being looked after by someone I trust very much. She is in a place without confusion, judgment, or hardship.

The hardship exists only here on earth. It lies in my accepting the changes this has caused in my life. This will be the most difficult transition I will ever make. To find a new normal is torturous and excruciating and feels impossible. That is why what this comes down to for me is not only dealing with the most profound loss a person can endure, but also digesting the changes inherent in that loss.

The ability to understand that change can be a good thing is something I have always struggled with, but now more than ever, it is something I have to address. Lauren and my relationship with her are now changed. It's not better or worse—she has just passed on, gone home, and our connection has fluidly evolved into a form that transcends space and time. I suppose we do all have to leave where we're at to get where we're going. Lauren knew that, and I will spend my life daydreaming of where her change took her.

For the past few years, Lauren has listened to Elton John's "Sacrifice" whenever she was lying in bed and couldn't sleep. She once shared it with me when I couldn't sleep—patiently holding the iPod, she stood gently over my bed in the dark until the song ended, just to make sure it worked and I'd been lulled to sleep. Her favorite line was "some things look better just passing through." She told me it was the sentence that made her feel best to hear when something good in her life had ended. *Some things look better just passing through.* She wasn't scared to let go.

But I am.

I'm scared. Scared to go through my life without my older sister. Scared for the inevitable moment when the shock wears off and this all sinks in and I actually realize what's happened; scared that I won't know what to do without her—or that it will cause me to do nothing; scared that I could lose someone else I love; scared I will lose confidence that she can hear me. But most of all, I'm scared for this day to be over, because tomorrow won't be just another day. And no day after today will be just another day.

So, I ask Lauren to please give me the strength not to let fear inhibit me from living the finest life I can. I ask her to guide me to do better, to care more, to reach higher, to use my gifts unabashedly and not feel guilty for being here to do it. A ship in the harbor may be safe, but that's not what ships are for.

I ask Lauren to lead me toward the good things that I hope will one day come from this, toward friends that wouldn't otherwise have come together. I ask her to lead me to ideas, faith, priorities, and purpose that will be inspired by her absence. Someone told me this week that I cannot appreciate a mountain from its foot. I have to do the work, and climb—many times struggling to climb, but when I reach the top, the beauty I worked so hard to see will be illuminated.

A couple weeks ago, Lauren and I had the silliest conversation about something. I was lying on my bed in New York and she in San Francisco, and we laughed and laughed until our bellies ached. About ten minutes after we hung up, she called me back and simply said, "Mick, I really loved talking to you just now."

Well, my Nana, I have always really loved talking to you. And I plan to every day until we meet again.

I love you, I love you, I love you.

Just a month shy of the two-year anniversary of my sister's passing, I look back on this piece I wrote and read at her memorial, and I'm carried away. I'd like to be able to say that even the brief time that has passed has healed my wounds, but I'd be lying. Anyone who has ever told you that time heals all wounds was trying to sell you on the aphoristic equivalent of a placebo. Time does not heal wounds, but in time, we do grow as people, and with that growth, we can hopefully see our wounds with a different perspective.

The truth is, some days I wake up with the theme song from *Rocky* in my head, and other days, I resign myself to ice cream for breakfast. Even now, when the finality of what's happened strikes me, it is a swift blow to the chest and nearly impossible to endure—more impossible still to endure with an open heart. The key for me has been compassion with myself, realizing that having ups and downs is no sweat—it's normal. It's weathering those ups and downs with grace that makes a real, quality life—makes a real, quality woman.

Part of my connection to Lauren now lies in my having absorbed some of her qualities into my character—which I feel are equipping me with the tools I need to live life without her in clear sight. I was born very free-spirited and starry-eyed; she—gentle, subtle, and knowing in a kind of unassuming way. Her spirit is and was realistic, yet still hopeful—she knew the best could happen, but she wouldn't fall apart if it didn't, like I've had a tendency to do. I've always been younger and less appropriate than her, but she let me feel like her equal. In looking at these admirable qualities of hers through the lens of her legacy, I can see clearly that having them in my life will ultimately make it calmer, happier, and more balanced. In life as in passing, Lauren showed me that although my penchant for wishful thinking is a sweet thing, you just can't build a sturdy life on it.

There is just no way to get used to the loss of someone so close to you. At just 22 months apart and consonant in voice and mannerisms, we were more like twins than anything else. Lauren was a part of every memory, conversation, and inside joke for the first 26 years of my life. Adjusting completely to the horrifying about-face of losing her is simply an impossibility. But, I am beginning to understand, there is a way to use it for good—both in her honor and for mine.

A tragedy like this levels a person. It flattens their mind, character, and soul right down into to the ground. What I try determinedly to do is to see that unmitigated demolishment as an opportunity to build myself back up better than I was before. How often will I get the chance to look at my base self with such honesty? How often will I get the chance to cultivate my character all over again from the ground up? I can be careful not to reintroduce flaws and misgivings that may have afflicted me before and mindful of new qualities that will be necessary to have as I face the world under more difficult circumstances.

Sometimes I miss my old life, as I call it, when I had less weighing on my mind and far fewer worries. The thoughts that come in the wake of something this traumatic incite ideas and insights that are so much larger than me, so it has had to be my effort not to let them cast a shadow upon me. I've realized, though, that sometimes life makes your decisions for you. If this hadn't happened, I wouldn't have moved back to San Francisco from New York, a decision that has ultimately been healthy for me. I wouldn't have spent so much time with my parents and brothers as a grown woman, creating an unbreakable family unit, stronger and closer than any I've ever heard of or read about. If this hadn't happened, Lauren wouldn't have literally reached down from Heaven to guide me to a job I find fulfilling and fun on a daily basis. I can feel the metaphoric tectonic plates beneath my life sort of subtly shifting into the place I'll need them to be for the rest of my life, and that feels good. There is a real pride that comes with making strides through something so difficult.

My heart just feels differently since Lauren moved from Earth to Heaven. I suppose that is the best way to describe it. Two years ago, I thought that was because my heart was broken. Today, I think, maybe it only feels differently because Lauren and I are sharing my heart now and I'm not quite used to the feeling. I hope the latter is true. I'd share anything with her.

It is because Lauren set such a potent example that I have some semblance of an idea what the next step is. It is with the profound support of my stand-in sisters (you know who you are)—who miraculously always seem to be one step ahead of my needs—that I still have confidence when I don't know what that next step is.

Mickey Nelson

Since graduating with a degree in Creative Writing from UCLA, Mickey Nelson has remained true to her singular passion of writing—working in the editorial departments of a string of high-profile publications in genres ranging from lifestyle and fashion to more serious research journalism. After turns in Los Angeles, California, and New York City, she is happy to be working as an editor in her native San Francisco, California, near her magical family, her unequaled dogs, and her beloved Lake Tahoe.

Joy Along the Rough Road

Joy M. Nordenstrom

Can you imagine being named Joy Time, my birth name, and being informed that there is a 25 percent chance you could lose your ability to smile? Scary, right? That's what happened to me when doctors stumbled upon a tumor in my head.

It had already been a challenging year, to say the least. My fiancé had broken off our engagement and a day later declared on Facebook he was "in a relationship" with another woman. The following day, while I was sitting in traffic, I was rear-ended by a guy driving 45 miles per hour, which resulted in a concussion, whiplash, and nerve damage causing me to have facial and tongue numbness. The day after that, I had a cervical biopsy which came back positive. At times like those, you learn not to say "It can't get any worse."

As I was viewing the MRI with my neurologist, watching my tumor gradually increase to the size of a ping-pong ball, he admitted he'd fibbed when he'd originally told me it was small. He hadn't wanted to scare me while I was driving. The good part was that none of my current symptoms—facial and tongue numbness, severe headaches, and neck and back pain—were related to the tumor but instead, were resulting from injuries I'd incurred during the accident. In fact, it was a miracle that a tumor this large was not yet showing any symptoms. It had probably been slowly growing for ten years. The general consensus was that it was benign because the edges didn't look "angry," but they wouldn't know with 100 percent certainty until they removed it. One thing all the doctors agreed upon was the high degree of risk involved with the tumor's removal or radiation.

My poor mom, 2,000 miles away in Minnesota, went silent when I called her and told her the news. She is a nurse and knows much more about medicine than most people. I, on the other hand, had the luxury of being ignorant. At one point, I left her a very stern voicemail emphatically declaring, "Mom, I told you not to worry. So don't!" Funnily enough, she still has that voicemail on her machine and plays it back when she needs the reminder.

I'm the kind of person who takes things one day at a time. I don't like drama. I see the glass half full. However, the magnitude of what was happening hit me suddenly one day when I was talking positively about my life to a friend. She brought the conversation to a screeching halt by not-so-subtly reminding me, "Yes, but you have a brain tumor!" *Oh shit! You're right,* I thought. Suddenly, I felt like I was essentially alone in California, struggling with a start-up company in a bad economy; just trying to survive. I didn't have a safety net. *Oh no! I am not in a loving, supportive relationship. I am not where I thought I would be by this time in my life. I am so not in control.*

After having a good cry and taking a deep breath, I knew I would get through this, too. This is the only life I am blessed to have and I was ready to live it to the fullest. This challenge was simply another interesting part of my life story. In fact, it was a miracle that I had that car accident, as it enabled me to discover the tumor in the first place, study different courses of action, and find the right team of doctors. It is funny how life works out.

I went to see three teams of doctors. The first two were gung ho to Gamma Knife and radiate the tumor. I came to find out that studies were being done on the Gamma Knife and apparently doctors wanted more subjects. The third team reasoned that since I wasn't experiencing any symptoms, I could actually safely wait up to two years to take action. That sounded like a better plan to me.

I was ready to live my life to the fullest—write my book, get my business funded and take it to a place it could survive without me at the helm everyday, find the love of my life, start a family, and—oh yeah—finally get those boudoir photos taken. Then, all the symptoms doctors said would occur over the next two years happened within six weeks.

The doctors speculated that the trauma of the car accident kicked the tumor into overdrive. The first symptom, vertigo, hit me while I was teaching a class. The second started while I was house sitting. I chased a buzzing noise all around the house, only to realize it was in my own head. Shortly thereafter, I started having severe headaches and the hearing in my left ear rapidly diminished.

Being so out-of-control drove home the lesson that I was never really in control. So again, I surrendered to the universe. The need to do, do, do gradually subsided, and I knew what needed to get done, what could wait, and what really didn't need to happen at all. It was the way it was meant to be, in the flow and wonderfully perfect.

Unfortunately, my mom had spent the previous two years battling her own health challenges—back surgery, three types of cancer, various infections, and torn ligaments in both of her knees. In fact, when she found out I had to go in for brain surgery, she was just days out of a partial knee replacement surgery. I waited five weeks to schedule my surgery to give her some time to recover.

Thank goodness my mom was able to be by my side for the surgery and during the recovery period. There was truly no one other than my mom, my best friend, who I would have wanted to be with during that painful and challenging time. One of the biggest upsides of that crazy time was that I was able to spend so much quality time with her.

My mom and stepdad arrived two days before my surgery. We traveled to Stanford University the day before, for my pre-operative care, and stayed in a nearby hotel. The night before the surgery, I did not sleep. I knew I would have many days of sleep on the other side of it, if all went well, so I wrote an email to my friends, many of whom didn't know what was about to happen. The last words I wrote in the email were, "Life is short no matter what age you live to. Each day is precious. I encourage you to catch as many sunrises and sunsets as possible, regularly tell the people in your life why you are grateful for them, and live life with your heart wide open."

I went into surgery at 7:30 a.m. and stayed under the knife for a little over ten hours. I can't imagine how difficult it must have been for my mom and stepdad to sit in the waiting room all that time. When I woke up, I was happy to have passed the scariest part and have gotten through the life-threatening surgery, but my head hurt like hell and felt heavier than a bowling ball. I literally had to use my hands to lift my head when I needed to throw up, which was often. All the pain aside, I was ecstatic that some of the big questions were behind me. I survived the surgery, the tumor was 100 percent removed, and my facial nerves were minimally impacted, meaning I could still smile.

In the hospital, the nurses and doctors came by every two hours, woke me up, and asked me a series of questions. The last day in the hospital, one of the surgeons asked me what procedure I'd had and I responded with a straight face, "You gave me a lobotomy." Apparently my sense of humor was a sign that I was doing well enough to leave the hospital. Since my mom was a nurse, my doctor released me in her care with the condition that we stayed nearby for a few more days. Originally, they said I would be in the hospital between seven to ten days, so leaving on the fourth day was impressive. My head still felt awkward and heavy atop my shoulders, but I was happy to be out of the hospital in a place where I could finally get more sleep.

My mom played a very hands-on role. On our second post-op visit to see the surgeons at Stanford, they said the 14 staples weren't quite ready to come out. Not wanting to make the long trip back three days later, my mom asked if she could take the staples out herself. I thought she was kidding, and the surgeon said "Oh yeah, you're an RN, right?" When she said "yes," he whipped out a pair of staple removers and gave them to her. I was too nauseated to put up any resistance. I am glad she did it because I'm sure she was much more gentle with me than the doctor would have been.

Anyone who knows me at all knows that laying low is not an easy state for me. On the days I felt well, I wanted to keep going, but my mom did her best to keep me rested. She was constantly by my side even when there wasn't much I could do but lay around, talk, giggle, and watch movies.

Since I had to take it easy, I was able to observe life differently. When our lives are going a million miles per hour and we are all doing our own things, it's sometimes hard to see our interdependence. Keeping such a fast pace makes it easy to rush through life's magic moments. In my correspondence, I encouraged friends to stay present in each moment and not to let the precious times shared with family and friends stream by them without gratitude. Let your presence be a present, I told them.

Through this experience, I relearned several lessons. It is clearly the journey—not the destination—that makes it all worthwhile. It's important to acknowledge the simple joys in between the highest highs and the lowest lows—going to the grocery store, smiling at the people you encounter, preparing a meal to share with loved ones, watching the sunrise, spending time with friends, finding ways to show your appreciation and gratitude for all that you are blessed with in this life. I experienced one of those little joys every night my mom was with me. Since I lived in a loft, my mom slept in my bed up a tall metal ladder while I recovered on the couch downstairs. Each night, we would smile as we played out the last scene from *The Waltons*, "Goodnight, Mom." "Goodnight, Joy."

During my recovery, I had to learn how to do the simplest things again—read without feeling carsick, stand on one leg, drive, and walk without feeling dizzy. During those months, having the encouragement of my friends and family was paramount. Without them, I wouldn't have gotten through it as gracefully. My relationships are my most treasured asset in life.

My mom and I were both relieved when the doctor said I could start driving on side streets, only during the day and while chaperoned. I felt like I was back in high school and had just received my driver's permit. Things that were once taken for granted were now major milestones, and my mom helped me celebrate each and every one of them. I asked her to make sure we were both careful with the way we phrased things, so I wasn't personalizing the pain or weaving a story around it. Instead, it was just something to get through. Our attention went to the progress, the little joys.

All in all, I wouldn't trade this life experience for the world. It's not often that, at the age of 36, a daughter has the opportunity to spend so much time with her best friend . . . her mom. When I asked my mom what the most important thing she learned during our time together was, she said, "I appreciated being able to be there for you and to see firsthand that I raised you well."

Joy M. Nordentrom

Joy M. Nordenstrom is founder of Joy of Romance, Inc., and is a certified matchmaker, relationship coach, wedding proposal planner, and special romantic event and vacation planner. Joy emphasizes making relationship maintenance fun, sexy, and intelligent by educating individuals on a practical, scientific and passionate approach to maintaining their romantic relationships. Joy received an MBA in Entrepreneurship, a BA in Communications and Economics, and a minor in Psychology from Mills College. She is a certified matchmaker from the Matchmaking and Behavioral Science Institute in New York City. Joy is a new mother and lives with her fiancé and their son in Sausalito, California.

Warriors

Amie Penwell

It was February of 1974, in the western part of Massachusetts, in the town of East Longmeadow. I was born into what was already shaping up to be a perfect storm: a deeply loving, recently bankrupt, unreservedly affectionate, manically depressive, unabashedly loud, religiously fanatical, beautiful Irish-Italian family, with alcoholic undertones budding on the young branches of its children. Our collective light and dark were as distinct as my father's blue Irish eyes and my mother's black Italian hair, both of which I inherited.

My parents were considered old to be having a fourth child in their mid-thirties, but had me they did. I was a new opportunity for the family, a place of solace and distraction amidst the loss of my father's dream to build beautiful houses during the economic crash of the mid-1970s. My family lost everything, heightening my mother's need to find a spiritual path and my father's depression. For the first six years of my life, even in the midst of all of this, I had come to know a sense of security, consistency, and family harmony . . . though it was slightly out of tune.

We ate dinner together. We went to Episcopalian mass every Sunday, followed by homemade pancakes and listening to records in the living room. The music was of my parents' choosing: we listened to anything from Rita Coolidge and Kris Kristofferson to John Denver, Fleetwood Mac and Neil Diamond to Pavarotti. We played the piano, board games like Uno, had puppet shows, dance recitals, and read aloud to each other. We took rides in Dad's truck to donut shops and on adventures to get soft-serve ice cream. Big deals were made out of birthdays, hockey, theater, and soccer victories. We were loaded into the wood-sided station wagon every year for our vacation to Cape Cod where we sang songs around campfires, walked beaches at low tide, and got sunburns. But between Mom's increasingly radical spiritual appetite and Dad's growing resentment and subsequent silence from an unwillingness to face much of anything, life as we knew it blew up like a slow-motion bomb landing us all over the fine state of Massachusetts.

My parents separated. My childhood home was empty and on the market with everyone living in different places. The family cat Benji was put to sleep. After my father sent us packing in an old white Datsun, Mom and I went around the outskirts of Boston from one spiritually-based communal household to another. I was sleeping on a mattress on the floor in a room I shared with my mother, absent of all regularity, familiarity, security, television, or treats, in the hell of homeschooling.

After a few months, I reached my breaking point and moved back in with my father. He had fallen in love and was living with a woman from our hometown church whose spirituality didn't involve a guru proclaiming to be God, ashram living, or vegetarianism. Dad's gal kept a clean house, baked fresh pies, and read *The Good News Bible*. Neat and tidy was what he got for the last five months of his life. He died of a massive heart attack on May 11th, 1985, causing our lives to hit bottom harder and deeper than any one of my family members thought life could go. My mother and I moved back into my empty childhood home, which was still on the market, in East Longmeadow.

We were still camping out, but now it was in the shell that used to house our past life. We remodeled the kitchen and bathrooms and repainted and refurnished in the way I had always fantasized about. I felt great relief inviting other children over. My mother was buying me potato chips and hot dogs. I felt like my home finally represented us: clean, simple, and elegant. Little did I know the upgrades were merely in preparation to sell the house and move into another communal living situation, far away from my newly replanted roots. There were five moves and six schools in the next two years—finally landing us in Wellesley, Massachusetts. By then, I was 13 years old. I had become a smoker. I was getting drunk, smoking pot, and growing more disillusioned and pissed off by the day.

On the first day of eighth grade, I found myself in unfamiliar territory yet again, scanning another classroom for islands of safety in the form of possible new friends. Searching for girls who might understand, who would accept this foreign, nervous, pubescent, U2-obsessed, shell-shocked alien who wore black all the time. I needed a girl who would like me even after she came to my embarrassing home with a living room full of framed pictures of my Mom's guru, mismatched furniture from all of our roommates, and ugly, brown shag carpet instead of the neutral wall-to-wall I loved so much. Someone who wouldn't make fun of the bulk soy cheese we ate instead of Kraft Singles, the granola instead of Captain Crunch, and our old Ford Escort in the driveway instead of a BMW. I needed someone who would see in my eyes what I was surviving, recognize the warrior in me, ask me to hang out during lunch, and trade my sprouted wheat crackers with almond butter for their package of Ding Dongs or Ho Hos.

I had purposely forgotten my gym clothes and had to sit on the sidelines during my first gym class. I hated sports almost as much as I hated showing my legs. I later accrued so many detentions for skipping gym class that I had to change schools to avoid them. After class, while all the other girls were changing, a soft-spoken girl with a tamed Jewish-fro approached me in the locker room. She looked older, exotic, gentle, and sturdy. In a sea of straight blond hair and polo shirts, strange looks, and little whispers, she was exactly who I was looking for. She was all hippie and since I looked like I was in terminal mourning, dressed in black with dark red lips and too much eyeliner, we were somehow a perfect pair.

After asking my name, introducing herself as Madeline, and welcoming me, one of the first questions she asked was:

"Do you like the Grateful Dead?"

All I knew about The Dead was their song "Touch of Grey." I

hated it. The Dead looked old and crusty and sounded watered down to me.

"Not really. Do you like U2 or Sinead O'Connor?" I asked.

"No," she responded kindly. "Do you smoke?" she asked.

"Yup," I said with a tone of relief. Off we went behind the school to smoke a butt before the next period.

Somehow, through the uncomfortable and awkward reaction of disdain for each other's music, there was a connection. Madeline possessed a darkness I recognized that was just as potent as her light. Right behind her gentle green eyes and wide smile, I could sense another wounded warrior. I had found my island.

We spent the majority of the next few years on her porch or hanging out behind buildings near the train tracks eating stolen donuts, smoking cigarettes, and having deep spiritual conversations. We were living through teenage trauma, digging deeper into the caverns of our budding souls to excavate and discuss the possible blessings of our wars. I'm not kidding when I say deep; there was no small talk between us. Some of those talks we had so many years ago have yet to be rivaled in my experience. We knew what we shared was rare and also essential to our finding our way through the sea of shit we'd experienced and were still wading through.

There was an unspoken bond of safety between us and, more often than not, the rarest gift of all—acceptance. There was no subject we couldn't broach if it had heart and meaning to us; there was nothing we could admit that wasn't met with some spoken or unspoken understanding. No one could break our bubble of protection when we were together on that porch in a sea of smoke and spirit.

Taking conversation, cigarettes, drugs, and humor as our blunt tools for craft, we began to build jagged new beginnings. We were trying to transform our pain and confusion into lives that made any kind of sense. We shared experience freely and without pretense, with the intention for the other to reach for the highest good. With Madeline, I began weaving my pain into song, recognizing and stringing together small graces into a new kind of history. We were planting tiny seeds recovered from the rubble of our devastations in hopes that they would one day become the fruit of victory. For each other, we could become a fair witness who'd see the wider frame of why we had to survive all of it. We were cultivating the courage to see and live through things as they were, rather than some fantasy of what we wanted them to be. Objectivity.

My bar for female friendship was set forever high during those few years. I didn't know at the time, but with Madeline I was intentionally creating a friendship consisting of the practice of love, loyalty, forgiveness, safety, laughter, compassion, honesty, fun, deliberate listening, reliability, generosity, and authenticity. Though I have stomped all over these qualities and people at times in my life, I come back, however clumsily, to remembering again, forgiving and asking for forgiveness again, choosing compassion with myself and others again, giving myself permission to start over, to keep practicing, and to keep showing up for myself and for the people in my life.

For this precedent, I am forever grateful.

Amie Penwell

Take the voice of an angel and drop it one octave, like a lover's moan, that's the sound of Amie Penwell. Once a newcomer from Massachusetts to the San Francisco Bay Area music scene, Amie Penwell has since made quite an impact. "Penwell is regarded by many in the Bay Area to be one of the next big heavyweights," said Mark Langton of the *Marin Independent Journal*. In 2012, along with her third release *Under City Lights*, Amie's song "Mercy" was featured in the documentary, *The Eyes Of Thailand*, which won Newport Beach Film Festival's 2012 Humanitarian Award. Penwell will appear as a featured vocalist on composer Jack Perla's next full-length record.

My Abortion Brought Us Together

Aspen Baker

Three drugstore purchased tests had proved it without a doubt. I was pregnant. Sitting on the toilet, looking at the tests lined up side by side on the tub, it was a typically cool and foggy summer day near the beach in San Francisco. I stared at the tests and saw my future as a mother.

It wasn't until later, when the guy brought it up, that abortion became an option. Even then, when I knew we wouldn't be together forever and faced that parenting would be mine to handle alone, I could better imagine myself as a struggling single mother before I could picture myself as a person who had an abortion.

It was just a few days after I took the pregnancy tests that I revealed my secret to Polly. Polly has more tattoos now than she did back then, but her natural charisma was as strong as ever. It was past 2:00 a.m. when we'd finished counting our tips and closing the downtown Berkeley bar where we worked. I declined our customary end-of-shift drink and told her why: "I'm not drinking because I'm pregnant. I don't know what I'm going to do yet." I don't know what I thought she'd say or how I hoped she'd help. But, I'll never forget what she revealed: Without hesitation, she said, "I've had an abortion."

Everything changed in an instant. I remember how that moment felt to this day. It was like a veil had been lifted and I finally saw the world as it truly was, behind all the secrets. I saw how much I didn't know about other people's lives, the challenges they face, the choices they make. And I thought of my own life. Here I was working all night behind the bar, making jokes, keeping things light when I felt anything but, and wondering, *can they tell I'm pregnant?* Did these customers, our regulars, know that I was different than I was last week? Did they know I had a secret? Could they tell I was in pain and dealing with the hardest decision of my life?

It's strange to have something so potentially life changing happen and not feel like you can talk about it with anyone else. I'd soloed my first airplane when I was 16, had driven by myself from Alaska to California (over 3,000 miles in ten days) at age 20, and had been the only woman selling bikes and skis with the guys at a Berkeley action-sports store just the year before, but this was the first time I'd ever felt truly alone. I was 24 and I felt heavy with the weight of the choice.

Polly's admission was a revelation. The old saying that you can't judge a person until you walk a mile in their shoes came alive. It would become my credo, shaping my future leadership. But that night at the bar it was exactly what I needed to hear. Polly gave me a gift in the knowledge that I was not alone in my experience.

Others had been through this too. Polly taught me that abortion is something that we can talk about. I realized then that there were probably many more women who'd had abortions than I'd ever considered. Much later, I would look at the facts and find out that nearly half of all women in America would have an abortion and that worldwide the average was even higher, at one abortion per woman. The ratio in the United States has gone down since then, but it's still high: today, one in three women in the United States will have an abortion in their lifetime. This figure shows that abortion is incredibly common. In fact, it's one of the most commonly performed surgeries in the United States. All the myths and stereotypes I'd held in my heart about people who have abortions started to fade away in the light of my new reality.

Soon after talking with Polly, I had an abortion. I wouldn't let the guy come with me. We were still talking, barely, but I was starting the next phase of my life and he wasn't going to be a part of it. I asked my friend Heather to go with me. I told her that I might back out at the last minute, unable to go through with it. I said this remembering a beautiful surfer girl from high school who had told me one day while we were

out in the waves off San Clemente that she was alive because her pregnant mother had walked out of an abortion clinic.

I didn't walk out and no miraculous spontaneous miscarriage
occurred. I went through with the abortion just like so many women
before and after me have done.

I didn't go through it alone. Heather was with me every step of the
way. Afterwards, we even tried to walk home together, but the Berkeley
hospital where I had my abortion didn't let patients walk out the door
on their own two feet, since they treated abortion like any other surgery and I was put under local anesthesia and went through pre- and
post-operative procedures laying beside other people who were having
their knees and organs fixed. So Heather wheeled me to her car in the
requisite hospital wheelchair and drove me the two blocks home.

At the time, we'd only just gotten to know each other. We'd met,
of all places, in a Women's Studies class at UC Berkeley. We were both
transfer students, a little older than everyone else, and looking to make
new friends. It's been 15 years since I first met Heather. We've gotten
to know each other a lot more since then and we've supported each
other through life's highs and lows. She has become one of my closest
friends.

While I was home recuperating from my abortion, I opened my
front door to find a short ceramic vase overflowing with purple flowers
and a card with my name on it. "Thinking of you," Jodie signed. I didn't
realize that it was okay for your friends to acknowledge or show they
cared when an abortion was involved. Polly and Jodie had been friends
for a long time and we all worked together as bartenders. I was the Bay
Area newbie and they knew everyone. I felt cared for and acknowledged by people I had just met. They taught me a lot about what it
means to show up for your friends.

Polly, Heather, and Jodie made me realize I wasn't alone. Polly
had been through her own abortion, Heather was with me through
mine, and Jodie wasn't afraid to reach out to show me that she cared. I

want every woman who experiences abortion to have a team like mine: people in their life who show up when they're needed most. At the time, I thought that my abortion would feel like one of the most isolating experiences of my life, but in reality, my abortion actually brought us closer together and turned my new acquaintances into lifelong friends.

Not long after that, I founded Exhale, an after-abortion talk line where women share their stories. At Exhale I have seen again and again that sharing and listening without judgment to stories that had previously been secret can bring women together, create new relationships, and strengthen existing ones. At Exhale, we call this storytelling approach "pro-voice."

For a dozen years, as Exhale has continued to grow, I've been telling my abortion story. I've shared it in almost every venue imaginable, in coffee shops and at cocktail parties, on national TV and radio, with journalists and activists, at conferences and on YouTube, and with family and friends. It's never been easy. To share openly about abortion is to open oneself up to misinterpretation, judgment, or worse.

But it's also transformative to share my real, human story about abortion, a subject that is often reduced in public conversation to simple talking points. I've told my story hundreds of times, and my story comprises many stories. My story is full of loss, love, challenge, and triumph. I could tell you the medical story and describe the hospital, its staff, and the bloody pad between my legs. I could tell you my decision-making story or the story about the guy. One day I may tell the story of how I healed my abortion pain by bringing home an abandoned furry girl (a Rottweiler I named Lucy, for Lucy Lawless, the real woman behind Xena the Warrior Princess) who was my constant companion until she died last year in my arms. All these stories and yet, I've had just one abortion. My abortion stories are as layered and nuanced as any human experience. Not made for easy consumption or political talking points. Despite the real risk of being judged or misunderstood, the result tends to be the opposite: the listener glimpses a deeper understanding of a real experience of abortion. We make a human connection.

Through my work, I hear stories of relief and regret, grief and happiness, and more. All of those stories are as real, complex, and human as my story, and together they illustrate a community of women who have had abortions. I believe that these women's real stories and voices are what can reshape public discussion about abortion.

When the voices and stories of women who have had abortions, along with the stories of our loved ones affected by abortion, are at the center of the public discourse and political decision-making around abortion, I believe we have the potential to transform the political debate from one of heated talking points to one of understanding. I believe we can usher in a new era of peace around the subject of abortion.

There are challenges to this vision. Our personal stories can be used to divide us—others can use our stories as evidence on either side of an argument—or they can easily be dismissed as just another tactic in the political debate. But there is a real value to storytelling that can't be taken away. As women who have experienced abortion, we can share our stories to be sure that no woman ever has to feel isolated or alone, we can share to offer our support and respect, and we can share to build connections and open new ways of thinking about a decision that affects so many people. That's what's so important to remember: stories have the power to bring people together, to move our collective discussion about abortion outside the expected rhetoric of politics.

This has been my abortion story of friendship and love. I share it to honor my friends, to say thanks to Polly, Heather, and Jodie for what they did all those years ago. I share it with the hope that others might relate to what I experienced. I share it as a reminder that sometimes the thing we fear we must keep secret is exactly the thing that, if revealed, can bring us together. I am pro-voice, and I am part of a growing movement of people who have experienced abortion who are shaping what's next in our own lives and our communities. I hope you join us.

Aspen Baker

Aspen Baker is the nation's leading voice on the personal experiences of abortion among women and men. The Founder and Executive Director of Exhale, an award-winning pro-voice organization changing the social climate around abortion, Baker has been featured in a variety of media outlets across the country, including CNN Headline News, Fox National News, *Ladies Home Journal*, the *New York Times*, National Public Radio, and many more. She lives in Oakland, California with her family and serves as a member of the Public Ethics Commission for the City of Oakland.

Far From Shore

Margaret Kathrein

We learn to know ourselves as we move through life's experiences. Sometimes the lessons are unforgettable.

The day began as any summer day, as I rushed into my routine without taking time to reflect on how special life was or how much I treasured my family.

That afternoon, I received the call that every mother dreads and my world came apart. My son had been in an accident.

"Your son's been attacked by a shark!" The words echoed in my ears and my heart pounded, "A great white shark attack . . . at Stinson Beach. He's lost a lot of blood."

I couldn't comprehend the words I was hearing. Shark attacks don't happen in normal life. This was no longer an ordinary day.

Suddenly everything changed and my world began to collapse. Jonathan, my 16 year old son was airlifted to a trauma center and was fighting for his life . . . and I was far away. Immediately, I blamed myself. I should have been there. Why wasn't I there when my son needed me? I imagined the pain and the fear he must have felt, so young and innocent and alone in the ocean, in the jaws of a creature so terrifying.

I could endure almost anything, but I could not handle losing my son. I knew I could not live without him. I had to get to Jonathan, to be with him and comfort him as I'd always done whenever he skinned a knee or fell from his bike as a child. I didn't want him to be alone or afraid. I was caught in my own panic; everything looked pale and ominous in the white heat of the summer afternoon.

I raced across San Francisco Bay to the hospital with my younger sons Michael and Eric beside me, helping me find my way and urging me to be strong. "Mom, you can't drive with tears in your eyes,"

Michael said, while every moment I feared we might lose someone so dear to us. Reed, my husband, met us at the emergency room door. Together we rushed inside, frantic to see Jonathan, only to spend seven long hours in the waiting room while a team of doctors worked on him. I prayed they could save his leg and his life. Finally the surgeon appeared to speak to us. "His leg looks like it's been through a chain saw accident," he said. "We're doing our best, but it's going to take longer than we thought."

I was numb, thinking only of Jonathan and what he'd endured in the ocean. I didn't want to cry, but the tears rolled down my face. Reed held me in one of those long, tight hugs. "C'mon, Marge," he said. "You're the glue that keeps us together. We all need you to be strong." Inside, I felt everything coming apart.

Finally, hours later, the doctor appeared again. "Jonathan is in the recovery room. You can see him now. It might be difficult for you to see him. He's been through a lot." As we stepped through the doorway, my eyes wandered over the shadows of the dimly-lit room. Fluorescent lights cast a hollow glow while doctors and nurses came and went, busily checking things I had not yet begun to comprehend. Everything looked unfamiliar. Then I saw Jonathan, motionless in the narrow bed, surrounded by equipment, tubes, and IV bottles. Red lights blinked and needles twitched on the gauges near his bed. Monitors flashed with colored messages. A silence hung over the room, interrupted only by the soft voices of nurses and doctors. They leaned over him, showing their concern even now, after the surgery was over.

"Our main concern is to avoid infection deep inside," the doctor whispered. "We're giving heavy doses of antibiotics, but we don't know for certain what's in the mouth of a shark. It's going to be touch-and-go for a while until he's out of danger."

We tiptoed closer to the bed where Jonathan lay asleep, drained of strength and energy. I could hear his shallow breathing. A confusing array of bandages and tubes crisscrossed his body. His leg was a web of stitches and staples. Long plastic tubes came from inside the skin, draining fluid out of his leg. His skin was stretched tight to pull together the gaping wounds and torn muscles.

Despite my efforts to contain my emotion, tears welled in my eyes. I held Eric's hand and I saw the tears in his eyes, too. His big brother, the one who'd always been so strong, the one who'd always helped him, was flat on his back unable to move.

I looked at the rows of tiny black threads tied in knots, protruding everywhere. Teeth marks punctuated his leg, with a maze of lines where the skin was torn in the shape of the jaws. Large staples held his knee together and a screw inserted below his knee reattached his tendon to the bone. His knee was swollen to many times the normal size, red and puffy where it was pulled and stapled together. He was a jigsaw of stitches and staples. One painfully long gash ran all the way up the side of his leg to his hip. I watched and listened, afraid to say a word.

"Jonathan . . . " Reed spoke softly, hovering over his injured son, tenderly touching his hand. Jonathan recognized the familiar voice and slowly opened his eyes, looking up into our faces. His eyes moved from one face to the next. When he looked at me, his smile lit up my life. We were a family—teary, proud, worried, and thankful. Our lives were so intertwined with his that nothing else mattered. His face and eyes looked puffy and swollen. My heart sank to see my son so injured and weak. And yet, seeing him alive was the most wonderful gift in the world.

Jonathan searched the room trying to make sense of his surroundings. He studied everything, as if he were a little boy again, trying to absorb where he was and what was happening. His face looked pale in the eerie light but his deep brown eyes were strong. He raised his arms, inviting our hugs and wanting us to be close to him. We encircled him with hugs and love, taking care not to bump his battered body. We were all there for him just as we would always be there for each other. I could see the gratitude in his eyes. "What can I do to help you, Jonathan?" I asked. "Just being here is good, Mom."

I smoothed his tangled, salty hair. I felt his feet to see if they were warm. "Your cool hands feel good, Mom," he murmured. "I'm glad you're here with me."

"Me too," I said. Staying close to him made me feel better, too. I brushed away the grains of sand still clinging to his face and hair and even inside his ears. I was surprised how sandy he was, even after all the hours of surgery. I thought of the swirling sand and water, and the struggle he must have endured fighting for his life in the jaws of an animal so powerful. I couldn't imagine how violent it must have been.

"I guess you beat the shark," Eric said. "Good job fighting back."

"Thanks." Jonathan reached out for Eric's hand and held it tightly.

"I'm really mad at that shark for trying to eat you," Michael said. "I'd like to go out and hunt it, like the ancient Hawaiians used to do, but I guess I'll forgive the shark for making a bad choice of meals."

Jonathan smiled at his brothers' remarks. Finally, after all these long and anxious hours, Jonathan's smile was the answer to my prayers. I was able to breathe again. His life was our miracle. For the next seven days in the hospital, I couldn't leave his side.

Over the coming days, weeks, and months, friends, neighbors, and our community members came to be with us, helping in every imaginable way. They cheered us with smiles, shark toys, mementos, flowers, food, cards, and prayers. Friends called Jonathan "Shark Boy" and "Shark bait." They teased that he must not have tasted very good to the shark, and praised him for his presence of mind. Jonathan smiled with pride, yet somehow he always managed to keep it light. "I'm not letting anything go to my head," he said, "I still have a lot of work to do to get better. And I'll need lots of help, Mom."

Jonathan's friend, Peter, and his mom, Nelly, brought chocolate from her homeland of Peru. "Last year when Peter was rushed to the hospital with a ruptured appendix and nearly died, you came," Nelly reminded us. "I remember what it's like when your child is in the hospital," she continued. "Every mom is very scared. Nothing can compare to the thought of losing a child." In that moment, I was reminded how vital friends really are, not just for our kids, but also for all of us.

Cecil, one of the moms from our playgroup, brought homemade muffins and a little stuffed shark. Jonathan's friends from swim team brought a big stuffed shark and stayed to visit. "Sharks are starting to fill my room," Jonathan laughed. Susan and her son Alan came with smoothies. Sean and his mom brought flowers and balloons. Vicky, my neighbor and constant sounding board, kept things running smoothly on the home front. Good cheer, stuffed animals, flowers, cards, and home-cooked meals reminded us that so many others cared for us and wanted to help. There was never a dull moment and I was glad for the calls and visitors. Our friends brought gifts from the heart, but their most important gift to us was just bringing themselves. I learned how the love and concern of others could heal us.

Even after Jonathan came home from the hospital, my lingering fears and concerns were relieved by the steady flow of friends and neighbors who helped in more ways than I could imagine. They helped to ease me back into my familiar schedule, so I could feel safe again and unburdened by worry. In that spirit, the next Friday my friends and I resumed our long-established tradition of Friday morning Moms' coffee day. We laughed and compared notes on raising our kids like we always had, shared advice about our lives and the funny things that always seemed to happen when you're already late for soccer practice. It was clear that my friends were a source of strength and spending time with them was what was most important. In a world that now seemed dangerous and unpredictable, their consistency reassured me and in turn, my friendships with them became stronger, giving me the confidence I needed to move beyond the attack.

The gratitude I felt for these relationships trickled over into every other part of my life. I began to find reasons to be thankful for everything and to perceive each day as a gift. On a run through the neighborhood, I noticed more than ever the sweetness of the air. I realized that all of life is now, before our eyes, and the people who support us make it richer. Until the day of the shark, I'd failed to grasp that; I hadn't treasured my family, my friends, and my life as if each day were my last.

Now that we've crossed the thin line back from the edge of peril, I recognize the fragility of life and how quickly it could be taken from me, and that has made me a more appreciative person. Life was presenting us with opportunities to meet people, to thank each other, and to grow closer to those we loved. I was in the right place. This was where I needed to be. I could see challenges ahead, but I couldn't let myself look upon the shark attack as misfortune because I'd learned to look at life in a new way. Jonathan was getting better and he wanted to get back to the ocean. With his improvement, I experienced my own. I could see life's majesty in the beauty of the ocean, and it was breathtaking. Finally, I could let go of fear and share my joy with others. We didn't know where our lives were headed, but with our friends, we'd get there ... all the while remembering that the hard times behind us expand our minds and make us stronger and better equipped.

I am better for this experience because it taught me to be more mindful of my connections with others—especially my female friends. Before, I hadn't stopped to think about how much they meant to me. I learned how awful it is to know the suffering of your child and to be powerless to prevent scary things, big or small, from happening. There were questions I could not answer and the world seemed out of control. When caring friends arrived, they lifted me to a new level where I felt more capable of coping because of their support. In this way, tough times remind us of the bounty of our relationships and prompt us to be there for others just as they were for us. Startling experiences remind us what's important in our lives and unimportant details melt away. I know now that when something happens to another, we mustn't wait to be invited, we must just show up. Each of us can make a difference for someone else in a time of challenge. Our presence, with a listening ear and an offer to help, can make more of a difference than anything else. Nurturing, caring, creating, and weaving together the strands of our lives with our friends' lives helps hold us all together. Somehow, when we stitch together the threads of our extraordinary lives, we connect with other people in the deepest sense. Feeling the bumps and potholes in the road as we travel together brings new depth to our relationships and richness to our appreciation for one another.

I still think about that day not so very long ago, when Jonathan was in a hospital bed, unable to move, hardly able to speak. He could barely open his eyes, but he really opened mine. When he faced the shark and fought back, he confronted a challenge he didn't know he could handle, showing us that we, too, could accomplish things we didn't know we could do. My shy son became a speaker, leading assemblies in schools to inspire children and to share the lessons he'd learned about life.

During his recovery, Jonathan and I spent many hours talking and writing about this experience, recording our thoughts, and what we'd learned. Our two books, *Surviving the Shark*, and *Far From Shore: A Mother's Memoir of a Shark Attack*, describe the details of our experience that day at Stinson Beach and beyond. Jonathan's children's book, *Don't Fear the Shark*, is a metaphor for our lives and treating others well. Our writing gave us an opportunity to reflect on what we'd learned from our experience: to nurture our relationships and to respect the world around us. We hope that sharing these life lessons will inspire others, too.

Looking back on our experience with the shark, I realize how scars have the mysterious ability to remind us of the stories of our lives, stories that become our family history. Our scars and memories, seen or unseen, represent experiences that have helped us grow and make us who we are meant to be. The battle scars of life awaken us to our potential and to the promise of each new day. Jonathan's scar dominates his leg, and is the source of endless questions and stories. It will always be a reminder of the path we had not expected to follow and the joys we found along the way.

I'm forever grateful for all of the women in my life who helped and supported me in countless ways throughout this experience. Until that day, I'd failed to recognize the true meaning of friendship and its importance in our lives. Each of us can truly make a difference in the lives of others just by being present.

Margaret Kathrein

Margaret Kathrein has written two books, *Far From Shore: A Mother's Memoir of a Shark Attack*, and *Surviving the Shark*, with her son Jonathan. She is also the author of *Crisis Management* and *Occupational Health Law*. Margaret is a director of E3, an educational nonprofit, former director of the Lucas Valley Homeowners, and member of the Cal Parent Advisory Board. She is a former international flight attendant for Pan Am and an attorney who specialized in food and drug law with a Chicago law firm. Margaret currently resides in Marin County, California, and is the mother of sons Jonathan, Michael, and Eric.

Friends, Strangers, Sisters, and Saviors

Medea Isphording Bern

Breast cancer is a scourge. My mother had it. Many of my friends have had it. Fortunate daughters and wives and colleagues survive lumpectomies, radiation, and chemotherapy. The unlucky ones die from aggressive cancer that takes them too soon, leaving their grieving husbands and children behind to navigate carpools, sports signups, and first dates without a mother's gentle and knowing hand. On select streets in my town, every woman has a lumpectomy scar, is taking Tamoxifen, or has reconstructed breasts that can no longer feel a lover's tender touch. For women today, receiving a breast cancer diagnosis can seem less a question of "if" and more a matter of "when."

It would be reasonable to expect that hearing, "You have cancer," followed by weeks of poking and prodding and testing would wear a person down and give her the right to scream and yell and spend hours and days wallowing in self-pity. Without the scores of women, friends, and strangers who spun a web of support around me, that is precisely what I would have done. Instead, their strength lifted me up and out of my despair.

My diagnosis arrived like thousands of others—out of the blue. No mysterious lump lurking beneath the skin. No unusual streaking or discharge. My cancer was sneaky. It grew in filaments as thin as gossamer that were undetectable on a mammogram. The radiologist found it only incidentally when she biopsied a suspicious cluster of cells. My cancer didn't live among those cells, but was hiding nearby.

I posted what I thought was a private message to a friend on Facebook because I lacked the pluck to call her and utter the paralyzing words "I have cancer." Within an hour, I heard from six women, a few of whom I had not laid eyes on for thirty years, offering support and telling me about their own breast cancer. These six had survived. They assured me I would too. The terror of this cancer diagnosis paralyzed me with its deadly implications, but their confident reassurances helped to relax its immobilizing grip.

My friend Karen, an erudite Texan and Episcopal priest, told me that women have an advantage over men because we learn early on that we lack control. The lesson is made clear during pregnancy. A life grows inside of us, pushing our bellies out, making us nauseated, wreaking havoc on our hormones, and all we can do is smile and wait. The same is true for breast cancer; although we eat right and exercise and think wholesome thoughts, it will still attack. It will toss us up high in the air, leaving us to fall back to earth without a safety net. But the women in our lives are watching and they will catch us just in time.

As word about my cancer spread, so did the flood of support. Women quietly living in their own private hell nevertheless put their issues aside to stand by me. Grace, a woman in her late seventies, had a double mastectomy forty years earlier and she held me while I fell apart. "You'll be fine, dear. Look at me!" Rita's sanity-saving gesture came while she was visiting her son, whose wife had just died, at age 54, from a brain tumor.

Wherever I went—cocktail parties, the supermarket, my son's sporting events, women who had heard about my diagnosis would stop me, offer a warm smile, an encouraging word, and relate their own story of survival. At one lacrosse game, there were five of us who either had a battle with cancer ahead or who were counting the months of survival post-treatment. Our immutable bond, born of disease and optimism, carried me through that long lacrosse season. Now, we watch out for each other's kids. We cry over the failure of the mammogram. We bleed together when another woman hears the words, "I'm sorry. You have cancer." We wait for a cure.

So many women rallied to support me in untold ways. A friend who cares for her fragile parents and whose husband has survived brain cancer, called every day after my diagnosis, just to check in.

An acquaintance whose mother and sister both died of breast cancer offered to come and sit with me for as long as I might need, so I would not be afraid. A colleague offered to host a lingerie party for me, as she understands my fetish for sexy underthings. One friend cut short her workouts so she could deliver me to doctors, labs, and finally, to the hospital. Two women whose sons grew up with mine insisted on setting up a post-surgery dinner delivery service for me. I will never forget the 30 women (and one special man) who took time to plan, shop, prepare, and deliver nourishing meals so my family would be free to rest and recover with me.

Dozens of high school friends, now dispersed across the country, sent prayers and words of encouragement every few days. Old babysitters, neighbors, friends of friends, my hairstylist, people I had known forever and those I barely knew at all came through with cards, care, hope, and love.

Our mobility has cast us far from our birthplaces, the familiarity of the streets we roamed as children, and the security of our families. We learn the nuances and contours of our adopted towns and reach across fences, lunch counters, and playgrounds to find new emotional connections and to give and receive the solace of women we know will form our new foundation, just as we will form theirs.

None of this is meant to discount the love and support offered from the men in my life. My teenage son stayed with me in the hospital, slept intermittently between my nurse and doctor visits, and lived on hospital food. A new friend drove an hour to deliver a home-baked, Southern comfort-food feast: his famous fried chicken, greens, and buttermilk biscuits. My best buddy who lives in Guatemala wrote to me every single day, sometimes three times a day, to let me know he held me close in his heart even though we live two thousand miles apart. My husband, though scared senseless, composed upbeat email reports about my status for family and friends.

But only a female friend truly understands the significance of our breasts: how we wait for them to bud as young girls, how we marvel at their power as we mature, and the pure joy and delight that comes from nursing our babies. Only a female friend can sit by our side, strong and quiet, as we mourn their loss. Only a woman can grasp the grief that comes from losing a part of ourselves so intrinsic to our concept of femininity. Of course a woman without breasts is still a woman. Isn't she?

My breasts had served for years as faithful stewards of my sensuality. I forgave them their droop—they'd earned the right to relax. Breast cancer would at best leave them with a scar and at worst, it would take them from me forever. One friend joked that the silver lining would be a boob job paid for by insurance. It's hard to argue with that logic, but still, the thought made me cry.

I agonized over whether or not to remove my breasts. Women I knew and women I had never met spent hours with me on the phone, in coffee shops, and walking the hills as I weighed the pros and cons of the decision. One friend cancelled her own doctor's appointment to talk me through her decision to have a mastectomy, describing the intricacies of the operation and recovery in terms my doctors had never used. Another friend drove thirty miles to answer my questions face to face. A third showed me her scars and her tattooed nipples, full and vivid disclosure of the way my own chest might look if I went ahead with the surgery.

Thinking about kissing my breasts goodbye left me desperate. I knew a mastectomy meant losing all sensation in my chest. My doctor could not promise he could save my nipples. I might develop a particular complication (lymphedema) that permanently disfigures one's arms. None of these frightening prospects existed with the less aggressive treatment, lumpectomy and radiation. Without removing all of my breast tissue, this sneaky cancer could recur, undetectable and lethal. The thought of missing my sons' graduations and weddings for vanity's sake seemed selfish and shortsighted. After weeks of studying websites, statistics, lab reports, and my own soul, I decided to undergo a double mastectomy. As the surgery date approached, I hatched a plan to hold on to my breasts forever by casting my chest in plaster.

Two days before surgery, I mentioned my casting plan to a close friend and fellow breast cancer survivor. She knew of yet another breast cancer patient, one who had cast scores of breasts for women stung by our disease. She promised to contact a mutual friend, Laurel, who could put me in touch with Haley, the caster.

By noon the next day, with 18 hours to go before surgery, I had yet to connect with either Laurel or Haley. Panicked, I called an art supply store in San Francisco and found it carries casting kits. I could just get there, get home, and get plastered before bedtime.

The clerk gently explained proper gauze casting technique: "Cut the gauze into one-inch rectangular strips, soak them in warm water, layer them six-deep, rig a cord round your neck to hold the cast taut while it hardens. It's pretty easy, just messy." Just like cancer: easy to get, messy to fix.

On the way home, my friend phoned to let me know she had found Laurel and given her my number. Laurel and I traded phone and text messages. The clock was ticking. They had a yoga class at 8:00 p.m., so the chance of getting together was growing slim.

I sped home and dumped the gauze on my cold, stainless steel kitchen counter. Time was running out. Cutting the gauze with shaking hands, teary eyes, and knots in my stomach left me with strips resembling waves, not rectangles. Not casting tonight was not an option; tomorrow my breasts would be gone. The doorbell rang. It was Laurel and Haley. They had found my address and swooped in like guardian angels to make sure I had my keepsake. I whipped off my shirt and these two strangers went to work layering wet gauze across my naked chest.

Haley and Laurel showed trademark female compassion. Their selflessness and calm allowed me to enter the surgical suite the next morning with my breasts cast and my mind free from fear.

Fortunate is a pitifully insufficient word to describe how lucky I am to have been warmed by the superabundant light from the grace of so many empathic women. They created a tsunami of generosity that rolled in day after day, month after month; a tidal wave of unselfishness that still continues. They have given me a priceless gift: the chance to live each day of the rest of my life out loud.

No one can predict the course of this disease. All of the reassurance and buttressing in the world does not ensure survival. Yet as I entered this maze of fear and dread, the hands of friends and strangers held my salvation; their faith gave me the power to fight and, at least for now, to win. We may lack a certain control, but our drive to serve as a rudder when a sister snaps her mast is undeniable, unrelenting, and unmistakable.

Medea Isphording Bern

Medea Isphording Bern is a writer/essayist who lives in California's San Francisco Bay Area with her husband, two sons, and three cats. When she isn't writing, she loves concerts, travel, cooking, scuba and sailing—common themes in her work. She also roots loudly for the San Francisco Giants. She is studying writing through Stanford University's Creative Non-fiction certificate program. Because she lives in a house bursting with testosterone, Medea keeps in touch with her feminine side through frequent visits with her treasured girlfriends.

Taking Turns

Janine Kovac

In the photo album of my memory, alongside the list of my children's firsts—first words, first steps, first solid food—is Room 1022, the play-group where I brought my twin boys every Tuesday for the first year and a half of their lives.

On this particular Tuesday, Michael is exploring the steps of a toddler-sized slide while Wagner scoured the floor for Cheerios. I strategically place myself between the two, ready to attend to either in a single bound. The boys are 15 months old, not quite walking yet. As Michael loses his footing on the steps, I reach out to catch him. When I return my attention to Wagner, I see that he has crawled across the room to sit next to Cathy Coggins, an early intervention specialist. Cathy facilitates the playgroup for babies who were born prematurely or have other physical problems such as cerebral palsy, under-developed lungs, or weak hearts.

Cathy is like a lantern, not a spotlight. Her perspective is broad and takes in the entire context, not just pointed specifics. She has this magnetic energy that coaxes out the inner calm you didn't even know you had. She's like a kind, forgiving conscience.

Sitting on the rug next to Wagner, Cathy looks at him, smiling. He looks at her, not smiling. She taps her hand twice on the floor between them and then rests it in her lap. Wagner watches her hand and looks back at her face, waiting. She does it again, *tap, tap, rest, look*. And again, *tap, tap, rest, look*. She is teaching him how to talk. In developmentally delayed children such as mine, the first lesson isn't sign language or baby talk. The first lesson is teaching them to focus on a single inter-action. It's what infant development specialists like Cathy call "joint attention"—and it's what parents of normally developing children take for granted.

Cathy taps, rests, and repeats the game several times. Then it happens: Wagner thumps his pudgy hand on the floor and looks at her, expectantly. Just like that, he has learned the second lesson of learning how to talk: taking turns.

At 15 months old, my boys should have a minimum of six words in their vocabularies. At the very least they should know that I am Mama or turn their heads when I call their names. But my boys are micro-preemies born at 25 weeks' gestation—a full three months before they were due. So while their chronological age is 15 months, their developmental age is 12 months or even younger.

Micro-preemies usually spend the first three or four months of their lives in the newborn intensive care unit—the NICU. My boys were no exception. For the first two months, they had machines to breathe for them and were fed through IVs and feeding tubes. Both boys needed surgery to repair a faulty arterial valve (a condition common in micro-preemies). These surgeries were followed by several blood transfusions. A year after their multi-month hospital stay, the boys are relatively healthy, but they are still developmentally delayed. At 15 months, they still do not walk or talk.

Every Tuesday, as we navigate our way through the hospital to Room 1022, I field the same questions.

"Twins?" people ask, as if it weren't obvious.

"So big!"

"So cute!"

"What do you feed these guys?"

The twins are quite chubby now. One would never guess that Michael, the bigger one, was born weighing just one pound, 12 ounces.

Sometimes we get different questions: "Are they walking yet? Talking? Climbing? You must have your hands full!"

I used to tell the truth: "No. No. Maybe soon. Yes." I'd explain that my boys were delayed because they were micro-preemies who were born very small and very early.

"How early?" they'd ask.

"Fifteen weeks early," I used to say. And then I'd watch the color drain from their faces.

"Oh, how awful!" they'd exclaim.

These days when asked about the twins, I just lie. After all, those people are just strangers. A little fibbing won't hurt anyone and it saves me the looks of horror and pity.

"Oh, yes! They climb like little monkeys!" I lie cheerfully.

Hopefully the twins will catch up, but it's also possible that their delays will become disabilities. We come to Cathy's playgroup because early intervention will give my boys the specialized attention that could make the difference.

The class meets every week and offers parents specific exercises to improve their babies' gross motor skills (sitting up, crawling, walking), fine motor control (used for grasping toys, stacking blocks, or holding a cup), and language acquisition.

Nearly every mother arrives late, huffing and puffing, pushing a stroller and dragging a diaper bag, trying to shake the idea that we are all here because something is wrong with our babies.

"We're just glad you came," Cathy always says with a smile, adjusting her black-rimmed glasses and pointing to an open spot on the floor where we can join the circle on the rug.

During the playgroup, Cathy invites the mothers to share their stories, prompting us through various icebreakers such as, "What was your favorite toy as a child?"

Most of the families have been through a lot: surgeries, health scares, hospitalizations, and we all face uncertain futures. Cathy's prompts are always positive, though, and seem to find the common thread between parents of different cultures, religions, and ages, regardless of economic or marital status. After each mother introduces herself, the connection we feel to each other is palpable. It becomes an invitation to open up even more.

Some kids, like Julia, are doing great. Their moms often hear, "You'd never guess she was a preemie!"

Then there are babies such as Kikiko, who is four months old and still only weighs seven pounds. He weighed three pounds at birth—even though he was born at full term. Kikiko's mother lies to strangers, too. She tells them that her son is only a few weeks old. She got tired of explaining why her son is so tiny. No doubt, it was just curious bystanders making innocent comments, but to Kikiko's mother, their small talk felt like hailstones.

Kikiko has a vacant stare and his eyes don't track moving objects, even when they are dangled right in front of his face. But when he hears his mother's voice, he turns sharply in her direction and flaps his arms excitedly like a baby penguin trying to fly. This is the story Kikiko's mom shares with us when she answers Cathy's question of the week: What new thing did your baby do this week? As if on cue, Kikiko turns to look at his mother when she speaks.

"You know your Mama, don't you Kikiko?" says Cathy to the little baby.

But Kikiko is still flapping at his mother. He adds a couple of kicks and squeals.

"Only has eyes for Mama," she says to Kikiko's mother, whose gaze is fixed on her son.

Cathy points out that while it looks simple, the locked mother/baby stare is actually a developmental milestone. I know from experience how proud (and relieved) Kikiko's mom must feel now that she can mark this milestone off the list.

Next to Kikiko and his mother is Donna. Her twins are identical, but only one baby is showing signs of cerebral palsy. Donna's sick of hearing the question, "What happened?" She'd rather concentrate on how she can get her baby to turn his head evenly to both sides. Or how she can prop him up in the sitting position that's good for his tiny hip sockets. After the physical therapist shows Donna how to arrange pillows around her son, Cathy points out that while the baby prefers to turn his head to the right, Donna can get him to exercise his neck muscles by holding him on her lap and using her right arm like an over-the-shoulder seat belt. If she dangles interesting baubles to the baby's left side, he'll turn to look at them.

This gives Donna some ideas. "I could call his name from behind his left shoulder!"

"That's a great idea," Cathy confirms in her soft, velvety voice.

"Maybe I could just nurse him on one side so that he always turns his head to the left to nurse."

One of the other mothers chimes in. "You could nurse him in a cradle hold on one side and then in a football hold on the other. Then you could nurse from both sides but he always nurses to the left."

The group brightens and buzzes, nodding in agreement as if we've solved the climate crisis.

One Tuesday, a new mother comes into Room 1022 with her daughter, Celeste, who was born at seven months' gestation and spent ten weeks in the hospital. On her fourth day home, Celeste suddenly stopped breathing and was rushed to the emergency room. The doctors determined she had a respiratory virus that is nothing more than a common cold for most children but is deadly for micro-preemies. Celeste spent a week in the hospital. The mother tells her story, not for sympathy, but by way of excuse as to why they had to miss the previous two weeks of the playgroup.

Oh, how awful, I want to say. But I don't. I have no idea what this mother has been through with her baby; I only know what I went through with mine. I know that when people hear your story and say, "Oh, how awful!" it makes you feel even worse. But I don't know what else to say. Fortunately, Cathy does. She reaches toward the young mother, placing her hand on the floor.

"That must have been scary for you," she says.

The young mother nods solemnly. She tells us how her boyfriend, the baby's father, was home at the time. As soon as he saw Celeste's lips turn blue, he revived her with mouth-to-mouth resuscitation and rushed her to the emergency room.

"I could have never done that," I want to say. But again, I know from experience that this will not make her feel better. People constantly tell me, "I could never have done what you did." Translation: I'm so glad I didn't have to do what you did. I have to admit, that's exactly what I'm thinking about this young mother's situation. I'm so glad I've never had to give mouth-to-mouth to my newborn.

Cathy has a better remark. "Your boyfriend responded quickly and knew just what to do." She says it matter-of-factly, without any exclamation points, as if she is narrating the event.

The young mother's face lights up. "Oh yes!" she says, proudly. "He was with her everyday at the NICU. Doctors said they never saw a more attentive father. He went to the CPR class and everything. He knew just what to do."

I nod knowingly. The sight of mothers at their baby's bedside is commonplace but the sight of fathers is rare. I want to pipe up and say that my husband was at my boys' side everyday, too. But I don't. Instead, I watch Cathy to see what she will say.

"We were just talking about our babies names," Cathy says in her soothing, calm way. "How did you come up with your daughter's name?"

The young mother smiles broadly. Her daughter is named after a favorite aunt. The tension in her face melts away as she shows off the matching cap and booties the aunt knitted for her namesake. Watching her mood shift changes mine as well. Suddenly we are all just proud mothers again, glowing as we show off our babies.

A month later, I'm at the library with the twins. We're sitting on the floor reading a book when a woman comes up and asks, "How old are they?"

This is a tricky question. My boys are now 16 months old but they still don't look it. I don't want to give any answers that might solicit follow-up questions and lead into the territory of "Oh, how awful!" So I tell her that they are one year old.

"My son's one year old, too! When is their birthday?"

I'm trapped in my lie. I don't really want to tell her that my babies are nearly four months older than they look and act, but I can't think quickly enough to make up a fake birth date. I come clean. Backtracking, I tell the woman that my sons are actually 16 months old but they were preemies. She asks more questions. How early were they? How long were they in the hospital? What did I do?

I smile mechanically and answer her questions. To which she responds, "I could never have done that." Maybe I should have stuck to my lies.

After a pause the woman continues, "My son was a twin." And then for emphasis, she repeats, "Was."

Now she's the one with the mechanical smile. I imagine what Cathy would say. One of my homework assignments as I try to help my sons with their language delays is to observe their gestures and copy them. The gestures come before the words; they communicate a lot, Cathy tells us.

And so, because I don't have the words to say to this stranger, I communicate with gestures. When I want to ask her how it happened that one of her twins died, I put my hand on the floor toward her, reaching out to her instead. When she tells me that she is so grateful for little Blake—he's such a blessing—but sometimes she wonders what it would be like to have two . . . I realize that this is what she pictures when she looks at my boys toddling around, chewing on books, and grabbing them from each other. I can't think of anything to say, so I put my hand on my chest and nod. And when she forces her smile, I don't smile back. It's my way of saying, "I know what it's like to pretend that everything is ok."

At the end of our conversation—even though I haven't said a word—the woman thanks me.

The following Tuesday I push my stroller through the doors of Room 1022. When I unbuckle Wagner from his seat and put him on the floor, he immediately crawls over to Cathy and taps on the floor. He looks at her and smiles proudly. I smile, too. Cathy's playgroup has taught us both how to communicate.

Janine Kovac

Janine Kovac writes about her experience as a NICU mom for the science-based parenting site *Raising Happiness.* She is an alumna of the Squaw Valley Community of Writers, blogs for The Writing Mamas, is the editor of the *Community Gratitude Journal* at the Greater Good Science Center, is program event coordinator for Write On, Mamas!, and is a database architect for Litquake, San Francisco's annual literary festival. Janine lives in Oakland, California with her husband and three children.

Common Sense

Susan Blankenbaker Noyes

Once upon a time, Joan earned her MBA at the University of California, Berkeley, where she met her husband, Brent. Fast forward ten years and Joan is now raising their two children, running their household within budget and without full-time help, and holding down a part-time job. She also donates a significant amount of her time to her children's school and to other nonprofits that align with her values. Despite these many commitments, Joan still manages to prioritize her girlfriends; sharing time, joys, and frustrations with them has always been a focus of hers and that hasn't changed in the shadow of her increased responsibilities. Joan can get all of this done—and done well—because she is a woman.

Until 2010, Brent was too busy at a boutique investment firm to help Joan with their domestic responsibilities. When the economy crashed under a mountain of debt created primarily by males using obscure financial instruments like derivatives that were supposedly being regulated, Brent was laid off. His next job—risk management at JP Morgan—demanded fewer hours of work, but his ego was still so bruised that he couldn't summon the energy to help with family responsibilities, let alone to nurture his relationships. Unfortunately, Brent's new job also disappeared, this time under the tsunami of loss and disappointment caused by the London Whale and the bank's risky trades.

The point of this tale is not if Joan and Brent lived happily ever after. The point is to contrast the qualities of Joan's that make her successful in her many roles with the qualities of Brent's that render him unsuccessful in his. The innate values by which most women live—particularly well-educated, multi-tasking mothers like Joan—would not have permitted the myopic, selfish course chosen by Wall Street titans who piled debt on debt using specious mortgages in transactions they didn't really understand. Women are too fair, aware, and empathetic for that. Most women wouldn't let their friends take such imminently disastrous actions, either. If only Joan and her friends had been running our financial system, instead of Brent's cohorts, perhaps our country wouldn't have suffered such arduous economic times, and Brent would likely have more meaningful relationships and better professional standing.

Women make their resources go a long way. As CEO's of their households, they not only balance their checkbooks, but they use their time and money in ways that help others, too. Women innately create and support win-win scenarios that strengthen their family and help others, without losing sight of their personal goals. A glimpse into Joan's before-school routine provides a good example of this dynamic.

"Bobby, don't forget to take all our Box Tops For Education to school," she reminds her son, as she finishes the sack lunches and organizes the dinner she volunteered to make for a local family fighting cancer.

"Also, we need to leave for school early so I can drop off a dress that Jacob's mom is borrowing for her opening party tomorrow night," she calls over her shoulder while changing a load of laundry. Joan is smart enough to create derivatives; she's just too busy and other-centered to do so. That's normal for women: they don't obfuscate, they collaborate. Women build relationships and connections, not houses made of cards.

Although it's too late to avert the financial meltdown of 2008 and subsequent global recession, it's not too late to build a sustainable recovery around the example set by women like Joan. Aligning investment and hard work with decent, understandable values is the most obvious path to a better world and a strong financial future. Because of the connection women feel with one another and the responsibility they feel for their families, women would be inclined to choose this smart, dependable, balanced course of action. In fact, there is substantial evidence that this is already happening.

Amanda Steinberg founded DailyWorth in January 2009, four months after the market crash, in order to give women "practical tips, empowering ideas and . . . key insights into building real net worth." It's now a booming business with over 300,000 subscribers. The female staff uses refreshingly honest self-deprecation to foster an emotional connection with the reader, before delivering easy to understand, helpful advice. For example, in her bio, editor in chief MP Dunleavey confesses, "It has been (cringe) a full year since I discovered that . . . my life insurance policy lapsed. And yet, I've done nothing about it. But I swear to fix it before tax day. If you don't get a post from me saying it's done, hunt me down and beat me to shreds."

Contrast this clarity and candor with JP Morgan's more obtuse online advice and their tagline, "Managing Risk and Utilizing Volatility." Can anyone really feel good about using this ostensibly abstract risk management strategy? Women-owned DailyWorth is growing a smart business with its transparent girlfriend-to-girlfriend advice at the same time it's helping its audience grow financially. Win for the readers, win for DailyWorth, and win for the world.

Female-owned small businesses like these are on the cutting edge of current economic growth. And clearly, they have the right idea. According to the United States Small Business Administration, *Forbes Magazine*, and American Express, women are starting new small businesses at a faster pace than men. American Express estimates that there are more than 8.3 million women-owned businesses in the United States, generating nearly $1.3 trillion in revenue and employing nearly 7.7 million people. These businesses exceed the growth rates of all but the largest publicly traded firms.

In less-developed countries, microfinance and social enterprise projects repeatedly show that women working together create the surest route to economic development and better lives. Through the microfinance site Kiva, women consistently make a little money go a long way in countries around the world, just like Joan does in her own household. They borrow a small amount to start a business—like weaving baskets, creating sewing cooperatives, or growing a small plot of vegetables—then spend their profits on health care, education, and improving life for their families. They also reinvest to grow their businesses and quickly repay their loans.

In Afghanistan, Arzu Studio Hope provides social support and jobs to female weavers and then sells their beautiful rugs internationally. The company launched in 2004 with 30 women weaving on the outskirts of Kabul. It's grown to 600 weavers in nine remote villages and now also offers education and health care. Arzu's most recent success is a new women's community center in Bamyan, with flush toilets, a laundromat, tearoom, solar power, and classrooms where both the women and children are educated.

It will come as no surprise that Arzu Studio Hope was the brainchild of a woman. Connie Duckworth, an American mother of four who was also a trailblazer at Goldman Sachs, founded it. She was the first female at Goldman Sachs to run a desk, then a division, then to make partner in sales and trading. Duckworth also served as a US emissary to Afghanistan. "When I saw the horrible conditions that Afghan woman suffered," she said, "I just knew I had to help." Behold: empathy at no cost to financial awareness. These two qualities are simply not mutually exclusive for a woman.

Even more evidence that women are powerful: Their intuitive urge to help probably accounts for the success of cause-related marketing. 92 percent of American women in Joan's demographic—educated, affluent women over the age of 25—will change their brand loyalty if they think the decision will make the world a better place. Women will not only change brands, but they will spend more money when they believe those dollars are helping others as well as themselves. Think Starbucks, where proceeds for an expensive cup of coffee also provide a better life for small coffee growers in Africa or South America; think Whole Foods, which promotes organic, locally sourced food and resources; think Costco, which provides more benefits for its employees than Wal-Mart.

Women love to use their dollars in support of the women right in their backyards, too. Across the country, women host shows of all kinds—jewelry, art, fashion, kitchen, and lingerie, whatever—in their homes. They invite their friends, open a bottle of wine, and a vibrant micro-economy flourishes for the evening. Local economies improve when women believe in the values or a cause underlying their purchases. Shop for the Cure, Ladies Night Out, and Grocery Dollars for the School are great examples of this. The shopper gets what she needs, helps a cause important to her, and often, she is doing this while visiting with a cherished friend.

"Real estate got us into the 2009 recession and real estate will lead us out," said the CEO of Coldwell Banker Real Estate, Jim Gillespie. If that's the case, the United States would be better served once again if we replaced some of the Brents with some of the Joans: Turns out, women drive the residential real estate market, too. In a vast majority of real estate transactions, women hold the deciding vote for which homes to purchase. Pricing and marketing home sales to women with common sense has been proven to sell more homes faster than any other residential real estate practice.

If Wall Street, our government, and our real estate practices were adjusted to operate with the same characteristically female values of fairness, open-mindedness, and compassion that Joan does, our economy, our country, and our world would be a much better place.

Susan Blakenbaker Noyes

Susan Blakenbaker Noyes is the founder and president of *Make It Better Media*, the most trusted, user-friendly online community resource and print magazine serving Chicago, Illinois' northern suburbs. Her board memberships include the Harvard Graduate School of Law, the Children's Memorial Hospital, the Chicago Symphony Orchestra, and many more. Susan practiced law for Sidley Austin from 1983–1989 and then focused her efforts toward philanthropy and volunteerism while raising six children.

Section Three

Modern Motherhood

My Mother's Chutney

Joyce Maynard

When my mother died, she left lots of stuff behind: soaps and shower caps (and the occasional towel) from every hotel she'd ever visited; packets of glitter and rhinestones and interesting bits of rickrack she'd set aside to use in craft projects with my daughter, who, more than anything, loved spending a weekend with her grandmother. A child of the Depression, my mother could never abide waste or throw anything of quality away, and so, if an outfit went out of fashion, she salvaged pieces of the fabric for doll clothes first, and always cut the buttons off to put in her button jar. Defrosting her freezer after her death, I found a couple dozen packets of chicken necks, hearts and livers—enough giblets to make broth for five hundred meals, I bet.

But it was in her cupboard that I found my mother's greatest stash. I'm guessing that at some point, a friend's tree must have yielded a great quantity of peaches, and the friend had known just who to call. There were 31 containers of peach chutney canned, according to their labels, just a few months earlier, in the fall of 1988. Until the diagnosis came that she had an inoperable brain tumor, anyone who knew my mother would have supposed she'd be around for decades. I disposed of the giblets and plenty besides, but I packed those 31 jars into a cardboard box and brought them home with me.

At first, I used my mother's chutney liberally. I spread it lavishly on toast. I set out a big dish of it at Thanksgiving. I even gave some away. But mostly I used the chutney in a particularly fine recipe my mother had taught me for curried chicken salad.

Years passed, and the number of chutney jars on my shelf dwindled down to the single digits. Sometimes, I'd make my turkey curry salad with Major Grey's chutney, rather than opening up one of the few remaining jars that still bore a label in my mother's handwriting. Other times I'd combine a couple of dollops of my mother's chutney with the store-bought stuff. I can't truthfully tell you that my mother's chutney was better: the chutney was made by my mother . . . that's all.

Of course these moments when I opened up the chutney were hardly the only occasions in which my mother came to mind. Now and then, out on the street I'd see a woman in her mid-sixties—the age my mother was at her death—and something about the purpose of her stride or the way she stopped to inspect a bargain would summon my mother back, and I'd feel the way I can imagine a landlocked sailor might, suddenly catching a gust of wind that smelled of the sea.

One time, I took the older of my two sons to a jazz concert in New York in which the singer Ruth Brown was appearing. When she stepped onto the stage and began to sing, tears streamed down my cheeks. Though Charlie was only ten at the time, he didn't need an explanation. Although Ruth Brown was much better at staying on key than my mother ever had been (not to mention that she was black, where my mother was a Russian Jew), something about her style and manner and her command of the stage reminded us both of my mother. After that, I took to buying tickets to see Ruth Brown whenever she performed near me. Every time I hear her sing, I cry.

In moments like those, it's as though I'm catching hold of my mother for a moment. But as the years pass and more distance lies between where I am now and where I was when she died, this has been getting harder. If my mother showed up on my doorstep this afternoon, she would no longer know me the way she used to. I'm not the same person that I was seven years ago.

It's been a few years since I've reached into the pocket of some garment of hers (that used to smell of her perfume, but no longer does) to find a coupon from a store in Toronto or a scribbled shopping list. By this year—the seventh since my mother's death—what was left in the way of tangible evidence of her presence on this earth were a few pieces of her jewelry. Books. Photographs. Chutney.

This spring I made the decision to move from my lifelong home in New England to Northern California. It was crazy to haul my one remaining jar of chutney three thousand miles; the time had come to finish it off.

I didn't make a big deal of the whole thing. I waited until I had some leftover chicken hanging around. Nobody was coming over for dinner and my children don't like my mother's curry chicken salad. This meal was going to be for me alone.

I took the jar down off the shelf. I imagined my mother spooning this very chutney into the jar eight years earlier, maybe feeling the slightest twinge of dizziness or throbbing in her head, but chalking it up to some diet she was on in her perpetual pursuit of getting into a size 12. "If I ever get a brain tumor," she used to say, as far back as I can remember, "I'm going to give up counting calories."

I cut up the chicken and the green pears and the slivered crystallized ginger. I spooned in the mayonnaise and scattered the golden raisins on top. I sprinkled in chopped coriander and walnuts and curry. I opened the jar. Inside, mold. There was nothing to do but to dump the whole thing down the sink. I would never again taste food prepared by the hand of my mother.

That afternoon, I went to the store and bought an expensive jar of gourmet chutney. Stirring it into my turkey, mayonnaise, and celery mixture, I thought about another kitchen lesson from my mother. With store-bought food, she used to say, there's one ingredient that's always missing. The food may taste great, but it wasn't made with love. Simple as that. Major Grey makes terrific chutney all right, but I can't call him up and ask him what to do about lumpy gravy. Of course, I can't call up my mother any more, either.

Still, I feel her presence in my kitchen every time I cook, no matter which coast I'm living on. I hear her voice at my elbow—offering scathing opinions about baking with margarine or processed garlic powder, over-handled piecrust, or any recipe featuring cream of mushroom soup as an ingredient. I hear her voice when I clean the giblets out of a chicken I'm preparing to roast, wrap them in plastic, and stick them in my freezer for soup. I heard her voice as I cleaned out my closets before I moved. I got rid of my old clothes, but first, I cut off a few of the best buttons.

Joyce Maynard

Joyce Maynard has been a writer of both fiction and nonfiction for over forty years. She has published two best-selling memoirs—*Looking Back* and *At Home in the World*. Her seven novels include *To Die For* and *Labor Day*, which is being adapted into a film starring Kate Winslet and Josh Brolin. In addition to writing, Joyce performs frequently as a storyteller with The Moth in New York City, and with Porchlight in San Francisco, near her Marin County, California home. She runs the Lake Atitlan Writing Workshop, at Lake Atitlan, Guatemala, where her particular focus and love is assisting other writers in the telling of their stories.

My Many Mothers

Cristina Robinson

I grew up in a girls' boarding school in Brazil from the age of seven, after both my parents had passed away. As a result, I grew up without a traditional mother-daughter relationship. In place of that, the school's headmistress and my friends' mothers became my own mothers. Everything I know about life, men, family, and marriage, I learned from these kind women who reached out and helped me, giving me the gift of motherly guidance that every girl needs and deserves.

All my mothers knew that I longed to have a family of my own someday, so that I could give the mother-child relationship that I didn't have to my own children. I fondly remember the hours they each spent with me, talking and sharing anecdotes from their own lives, asking me questions, and making me read newspapers, books, and anything else that would expand my knowledge of the world.

I learned something different from each mother because they each had their own personality; it made for an interesting and fun childhood. I was brought up with respect for my elders and always looked up to the adults in my life. It was a privilege to listen to their stories and to learn from their life experiences. Rolling of the eyes was unheard of, even in the most uncomfortable circumstances; children in my community were always respectful. I paid the same respect to all of my mothers, even though some made more of an impact on me than others because of the time I spent in their homes and what they taught me.

Each of my mothers gave me an extraordinary gift as they passed me their special messages.

My Mama Maria was a woman of deep integrity. When I was growing up, she was a professor at the local university and I knew, whenever she got a hold of me, I wouldn't be leaving her presence for quite some time. She taught me about the value of being a woman of honor and about keeping my word and holding that sacred. She told me, "Never be afraid to express your opinion, even if people don't agree with you. Never stand behind anonymity when you have something important to say." From Mama Maria, I learned that it's important to have courage and to hold strong in my convictions, even when others disagree; real life is not a popularity contest. She also taught me that the world didn't owe me anything and that I would have to earn everything that I wanted out of life in order to deserve it.

My Mama Márcia was a rebel who ran her household like a commune. Everyone was welcome but you had to follow her rules. She was fun to be around, but if you didn't toe the line, you would hear it from her. She would gather us girls in one corner and talk to us for hours, telling stories about her life and sharing secrets about her friends' mistakes so we wouldn't repeat them. She was a strong woman with a sharp tongue, but she was fair and just in her assessments of people and situations.

She taught me the importance of being true to myself and told me never to be a "yes" woman. She said, "A person who acquiesces to everything is boring—nobody learns anything from them. A bee has more personality than that kind of person." She taught me to be fair and to neither expect people to take my opinions as gospel nor to be disrespectful of others' opinions because they were different from my own; everyone is entitled to their opinion.

Mama Irma had a huge, sunny attitude. She thought attitude was everything. Unless we were ill, nothing warranted a complaint—not even a minor one. She taught me to be a positive person and to make my daily life more cheerful by filling it with pleasant experiences. She said, "If you are happy, you have something very special to offer other people. A positive person is an attractive person."

My headmistress, Herta, was a woman of strong moral fiber and values. She detested the word "self-esteem" and said that the best way to acquire confidence was to live outside oneself and to do something for someone else. One weekend a month, she made sure that I was busy working to better someone else's life instead of contemplating my own belly button.

One thing that she told me almost daily from the time I was 13 years old until I left for college at age 18 was, "Don't sow your wild oats while laying on your back." If I did that, she said, "years down the road you will realize that you have hurt your heart and your soul and will become crass about men." She taught me to be a proud woman and to hold myself in high regard, so others would, too. She knew I wanted a family, so she stressed the importance of getting an education and learning to take care of myself before finding a husband.

She taught me how to like my own company and said, "A lonely woman will accept any bum who shows up at her doorstep simply because she doesn't want to be alone. It is better to be alone than to be with the wrong person." I learned from her to be the chooser, never the beggar. She wisely said that if I had to beg for something, it was not worth having. In romance, she told me to choose a strong, kind, capable, mature man. "If you find that kind of man," she said, "you have found a true treasure." She often repeated, "It takes a smart woman to choose a great man because losers are everywhere."

I used to dream that my future husband would be just like my Mama Ermelinda's husband. Wherever she was, her husband Victor wasn't far behind. When she started a sentence, he would finish it for her and she would smile. Either that or Victor would start a sentence and she would finish it for him. He always looked at her with awe. In my teenage years, I dreamed of having a man look at me that way.

Mama Ermelinda was very influential in the way I viewed men and her husband was the man I used to measure all other men against. She taught me that a man will try to get away with everything, but if I maintain my expectations and standards, a man who likes and respects me will rise to the occasion. She cautioned me that the time to learn about a man was before marriage, when we were just dating. She always said, "Dating is the time to be sure the man you want to marry will bring peace, joy, beauty, and love into your life and the lives of your future children."

One thing that she and her husband reminded me was that a woman has to be pragmatic when looking for a husband, because a mother has an obligation to protect her children. Being educated and smart was significant, they both said, but being warm, loving, caring, and compassionate was more important.

Mama Chiquita has six children and a lovely husband. She told me, "Woman have a greater responsibility in bringing children into the world because life starts inside our bodies." If I wanted a family, she said, I should find the best man for the job, not just some slob. She explained to me that there was no such thing as a perfect marriage, but that I could have a near-perfect marriage if I "saw marriage as a union in which the husband and wife love and adore each other, are willing to make sacrifices for one another, take care of one another, and try to make the other's life worth living."

"The most important thing," she said, "is to practice patience and kindness." She always emphasized that this was especially true with words because, as she said, "there is a distance between your tongue and your brain for a reason. Take time to think before you speak. Words are very powerful, and no apology, no matter how many times it is repeated, can delete the memory of angry, damaging, mean-spirited words." What I took away from her advice is that a successful marriage has to consist of two mature people with the willingness to make personal sacrifices, because they are truly committed to each other and to their life together.

All of these great and strong women, my wonderful mothers, were instrumental in shaping the woman and mother I am today. When I left Brazil 30 years ago, I knew that no matter where I lived in the world, I would always bring my children to visit their many Brazilian grandmas. Some of my mothers have passed on, but there are still five feisty grandmas alive and ready for me to visit. Seeing them is like returning to a giant family; I love that my children have many grandmas and grandpas to tell them stories about their mother as she was growing up.

I have been blessed in my life to have the lessons of my many wise mothers to share. I honor these women, my many mothers, by passing along their teachings to my own children.

Cristina Robinson

Cristina Robinson is a dating and relationship expert. She has a Bachelor's in Business Administration, and has studied Psychology and Anthropology. Cristina has moved 16 times and has lived in Brazil, Switzerland, Germany, Italy, France and the United States. She currently calls her beloved adopted city of San Francisco, California, home. Cristina is fascinated by human interactions and writes a blog related to affairs of the heart at her eponymous website. She's currently writing a book about love relationships, due to be published by the end of the year. She has two grown children who are her pride and joy.

The Book List

Marie McHale Drake

Between 1959 and 1964, Mom was pregnant five times and three of us survived. My brother was born in 1960, me in 1963, and my sister in 1964. Mom believed in education, formal and otherwise, and reading was a family affair. By 1971, she had thrown out the television and we read at night, often out loud, each kid reading a chapter or two from the book he or she was reading at the time. We were all great readers early on.

Beginning in the spring of 1976, our Mom issued us a list of feminist literature to read. I was 13. The following is a partial list of the books she had my sister and me read while we were in the sixth, seventh, and eighth grades: *The Feminine Mystique* by Betty Friedan; *When God Was a Woman* by Merlin Stone; *The Female Eunuch* by Germaine Greer; *Towards a Recognition of Androgyny,* by Carolyn Heilbrun; *Against Our Will: Men, Women and Rape* and *Femininity,* by Susan Brownmiller; *Woman On the Edge of Time,* by Marge Piercy; *The Bluest Eye,* by Toni Morrison; *Beyond God The Father: Toward a Philosophy of Women's Liberation* and *Gyn/Ecology: The Metaethics Of Radical Feminism,* by Mary Daly; *The Women's Room,* by Marilyn French; and *Rubyfruit Jungle* by Rita Mae Brown.

There were more, but I can't remember all of them now.

I do remember challenging my seventh and eighth grade history teacher and school principal, Mr. Shultz, about everything he tried to teach us. The more I read, the more I challenged him. I was admittedly a smart ass, but you had to be blind not to notice that he paid more attention to the boys in class and it pissed me off. I pointed out to him that he was a product of the patriarchy and that what he taught was slanted, chauvinistic crap. I told him football was inherently sexist, with the males pounding one another while the tiniest, bustiest, kiss-ass females waited submissively on the sidelines for a chance to mate with them. To his credit, Mr. Shultz told me to bring the sources for my arguments to school. When I showed up with an armload of my mom's feminist books, he turned reddish-purple thumbing through the first few. He didn't borrow any.

Our classes at my school were small—there were only eight kids in my eighth grade graduating class. I don't remember how many were in seventh grade, but our classroom consisted of the sixth, seventh, and eighth grades mixed together to make about 15–20 kids. Mr. Shultz often kept me after school, but not to talk about *herstory*. Instead, he kept trying to get me to confess things to him about my mother: that she was a drug dealer, that she was promiscuous, that she was a drunk, that she didn't feed us regularly, that she was crazy but refusing psychiatric care, that our heat kept getting shut off, that drifters came through town and stayed at our house (and did they molest us?), and that she could not hold down a job. Between my attitude during his lectures and the small matter of the neighboring school district obtaining a permanent restraining order against my Mom, I realized he was in touch with Social Services, maybe even law enforcement, and was concerned for our welfare. But it was his patronizing, patriarchal way of trying to get me to turn on my mother that irritated me. His concern was a direct attack on our family, which, although it was falling apart, was still *my family*. He got nothing from me.

The permanent restraining order against Mom resulted from an incident one morning on the high school bus that was relayed to me by four different older friends of mine who were at the scene. It had been a long night for Mom, who was coming down from her favorite combo of LSD and tequila. She flagged down the bus by standing in the middle of the road and waving her arms. The door opened and she boarded the bus already screaming at the bus driver, berating him over his harsh treatment of my brother. Mom's rages were extraordinary, but this one, I understand, was something for the record books. Not long after that, she could laugh at the permanent, court-ordered end to her attendance at parent-teacher conferences and other school functions, not that she ever went anyway.

But when Mr. Shultz sat me down in his office to talk about my mother, I denied everything every time. I told him he was a macho, sexist jerk and that he could take his attempt to get Social Services involved in our lives and shove it. He didn't cotton to that kind of lip from me and his face turned red, his forehead glistened with sweat, and then he just stared at me. He tried a different tactic, trying to persuade me that a nice foster home down-valley would be great. I responded that, "any placement with a patriarchal family who wanted their women to be secretaries or broodmares would be resisted with tactics I'd learned from reading *The Monkey Wrench Gang* by Edward Abbey." When he looked at me quizzically I explained, "Sabotage and explosives."

Mr. Shultz was the former football coach and assistant principal of a neighboring high school, a portly man whose condescending attitude toward the hippie kids of my school made him less than popular. It didn't matter to me what he said about my mother or that it was mostly true. My fierce loyalty to her didn't ebb because of chaos, neglect, or occasional violence at home. Instead of acquiescing to his reasoning, I pointed out that having a lot of lovers was not a crime and maybe he should try it instead of criticizing her for it. That always made him blush through his freckles and then I'd get to leave his office. I always denied the part about her selling drugs, of course. I wasn't stupid. Besides, nearly everyone in town was dealing something.

For all her non-traditional parenting, Mom was adamant that we should never be ashamed of our bodies, sexuality, or gender. She didn't want us to feel or be repressed, oppressed, or depressed because we happened to be born female. She did the best she could to impart a sense of pride in us, even though her feminist rants often occurred through a haze of drugs and booze. It was in the wake of her binges that her own self-loathing haunted her, and it fell to us kids to shore her up as best we could. We were rarely successful.

When she was on one of her rolls, she told us the Mother Goddess loved us, loved our female bodies, and wanted us to be happy. She wanted us to have a lot of sex, experiment, be safe but not afraid, and not to hurt anybody. Mom told us that when she was touring the Vatican in 1961, she strayed from the tour and came upon a vast hall that was roped off. She ducked under the rope to look at the statues packed in against each other. As her eyes became accustomed to the light, she realized every single statue was female. They were naked or partially so, muscular and strong, their glory captured in stone. There were so many stored against each other in that hall in the Vatican that she had to stop and stare. After a little while, the Italian tour guide found her and started yelling at her. She returned with him to the tour group, but never forgot the hidden hall of women. And she never wanted us to hide our power or strength from anyone.

She said the Goddess had many names and many faces, that She had never disappeared, and that Catholicism never really let Her go, even though it shoved Her aside when She should have been the center of the trinity. She said the Burning Times during the Middle Ages were attempts to stamp out the old matriarchal religion and in particular, wise women. She said we were young Goddess Dianas: athletic, virgin huntresses that would someday be like her, the Mother, and eventually age into wise crones. She told us that "virgin" was mistranslated and that in Aramaic it actually meant "single woman," not hymen-intact young female. Somehow, that mistranslation had morphed into an obsession with virginity over the centuries. She said we should honor each other and ourselves in all our goddess phases, because the Goddess was in us and of us and we were Her. She said the greatest gift of the Goddess was compassion.

She told us about a place in New Mexico called Chimayo, where the Goddess appeared in the early 1800s. She said that She visited a small church where miracles happened because the compassion of the Mother Goddess could still be felt there. She said the church, lined with crutches, was a tribute to the Goddess, and although the Catholics laid claim to the spot, many knew its true origin. She said we would go there someday to feel the sacred energy of that place, and to bring some of its magic dirt home. I wish we had.

She said we should pray to Mother Mary, the Virgin of Guadalupe, Diana, Brigid, Morgan Le Fay, Rhiannon, Frieda, Aphrodite, Daphne, Demeter, Hera, Persephone, Devi, Kundalini, Shakti, Tara, Luna, Venus, White Buffalo Woman, Anuket, Isis, Kali, and many others. She told us that She was all of them, in all their phases and all their faces. She said the Great Mother gave hope to the hopeless, milk to hungry babies, and protected young people on quests. She said the Mother Goddess, in her Death Mask, took away the suffering of the dying and that above all things, She was compassionate. It would be into Her arms we'd go when we died.

Even though I spent much of my adulthood denying belief in anything spiritual, what Mom taught us tugged at the corners of my atheism. Now I find a little, intermittent comfort in the Mother Goddess, in the honoring of the feminine, in being of service to others, and in listening. I even feel for Mr. Shultz, who, faced with trying to help us kids and completely unable to relate to the dysfunctional, outlaw lifestyle that permeated our tiny town, did the best he could.

Because I've survived into late middle age, which Mom did not, I keep hearing of tragedies: friends dying young and without warning, hearts broken needlessly, mass starvation, and wars without end. Almost every week I light a Virgin of Guadalupe candle. They burn for about six days. I say a prayer to our Mother to please enfold the suffering in Her arms and smother them with compassion. I find comfort in these small, whispered prayers over a lighted candle, like a tiny breeze on a hot day. And I always remember my Mother when I do it.

Marie McHale Drake

Marie McHale Drake has been writing since she was ten years old. Her first short story was published in 1994. Marie is an attorney and part-time judge in the Denver, Colorado area and prior to practicing law, she worked as a dishwasher, chambermaid, construction worker, horse-drawn carriage driver, prep cook, bartender, house sitter, house painter, artist's model, Electrolux vacuum saleswoman, receptionist, paralegal, dog walker, restaurant hostess, jewelry saleswoman, clothing saleswoman, waitress, cat sitter, business consultant, and had her own radio show on KBUT Public Radio in Crested Butte, Colorado. She lives in the Colorado foothills with her husband Fred and a very spoiled dog.

Rescue, painting by Susan Schneider

Susan Schneider

Native Californian Susan Schneider continually finds herself captivated by the natural beauty of the San Francisco Bay Area as well as the emotions and beauty of the people she meets. Her artistic antennae react to the light she sees in landscapes and the light she sees in people. When she sees a special moment of light, she uses her camera to capture it. She then works from the photograph to reinterpret the feeling of that moment. Her joy is in translating with paint the visual and emotional content of that point in time.

I Don't Need Ovaries to be Fertile

Rebecca Nelson Lubin

On July 25th, 1978, Louise Brown, the world's first "test tube" baby was born in England. I was 11 years old at the time, and had been infertile for three years, since the removal of my second ovary. My doctor had been totally bewildered when, just 18 months after removing my first ovary because of a cyst, he discovered that a second cyst had completely encapsulated my second ovary and had to remove it, too. I had thought then that the chance of ever experiencing pregnancy had been taken harshly from me.

"I've never heard of anything like this happening to a child," the doctor told my parents. That admission left me feeling as if I were the only person to ever experience the isolation, loss, and betrayal one's own body can bring them. But with the birth of Louise Brown, I realized that there was someone else who knew exactly how I felt: Lesley Brown, Louise's mother. She too had suffered from infertility, thwarted by blocked fallopian tubes and failure. She made history by agreeing to In Vitro Fertilization (IVF), which was at that time an unconfirmed and purely experimental procedure that had never resulted in a baby. She was my very own personal Neil Armstrong. Four years after giving birth to Louise, Lesley had a second daughter, Natalie, who was the planet's fortieth IVF baby.

Leslie Brown taught me something else when I was only 11 years old and trying to come to terms with what it meant to be denied the ability to have a biological child: no matter what the situation, there are always choices that remain. At age eight, I had bravely announced, "So what? I'll just adopt," when my parents explained to me that my second ovary had not been saved. But truthfully, even then, I longed for the babies that I hoped would someday be mine. (My mother nicknamed me Mother Earth when I was only three.) They would have my blue eyes, cute nose, and freckles and have really good singing voices and there would be ten of them. "Oh my little Mother Earth," my mom would laugh, "ten is too many."

My mother's voice had a different tone on July 25th, 1978, that monumental day—hoarse with emotion and longing for me to have everything I wished for when I became a grown woman. She held me close and told me that I would be able to get pregnant and have a child someday, if that was what I desired. She told me that if in England they could retrieve an egg through a blocked fallopian tube and whip up a zygote in a petri dish, science would evolve and I would be able to have the same done with a donor egg. On February 3rd, 1984, eight years to the month that I lost my second ovary, the first IVF donor egg baby was born and choices grew.

But my loss remains. Infertility is an extremely private and grueling struggle for a woman. In my own experience, I have had deep periods of depression attempting to deal with my inability to have a biological child. If what makes a woman essentially female is her power to give birth and create life, then is an infertile woman somehow less of a woman? I spent my teen years waiting to transition from childhood. I spent my twenties in complete denial of my infertility, and I know that I walked through my thirties with a major chip on my shoulder, feeling that I was damaged goods and unworthy of a positive romantic relationship. If I couldn't give a man a child, then what man would want me? So I stuck to the non-committal, substance abusing, man-child types who allowed me to feel as if I did have my own baby to nurture.

All women have body issues, but I had major ones that began with a medically induced puberty around the time that most of my girlfriends were already having sex. At that time, Hormone Replacement Therapy (HRT) was a new science, so doctors moved me through it extremely slowly. My teen years were a never-ending merry-go-round of blood tests, hand X-rays, and very invasive physical exams. "Your labia majora are developing nicely," one intern told me when I was 15.

I worried endlessly about my body and continually pleaded with the universe to let me grow taller than 4 feet 11 inches, let me grow breasts, let me get thinner, let me get my period, and to let me stop looking like a little kid . . . all that worrying and wishing at age 15.

I love that I look ridiculously young now, but I didn't love it when I was the flat-chested, 17 year old prom date of the shortest dude in the junior class and his mother squealed, "Oh my God! Look how cute she is! She looks like a 12 year old!" I wanted to shrivel up inside my lavender Laura Ashley gown, crawl into a hole, and not to come out until I was finally on the rag.

Finally, in my forties, I feel comfortable in my own skin, and I have to admit, it turned out to be really nice skin after all. Of course, I keep getting cute little validations: the really hot, really young supermarket checkout guy recently told me that I was "a blessed woman" while smiling sweetly at my breasts. I am 5 feet 2 inches tall, curvy, and disgustingly adorable with a killer D-cup. I still want to be thinner, but don't we all?

I also feel safe in my own skin because of the choices that I've made. I've lost the ability to have a biological child and see my mother as reflected in my daughter's eyes. I may never be in the financial position to give IVF a whirl, nor have the financial resources to adopt a baby. These options remain a great, big, hazy if—a blurry question mark hovering in the distant future. I'm not there yet.

But just like the skin I live in, it's all turned out to be so nice after all because I have more children in my life than I can count on three hands. Professionally, I have been raising children for the past 20 years; if it takes a village to raise a child, I am the mayor of many villages. I feel nothing but joy and validation from each and every child I have ever loved, sentenced to a time-out, snuggled with over cartoons, and smiled at as ice cream dripped down their hands. I have wiggled many first loose teeth. I have tenderly held many young people as they cried. Sometimes they cried over a minor punishment and the tears went away quickly with a firm hug. Other times, they cried about more permanent issues like the pain of divorce, the disorientation of traveling between households, or just feeling alienated by life, circumstances, and even their own parents. Once, I cried with two of the children I've loved the most as they cried over the death of their father. Experiencing my own loss at a young age has made me enormously empathetic to the emotional needs of the children I have had a hand in raising.

I have children all across the country, spread out from New York to California. I have changed their diapers, held them steady with my hands under their armpits as they attempted their first steps, doled out discipline with firm discussions of privileges and consequences, given many of them "The Talk," bought them their first bras, nursed them through heartbreaks, and raised a cocktail with them when they turned 21. They are represented with pictures in my wallet. They are the audience to my storytelling, their little, rapt faces in pajamas perched in a pile at the end of the bed. They are an ever-growing lot of lovely little beings that I have lulled to sleep with the same Paul Simon song over the years, "St. Judy's Comet." Of course, I change the gender of the child in the song to suit my current listeners.

My children are many. This May, Sienna sent me a text that read, "You raised me too. Happy Mother's Day." I have been telling Rose, Lily, Sage, and Sam an ongoing epic story for the past five years. Skylar is the suddenly stunningly beautiful co-ed who comes home for the weekend and wants to meet me for brunch. Rex told me, "You understand me so much it's like you have a Ph.D. in children." He and his little siblings Sasha and Callie are the cute little people who get buckled into the backseat of my Honda every weekday afternoon, asking me to play Tom Petty on my iPod, requesting chewing gum and orange Tic-Tacs, and calling me Betta.

For six and a half years, I have worked with their family as their nanny, house manager, and personal assistant (and CEO, as they like to say). Ours is a relationship that blends the boundaries of employee and employers into something that feels like family. My relationship with Bella, their mother, trumps any that I have had with all the other women who have entrusted their children to me. She has total trust in me and treats me like an equal; she has respect for all my experience with all the other babies I have helped raise before I began raising hers. Bella calls me her co-parent, the children's mommy number two, and her "real wife." She has anointed me as Sasha and Callie's Godmother. She has made me feel as if I truly have children of my own—ones that might actually have come from my own body. I am always thanking her for so generously sharing her children with me. The gift that she has given me, letting me love her children as a parent, is invaluable.

I have an especially close relationship with Sasha, her five year old son. When he was just three, I was getting him ready for his nap and he asked me, rather seriously, "Are you a Mommy?"

"I am a Betta." I said.

"I will make you a Mommy," he told me very earnestly. Then he had me sit on the floor while he waved his magic wand over my head. He then gathered up all of his favorite toys—his trains, soft monkeys, and his much loved books—and dumped them all in my lap.

"Now?" I asked.

"Not yet," he said, raising the wand high and smacking me square in the head with it.

"Now!" He squealed, "Now you a Mommy!"

It made sense. I was covered in crap, suddenly had a searing headache, felt a little dizzy and a little sleep deprived—very much like a Mommy. But I also could not help thinking of *The Velveteen Rabbit* and how it became real just because one boy loved and believed in it so much. I believe, too. And if I ever grow insecure in that faith, I will just remember how this beautiful little boy will lay himself in my lap and look at me with pure love whispering, "I am your childrens."

Rebecca Nelson Lubin

Rebecca Nelson Lubin is a writer and nanny who resides in California's San Francisco Bay Area. When not raising toddlers she can be found cooking, hiking in the Marin hills, getting her groove on in the local music scene, and working on her forthcoming memoir, *I Don't Need Ovaries to be Fertile.*

Labor of Love

Andrea Drugay

The announcement came as a complete surprise. It was New Year's weekend and a bunch of us without kids had rented a bayside house at Stinson Beach, just north of San Francisco. We spent a couple of days kayaking, walking the dogs on the beach, playing board games, and drinking beer—well, most of us drank beer, except for Beth, who was several months pregnant at the time. A single mother-to-be, Beth was equally close with the guys in our party as with the women. It was just like that. She left on Sunday morning, heading back to the city, so we hugged and said goodbye, eagerly awaiting the final countdown to her due date.

A few of us lingered, sand still stuck between our toes. We sat around the big coffee table in the living room unready to move. I lazily paged through a magazine, enjoying some time off from teaching yoga every day. Jeri sat on the couch nearby, her face buried in a novel. My partner Dave gazed out the window to the seagulls and houseboats. Kevin, Jeri's husband, casually dropped some papers on the table, black-and-white photographs of some kind.

"Ultrasounds," he said offhandedly. I pictured Beth, waddling down the gravel driveway to her old car, not yet in full nesting mode, but close.

"Aww, it's gonna be so soon," I said, leaning forward to check out the images.

"Not Beth," he said, with a sly smile. Jeri lowered her book and grinned hugely.

"Us," Kevin and Jeri said together.

Shrieks of joy! Then hugs, tears, questions, and glowing, contented sighs. When the air settled, Jeri and Kevin turned to me, their big eyes sparkling like sunshine on the Bay.

"We were wondering," Jeri said, "if you would like to be my prenatal yoga teacher. I'd like to take lessons at home instead of going to a class."

"I was going to give this to her as a Christmas present," Kevin said. "But that would have given away the surprise to you."

I'd completed my prenatal yoga teacher training a few months earlier as a way to expand my teaching repertoire. Little had I realized how much I would enjoy working with pregnant mamas and their full, expansive energy. I also hadn't realized how much I would learn about pregnancy, labor, and delivery—three experiences I had decided long ago would not be part of my own life's journey. Growing up, I never wanted kids or a domestic life. Instead of playing house, I played hotel. Instead of baby dolls, I had a tire swing and a bike. As I got older, the desire to be a mom, to have children of my own, simply never entered the picture. When people asked, I'd say, "Ask me again when I'm 30." In my early thirties, I honed my catchphrase: "I've never wanted kids, but I've always wanted books."

As my friends and my sister headed down the path of having progeny, Dave and I created a life centered on our shared growth and development—a partnership focused on two people, not three or more. I loved my niece and nephew, played well with my friends' toddlers, and even thoroughly enjoyed a short stint teaching yoga to preschoolers. But nothing sparked the desire in me to have a child of my own. The author Elizabeth Gilbert once described her experience of not having children by explaining, "I feel like there are women who are genuinely born to be mothers, and women who are born to be aunties . . . My childlessness makes me available to spread my care across the community in more far-reaching ways because my resources don't belong to my children, they belong to whoever needs them." I was, in Gilbert's terminology, an auntie.

When Jeri and Kevin asked for my assistance, I felt honored and humbled. These were two of my most together friends, in every sense of the word: in their partnership, careers, and ability to throw casual get-togethers with the panache and flair of a magazine spread. Over the years, we'd spent time in close quarters: camping, snowboarding, and one particularly memorable (though somewhat hazy) trip to Mexico. When I first started teaching yoga, they were my guinea pigs. I'd come to their house on Tuesday evenings and guide them through breathing exercises and gentle poses. They got some stretching and stress relief, while I stumbled over my words, held them in positions for far too long, confused left and right, and screwed up dozens of times—the natural path to building confidence via blunders. They refused my offer for free sessions. In gratitude, I assured them I would never, ever charge them even half of what I'd normally ask for a private lesson. To be invited to share this new path with them was truly generous. We set a schedule and started the following week.

Over the next seven months, I showed up every Sunday morning, post-coffee and pre-stretch. Occasionally, I'd run into Kevin on his way out the door, but he never stuck around—this was my time with Jeri. We'd sit and talk for a bit, catching up on life but also on her moods, sleep, and physical changes. I'd put on soft chanting music, roll out my mat next to hers, unload the yoga blocks, straps, and bolsters, and we would begin. We started with breathing exercises and visualization connecting her with her growing baby. Then we moved on to warm-up moves and standing poses, to build the strength and stability she'd need after the baby was born. Finally, we moved on to floor work, including poses she could use during labor and delivery. We ended every class in Corpse Pose (called *savasana* in Sanskrit). This relaxation posture is sometimes considered the most important pose in yoga, because it's when the body and mind finally have a chance to deeply relax. When followed by meditation and visualization, *savasana* can help the practitioner connect deeply with his or her highest spiritual self.

Jeri and Kevin had chosen not to learn the gender of their baby before its birth. During *savasana* one Sunday, as Jeri lay on her left side hugging a bolster, a lavender eye pillow draped across her face, I watched her breathe and focused on her belly, the slow rise and fall lulling me into a waking dream. Normally, I do not watch my students as they rest, not directly anyway. It's more of a soft focus, sensing their tranquility and drawing my own awareness inward. But this time, as I gazed dreamily at her belly, a flood of joy, delight, and what I can only describe as feminine energy washed through me. I knew right then that her baby was a girl. The feeling was nearly overwhelming, and I sensed without a doubt that this girl's birth and life would be filled with grace. It felt as though Jeri's daughter reached out to me directly to let me know she was a girl, and I have always considered that moment a blessing.

I've always been pretty good at guessing the genders of my pregnant friends' children. With my friend Beth, I sensed that she was going to get pregnant a month before she actually did—though I didn't find out until many weeks later. My sister and her husband kept both the gender and names of my niece and nephew a surprise, although I intuitively identified both. Our dad simply could not believe I knew they would have a girl and name her Lucy, but my sister, even more sensitive than I, remains unsurprised. So the experience of Jeri's daughter reaching out energetically never seemed odd or disconcerting, but natural and fun. Slowing down and retreating from the external stresses of modern life can reveal an inherent connection between our inner lives and the rhythms of nature. In the peaceful moments of *savasana* and meditation, intuition can flourish, revealing understanding of and compassion for others that might normally get ignored or buried. Enlightenment, some yogis say, is not a building up but a stripping away. Deliberately relaxing into the moment allows pretenses and defenses to dissolve, deepening our connection to others: without intellectual and emotional walls, we're just energy and light. In the moment she revealed herself to me, Jeri's daughter reminded me that we are all connected.

Five months later—a few months after Beth had her baby, and one month before Jeri and Kevin's due date—I sat talking with Jeri and a few other friends at a housewarming party. A few nights before, I had a dream that I was training to be a doula, that is, a labor and delivery assistant. I woke from the dream surprised because it was a path I had never considered, and yet the idea seemed perfectly logical. So I brought it up. Jeri and the other two women responded with wide eyes.

"You'd make a great doula!" one said.

"Totally do it," said the other.

"Well," I said, "It sounds like a good idea, but it's kind of different. I mean it's not like writing a book or learning to surf. How do you find out for sure that you'd want to be a doula?"

"I guess just attend a bunch of births," the first friend said. "If it freaks you out, it's probably not right for you."

"You could attend our birth," Jeri said so brightly that I actually pictured a cartoon light bulb above her head.

I think I swooned. The other women gaped, grinning. The birth room, I felt, was a sacred space. Being invited in was like being asked to perform a wedding, or give someone a tattoo: highly intimate and unique. Jeri and Kevin had attended the birth of Beth's baby boy, and their relaying of the experience was only positive and encouraging. It would be foolish to say no.

As Jeri's due date drew closer, we continued to practice yoga, focusing more on preparing for labor and delivery with calming breaths, useful poses, and as much relaxation as possible. We meditated and practiced guided visualization, connecting the hearts of baby and mama, reminding Jeri of her power and worth. We went quiet and found an internal rhythm, 90 minutes of breathing, flowing, and trusting. When the baby did not arrive exactly on the due date, we agreed that the upcoming new moon, which was to coincide with a total solar eclipse, would undoubtedly stimulate labor. And of course, it did.

I got the call at seven in the morning, Kevin slightly out of breath. "Hey," he said. "We're at the hospital."

A quick coffee and a kiss to Dave, and I was off to the hospital. When I arrived, Jeri was up and walking, strolling the halls with Kevin in her paper gown. Her ivory face was deeply flushed and her pale blonde hair was matted against her cheeks. Nevertheless, she was stunning. Surprisingly to me, she was not screaming, swearing, or otherwise fulfilling movie stereotypes of hysterical women in labor. She seemed practically calm.

Kevin and I helped her into various positions, typically ones where she could see his face and where I could assist with massaging her lower back and shoulders. She grinned dreamily at Kevin between contractions and stared at him during the intense waves when her blue eyes weren't squeezed shut. She did her yoga breathing. I gave her ice and fresh washcloths so she and Kevin did not have to break their gaze. We visualized cool waterfalls and light-blue oceans while the Buena Vista Social Club and Orchestra Baobab serenaded us with their worldly rhythms. I had no sense of time, hunger, or fatigue. The three of us found a groove, fully aware of nothing but the present moment. Gradually, as gently as she could, baby Amelia made her way into the world.

She was born two years ago to this day, as I write. Jeri says she remembers her labor and delivery as "a calm experience," and that there was "never any stress." I later learned in my doula training that the mere presence of another woman in the delivery room, whether or not she's assisting the birth, dramatically reduces emotional stress during labor and significantly increases feelings of peace and calm. It's nice to know my company may have helped ease Amelia's birth, but on a deeper level, it's a gift and a blessing to have been able to help my friend. I didn't help Amelia arrive because I wanted to see a baby's birth—I helped Jeri deliver Amelia because I wanted to see my friends filled with joy and peace.

Dave and I had a party a few weeks ago. Beth and her boy came, as did Jeri, Kevin, and Amelia. Two year old Amelia has a crush on another friends' 18-month-old son. They kiss each other all the time. They grow up so fast. My ten year old niece and I have an inside joke about adults who always tell her, "You've grown so fast!" She doesn't yet realize that growing doesn't stop, even when you're grown up. As I watch her, my nephew, and my friends' children develop so quickly over the years, I'm reminded that I can be present with them sometimes in ways their parents might not be able to: as an auntie. By remaining true to myself as a childless woman, I have more time and energy to devote to helping others grow, no matter the pace.

I eventually completed my doula training, although I decided not to pursue it as a career. But my time with Jeri and the other women I assisted during my doula training deepened my confidence as a yoga teacher and as a woman. Learning to be fully present with others and offering the time, energy, and space they need to thrive has also allowed me to grow up fast. As I learned in my experience with Jeri, I can be an auntie to adults, too.

Andrea Drugay

Andrea Drugay is a writer and copy editor in San Francisco, California. She taught yoga for five years and is also a wellness coach, Reiki practitioner, and trained doula. She has an MFA in Creative Writing and a BA in Communications. She has written yoga how-to guides, feature articles, essays, and web copy for magazines and newspapers, both online and in print. Her short stories and poetry have appeared in many literary journals, including the *Coe Review, Identity Theory*, and the *Santa Clara Review*. Several of her short essays appear under a pseudonym in the anthology *Burning Man Live*.

Conjoined Twins, sculpture by Colleen Joyce

Colleen Joyce

Colleen Joyce grew up in Los Angeles, California, as part of a creative family. After graduating from high school, she was employed as a garment worker where she learned to sew. While attending Santa Barbara City College she studied art, graduating with an AA degree. A few years ago she produced a life-sized plaster sculpture called "Conjoined Twins" at the College of Marin which ignited her interest in 3D design. In 2011 she studied at Apparel Arts, a San Francisco, California fashion design school, which lead her to create her clothing line, Wabi Sabi Couture.

A Girl's Best Friend Is Another Girl

Eileen Chao

It is a truth universally acknowledged that a married woman in possession of a husband and children must be in need of a few girlfriends. For after all, while husband and children are the sources of her greatest bliss and joy, are they not also the embodiment of a constant and perpetual challenge to her sanity?

Never having fathomed the art of multitasking, I ever so carefully acquired the one husband and the single child during my stroll through life, with the hope that they would be manageable for me. But even with such a spectacularly lackadaisical setup, I often find myself falling into the mires of everyday worries, whether puddle-like or oceanic, where I would sink rapidly until one girlfriend or another, whoever has had enough of my wailing and can bear it no more, invariably yanks me out of my misery, dusts me off (not always gently), and sends me sallying forth again.

If only I had enough wits about me after my son was born, I could have run for the most unnecessarily worried mother in the land and won without competition. Everything about this baby worried me. He was never ravenous at feeding time, so his apparent lack of appetite worried me. His eczema worried me. Even his growth chart, which charted at a perfectly even pace, worried me. Skeptical of the accuracy of the measurements, I even worried about the possible margins of error.

My son had been a well-behaved baby who hardly cried and happily slept through most of his early months. So, of course, his lack of crying worried me. A girlfriend who had her first baby a couple of months after I had mine, on the other hand, delivered a girl who saw fit to exercise her lungs at full capacity and cry relentlessly in her first three months. My severely sleep-deprived friend, who had tried everything under the sun and moon to stop her baby crying and failed, was distraught and told me she was at the end of her tether. I then told her my paranoia about my quiet, sleeping baby and the fact that I was so fearful of his sleeping himself into an endless sleep that I, naturally distrusting the inefficacious breath-on-mirror method, would shake him gently at least once or twice every night until he stirred in his sleep. Stirring meant he was alive and, short of the definitive gesture of crying, that alone would allay my fears. We listened to each other's grief, my girlfriend and I, and laughed at our pitiful state as new mothers.

While my friend obviously had an advantage over me in the whining department, in that hers was a genuine complaint compared to my imagined ones, we both seemed to have found strength and reassurance in learning of each other's completely different problem. I told her to persevere, that her daughter couldn't possibly keep up such feistiness for the rest of her life, and that she must stop crying at some point. She told me to stop disrupting my son's enviable sleep pattern and leave him alone. That was good advice . . . hers better than mine.

As life chugged along, full of a variety of minor pandemonium, my girlfriends and I kept each other even-keeled by regularly assessing and reassessing each other's lot. At times, when we found ourselves in choppy waters, felt the threat of capsizing, or when the sight of dry land seemed just a little too evasive, we reminded each other how fortunate we were not to have more troubles than those we owned.

Happily, having somehow managed to sleep and grow sufficiently despite his mother's interference, my son reached third grade at the age of eight. On his first day in third grade, I walked him to his classroom; he went inside and left me alone to read the new class list of names by the door. I took one look at the list, which included none of his close friends, and spun into panic mode. How would my son cope without a friend in the third grade jungle of twenty-odd children?

I called a girlfriend as soon as I reached home and with a tremor in my voice told her my fear of my boy's abandonment without an ally in his new class. My girlfriend, who had been in tears often enough about her own children's problems, performed her role impeccably. After a brief phone call in which she exalted my son's ability to forge new friendships and instructed me on what to do next, I obediently called the school and asked, in a much calmer voice by then, if someone could please check on my son. The reply from his school came soon enough: The class had been sitting on the floor in a working circle that morning and my son was seen with his arm around the shoulders of the boy next to him. He was clearly content and in good company. And so was I, I realized then.

The most common source of my and my girlfriends' exasperations pertained to the men to whom we—rightly or, as we sometimes felt, wrongly—promised, oh ever such a long time ago, to have and to hold till death do us part. In their own unique ways, our husbands unfailingly possessed the uncanny ability to raise our blood pressure at random in the shortest of conversations. On the occasions where I could positively feel actual steam about to come out of my ears, it was always one of my girlfriends who managed to dissipate my anger enough for me to calm down and eventually remember why it was that I married the man. After my tirades, it usually took just a quiet mention from my girlfriends, "The man acted like a fool, never mind what he said, did, or forgot. He did do 'X' for you" and I would deflate and humbly accept that his crime had perhaps been exaggerated and my anger overstated.

Besides the huge amount of amusement we afforded each other by way of the details in our daily grind, my girlfriends have always been invaluable in my attempt to navigate the daily slings and arrows thrown my way. These came in the fascinating guises of parenting issues, constantly vanishing household items (which everyone in the house swore never to have moved), conflicting calendar dates, inexplicably long chunks of my life spent in doctor's waiting rooms, missing brain cells (usually my own, occasionally other people's), lurking meter maids, pestering policemen with their wads of speeding tickets, and other unreasonable people who would insist on disagreeing with

me. It would have taken me far longer to simmer down or shape up and regain functionality if it weren't for the small group of reliable and levelheaded girls I call friends.

Someone once likened the momentous events that happen unexpectedly and topple one's life to turning soil. Such events happen without warning and one's life is forever changed: Things are lost and new things grow in their place. In such an upheaval, it would be unimaginable to be alone.

My need for girlfriend support was never greater than when my son unintentionally skied into a tree at the age of six and pirouetted our lives into chaos. The three of us, over two hundred miles away from home, had been on holiday, taking with us my mother and sister, who were visiting from abroad. My son fell to the ground and was airlifted within minutes to the nearest hospital, where a hole was drilled into the side of his tiny head in order to release intracranial pressure before he was entered into an induced coma for what seemed like an eternity, but was, in fact, two solid weeks.

From the hospital, my first phone call was to a friend whom I had known since we were both in fifth grade. She promptly left all her own plates spinning in the air—she, who, out of all my friends, had the largest number of those—and came to me. By her careful arrangements and tireless efforts, my mother and sister were tenderly ferried homeward and supplies of my clothes were ferried toward me in the hospital. She came as often and spent as much time with me as she could, and even more time alone on the road driving hundreds of miles of icy January roads, for no reason other than the tenuous one that I had asked for her help. After two long weeks, all of us left for home, I with the knowledge that the surgeons, doctors, and nurses saved my son's life and that my girlfriend saved my sanity.

Sanity being a prerequisite to happiness for me (not being particularly fond of the kind of happiness sported by the daisy-coiffed residents of asylums), my girlfriends are absolutely indispensable to me. Think of all the happy women you know, and they will most certainly have a network of other women close to them who act as a critical life-support system from time to time. Imagine if Pandora had a girl-friend at hand to give her a timely tap on her wrist: She would never have opened that blasted box and we wouldn't be bothered with the likes of measles vaccinations. If only Lady Macbeth also had a girl-friend to give her a few sharp words . . . she would never have come to such a sticky end.

Eileen Chao

Eileen Chao spent her childhood in Taipei, Taiwan, studied (mostly English Literature) in the UK, got married, worked in publishing and then computers, and finally swapped London for San Francisco, California, where she now watches her son study. Her most favorite pastime is reading, because it is easier than her second, writing.

Section Four

BFF and BFF-Less

Sister Soul Mates

Christine Bronstein

"Where is Mitra?" my aunt asked as I climbed out of the cab and onto a dark residential corner in Naples, Florida.

I was in Naples to help my family take care of my 90 year old grandmother who had fallen and broken her hip. I hadn't seen my aunt, Ginny, in over two years, but our conversation about my best friend started mid-sentence, as if we had been speaking about it just minutes, not years, before.

She threw her arms around me. "I know y'all are lesbians," she laughed in her southern drawl.

"Just because we love each other and lived together doesn't mean we are gay," I sighed into my aunt's ear as we squeezed each other.

This was not the first time Mitra and I had gotten the lesbian thing. After all, we had been friends for almost 20 years, had lived and traveled together for almost ten of those years, and remain each other's stand-in date when our husbands are not available.

We met in San Francisco on a Thursday night in 1995. I was having a cocktail party at an apartment I was living in with my boy-friend of the moment (BOTM) when this woman with huge curly hair and bright orange flowered pants came flying into the middle of the gathering.

My friend Derek had brought Mitra and, as a joke, he had pushed her into the party, staying behind in the hallway. Although it was an unusual scene, a laughing, big-maned, beautiful woman flinging her-self into our rather tightly-knit group, no one flinched. We just drank our vodkas, tilted our heads and gave her a practiced, we're-too-cool-to-look-surprised, "Hey."

Derek finally came in, but we had already swept Mitra into our group. From that time forward, we were like sisters, except that we'd chosen each other. It was love at first sight, and until I met my current husband, it was the deepest, safest love I would know.

Soon thereafter, I broke up with my BOTM. Mitra helped me haul my trash bags full of clothes out of his place and into our new apartment a few blocks away.

There were many BOTMs (and one ex-husband) that came in and out of my life during our first years as friends. Mitra even broke up with one of my BOTMs for me on the phone because our voices sound so much alike. There were also a few more moves around San Francisco but, aside from a short-lived marriage, for almost ten years Mitra and I lived happily together.

Right before I got engaged, Mitra had moved out of the house we were living in together in order to move to New York to live with her BOTM.

When I got married (the first time), Mitra tried to get me to run out the backdoor of my extravagant Napa wedding. "Come on. It isn't too late," she urged me.

"It's ok. It's a good practice wedding." I replied half joking and half knowing it would end badly. During the ceremony, Mitra shoved the ring so far into the box that when my soon-to-be-ex-husband went to reach for it during the ceremony, he couldn't get it out.

Nine months later, as I was getting divorced, Mitra and her BOTM broke up and she moved back home from New York, dragging her suitcases up the front stairs as my ex-husband was dragging his down. His floppy hair bounced in his eyes as he spat, "I know you two are lesbians," over his shoulder on his way out of my life.

She dropped her bags in the vaulted entrance and we plopped down on our respective spots on the big grey couch in the living room. We stared at each other and she said, "Life would be so much easier if we were lesbians."

"So much easier," I nodded thinking about the divorce I had looming ahead of me.

I was so relieved to have Mitra back. My house hadn't felt like home since she'd left. I missed sitting on the couch with her doing a lot of nothing but having a great time. I missed her messy room where she taught me that water glasses could indeed grow mold. She was my Oscar and I was her Felix, but there was never any fighting or jealousy. Although we have different tolerances for mess—I see it everywhere and she doesn't see it at all—we have always shared a love for travel.

We have had crazy misadventures all over the world—from traveling to Kentucky for my rowdy family reunions to bruising ourselves every winter in Aspen trying to snowboard at my dad's house with a myriad of family and BOTMs. We'd been lost for hours, literally driving around in circles on a Greek island. We almost drowned each other river rafting in the Czech Republic. We'd been stranded in a remote Turkish port. We flew over Africa and dive-bombed elephants in a tiny tin can of an airplane. We laughed and sometimes cried, but even in the most stressful moments there has just never been anything to fight about. We love being together, even if we don't always enjoy the same activities.

Once, in Kenya, I talked her into going scuba diving. As we went out into the ocean, Mitra's tanned Iranian face turned green. Her eyes crossed as her mask went under the choppy water, still murky from the tsunami in Thailand only days before. The dive instructor kept separating our clasped hands as we dove and we kept grabbing back at each other as soon as the instructor glided ahead.

In the boat on the way back to shore, Mitra looked over her shoulder at me between rounds of vomiting and said, "Fuck this. You need to get a sporty friend. I want to be that for you, but I just can't. I'm sitting on the beach the rest of the trip." I didn't want a sporty friend. No one else could be my Mitra.

So instead, I got myself a sporty husband . . . a great husband this time.

Mitra was even there on our first date, of course. She was there at our tiny beautiful wedding and for the births of two of our children, and will always be my sister soul mate. Even as our lives transformed from nightclubs and cocktails to kids' clubs and sippy cups, our connection hasn't wavered.

She was texting me every day of my trip to Florida, and was also in touch with my husband, who was taking care of our three kids so I could go see my grandmother.

"You're very lucky to love your husband and have Mitra," my grandmother told me over lunch at the hospital.

"But we are glad you are married, you know," my Grandmother continued, "We all thought you two were lesbians for so long!"

Christine Bronstein

Christine Bronstein is the founder of ABandofWives.com, a social network and information website for all women. Her writing has been published in the *San Francisco Chronicle*, *Huffington Post* and more. She was CEO of one of the few female run venture-backed health and fitness companies in the nation for eight years and president of a child-welfare foundation for three years. She is a graduate of the Columbia/UC-Berkeley executive MBA program and a member of the honor society Beta Gamma Sigma. Chris is married to The Center for Investigative Reporting Executive Chair, Phil Bronstein and mother of three.

Changing Friendship

Shasta Nelson

It's hard to say, "I need friends."

We associate loneliness or a sense of social disconnection with "those" people. We picture some angry, hurt, unfriendly, socially awkward, and unlovable woman sitting alone in a dark house with the curtains closed and maybe a dozen cats.

We don't rush to picture ourselves in need of new friends. Instead, our egos remind us how likable we are, how friendly and fun we can be, and how much we have to offer someone. With defensive speed, we'll begin to name a few people we'd call friends, brushing away the nagging voice that prompts us to admit it's been a while since we've talked to them. Our self-image equates loneliness with being unlikable, as though the two go hand-in-hand. They do not. The most beautiful, loved, respected, powerful, outgoing, social, networked, busy, famous, important, and wealthy among us know loneliness . . . sometimes more than you might imagine.

Nonetheless, the admission that we need new friends can be hard to confess. We're afraid that might somehow be misinterpreted to mean, "No one likes me" or "I have no friends." We don't want to look like we're lonely, much less actually be lonely. We don't want to have needs that aren't yet met. We don't want to risk taking it personally— perhaps making ourselves feel worse that it's our fault we're in this situation.

We're more at ease saying that we need more money, need to lose weight, or need to find balance in our lives. We're even perfectly willing to tell people we're single and looking for love. (I still remember when we hid the fact that we met our dates online! Today, we comfortably accept that twenty percent of all couples meet on online dating sites and there's almost more shame in someone being unwilling to try it than not.) But admitting that we might need more friends still stops most of us in our tracks. We are shy to admit when we're on the search.

But most of us are.

In fact, research suggests that we tend to replace half our friends every seven years. That means we have a bit of a revolving door in our lives—friendships starting and friendships shifting. Some will stay consistent with their friendships, but the vast majority will not.

We're called to a lifetime of friend making.

When I was new to San Francisco eight years ago, I still remember standing outside a café window on Polk Street watching a group of women inside, huddled around a table laughing. Like the puppy dog at the pound, I looked through the glass, wishing someone would pick me to be theirs. I had a phone full of far-flung friends' numbers, but I didn't yet know anyone I could just sit and laugh with in a café here and now.

It hit me how very hard the friendship process is. I'm an outgoing, socially comfortable woman with a long line of good friendships behind me. And yet I stood there feeling very lonely, insecure, and exhausted at just the idea of how far I was from that reality.

I knew I couldn't just walk in there and introduce myself to them. "Hi! You look like fun women, can I join you?" I would have been met with stares of pity. No one wants to seem desperate, even if we are. We don't have platonic pick-up lines memorized. Flirting for friends seems creepy. Asking for her phone number like we're going to call her up for a Saturday night date is just plain weird. All the batting of my eyelashes that I could manage wasn't going to send the right signals. I wanted to give them my friendship resume, my vast references from past friends who adore me, assuring them how lucky they would be to call me a friend.

But it doesn't work that way. And so, I turned away from the scene of laughter and walked away.

No, unfortunately, friendships don't just happen. It used to feel so easy, automatic, and simple.

My childhood best friend was Amy K. We'd race to the playground at recess, knowing that whoever made it to the swings first would save one for the other. We'd swing high in unison while we sang "Believe It or Not," the theme song for a TV show neither of us had ever seen. We were just two little girls, belting out the lyrics, knowing we did believe in us.

We'd soon giggle over inside jokes, whisper secrets about boys, and beg our parents for permission to spend the night at each other's homes. Playing all day long on a weekend never felt like enough time. We believed in the pact we made to be friends forever.

I no longer have a habit of swinging and singing with my friends, but something about childhood memories makes me wistful, wishing for that kind of time and loyalty that I don't remember ever working hard to create.

But even then my friendships didn't just happen.

We were required to go to school, we had to sleep in cabins with other campers, we couldn't play games in the streets by ourselves, and it was cheaper in college to live with a roommate. Repetitive time together is what happened automatically back then, not friendship. There's a difference.

But walking away from the Polk Street window I didn't even know who to be consistent with. And while I wanted friends, I wasn't sure I had the energy to start all over with new people. They looked nice enough, but I hate small talk, sigh at the thought of telling all my stories over again, and shudder to think of the dance we have to figure out together until things will feel normal: if we both like each other, how often we'll hang out, who does the initiating, etc.

The truth is, I just wanted Karen, J'Leen, Liz, and Krista—the friends I left behind in Southern California when I moved. It was too tempting to compare new friends against the comfort of a proven friend. Once you know frientimacy—intimacy with a friend—a coffee date with a stranger isn't going to feel as rewarding. I so wanted to believe that my friends from my past were enough. I loved them.

But life keeps changing, and some friendships end. Some friendships are still there, but time has changed them.

Amy K. moved away when we were in the fourth grade. Furthermore, I know nothing more about my high school best friend's life than what she says in her Christmas card each year. One of my college roommates and I have only seen each other once since graduation. My former neighbors on the eighteenth floor in Seattle have all moved to the far corners of the country. I lost one of my best friends in my divorce. I still grieve over that one.

My Southern California girlfriends became the friends I see once a year on an annual trip; meaningful, but not the same as when we were local friends. I know they would do anything for me and few people may ever know me as well, but being limited to phones, computers, and airplanes, our friendships had to shift.

I still know I could call one of them tomorrow, say I needed her here, and she'd be on the next flight. The problem is that even though I know she'd be on the next flight if, say, my husband was in a car accident, I'd feel silly asking her to fly out for an afternoon of shopping. We know we can call our proven friends for anything, but we end up reserving them for life's biggies: births, divorces, dream jobs, moves, or the scary diagnosis.

But life only has so many biggies in it, and we're still left with all the seemingly mundane moments that don't seem important enough to warrant the phone tag and eventual hour-long phone call. That's not to say we don't still want to share them with someone.

The fact that we replace half our friends every seven years serves as a beautiful reminder to us that our lives do have a revolving door, whether we want them to or not. As friends inevitably go out the door, it's our responsibility to welcome new ones in at the same time. No matter how good the friendships are that we co-create, it seems we often still have that sign in our window that says "Now hiring."

Indeed, needing new friends is normal, in the same way that needing to move to a new town to start school or a new job is normal.

Facing the fact that many of us will go through more than one significant romantic relationship even after we hoped we'd found "the one" is also normal. Life does change. Our relationships change. Our needs change. For all of us, no matter how good, balanced, or healthy we are, life changes are what we will experience. Life changes, in fact, seem to be the one constant thing in life.

No matter how much we want that one group of friends that will never change, we will still need to know the art of holding friendships with an open hand and allowing people to come in and out of our life with grace. Allowing the ebbs and flows doesn't detract from who we are, but adds to who we are. For whatever time our paths cross, we can be sure that those who have known us are better off for that time together.

Eventually, I reached a point where I wanted to make new memories with friends, rather than simply reporting my life events or reliving the past with those I used to be close to. I needed present friends. I needed local friends. I needed new friends.

I had to uncross my defiant little arms and mentally change my pouty expression that said, "Prove you're as good as they are," and replace it with a hopeful smile that said, "Let's make something new."

Anyone who hangs out with me for long will hear me say "hold it with an open hand." It's a hand gesture where each hand is cupped, palm up. The gesture is relaxed in a way, and yet intentional enough that I could bring water to my lips with those fingers if needed. The very act of making those open hands has become my own little mantra in life, inviting my heart to reflect the handmade sign.

When I see those open hands, I am reminded of all that they can do, and conversely, what they cannot. If my hands are open, that means they are not limp by my side, unwilling, unnoticing, or incapable of being ready to receive. If my hands are open, they are not clinging with fists tight, trying to hold, control, keep, or grasp. If my hands are open, my palms are not turned out, pushing away, putting up walls, resisting, defending, or refusing to let life in. If my hands are open, they are not flat and stretched, unable to hold anything of value or refusing to be a safe container for what is given to me in my life. If my hands are open, they are not trying to stretch the fingers ever wider to hold more and more, for as the fingers spread in greed, the gifts begin to seep out like sand through the cracks.

I want to step into life with gentle, but firmly cupped hands, not needing to grab, push, cling, force, or refuse. Rather, I show up with a readiness that says I will look for things to hold, people to love, life to relish, moments to enjoy, and gifts to appreciate.

Open hands remind me that I am deserving of goodness. I am worthy, willing, and capable. I refuse to let past rejection, fears, insecurities, and previous losses stop me from being ready to receive this time. I value living life fully and I will look for moments to cherish and love.

Open hands remind me that if I give goodness the freedom to land in my life, then those same gifts have the freedom to fly away in their own time. I can't control one and then try not to control the other. I can't force people to stay here longer any more than I can force time to stand still. I can't manipulate, coerce, charm, or trap gifts into lasting forever.

And should I ever be tempted to close my hand around something, I will inevitably close my hand to other gifts as well. The very gesture of trying to keep one thing can be the gesture that prevents other good things from coming our way.

Sometimes, we're so focused on refusing to let go of one thing that we miss other opportunities. With gripped hands, we squish the bug we were trying to save, melt the chocolate we wanted to have later, or find fingernail marks in our skin because we clenched too hard. That which we wanted to keep, we lost anyhow. And now our hands are just messy and sore.

Open hands remind me not to give up, to engage, expect, hope, and cherish. They teach me to let go, unclench, and find peace. They offer me moments of joy and loss, inviting me to find contentment in both. My open hands invite me to embrace, hug, and cherish the people in my life now. My open hands remind me to feel grateful for relationships even when they have flown away. My open hands are a visual promise that I can anticipate a future filled with more love.

Not everything is meant to last forever. Emotional growth means learning to hold gratitude for all blessings—those blessings that I have now, the ones I have had in the past, and those that are still to come.

Shasta Nelson

Shasta Nelson, MDiv, is the CEO of GirlFriendCircles.com, a women's friendship matching site in over 35 cities in the United States. This essay comes from parts of her book *Friendships Don't Just Happen: The Guide to Creating a Meaningful Circle of GirlFriends*. Shasta writes at ShastasFriendshipBlog.com and for the *Huffington Post*, speaks to corporations, churches, and conferences on healthy relationships, and coaches individual clients through the personal growth that leads to relational fulfillment.

BFF-Less

Mimi Towle

"Who's your BFF?" my eight year old daughter Natalie often asks. I always lie and say, "Your father." As I see it, my answer solves two issues. First, my daughter feels secure in the belief that her parents are best friends. Secondly, I don't have to tell her that I don't have and never have had a Best Friend Forever. (I also can't call my biological father "Dad," which is a topic for another essay, but demonstrates my tendency to shy away from labels.)

I think the root of my issue with the BFF label is that relying on just one friend to be there for every situation in life sets a person up for disappointment. Take my wedding, for example: two of my brides-maids were grumpy about their singleton status, and another brides-maid couldn't get her mind or hands off her boyfriend. And these were the best friends I had. Not one of them took me aside and told me how happy she was for me or said, "Hey, let's take a walk on the beach before you become a married woman." Is that too much to ask? Probably. And truthfully, I didn't do any of those things at their weddings either, so no hard feelings.

Perhaps my idealism was due to my lonely status as an only child yearning for that perfectly scripted and supportive buddy I'd seen and studied on the small screen. These girls and boys on TV would have great adventures with their best friends, and any prickly or awkward situation would always be neatly tied up within 22 minutes or less.

As an adult viewer, however, I am rather suspicious of these fictionalized best friend scenarios, such as *Sex in the City*. Who really believes that in real life, the over-sexed Samantha would have patience for the pretty and tart Charlotte? Who would believe that the straight-shooting lawyer, Miranda, would ever tolerate Carrie's silly blathering? Or in the wildly popular *Friends* series—why was Phoebe in the mix? In *Seinfeld*, who would actually tolerate George, let alone eat lunch with him at the diner? These sitcoms have done to friendships what anorexic models have done to our nation's body image: set unrealistic standards. For those of us who don't have a glamorous, trend-setting, impenetrable group of friends, there is still hope. In other words, don't despair if you don't have a standing lunch date with a BFF at a trendy café in New York. A study conducted by the beauty company Dove revealed that 91 percent of women feel that media and advertising should do a better job of representing realistic images of women over the age of 50; I feel that I could poll my Facebook friends and get the same results regarding fictionalized friendships.

Still, I hope we can take the pressure off of having these unrealistic relationships and enjoy the benefits of the relationships we do have. Friendships, however labeled or mislabeled, are good for our health. Much research has been done about the benefits of friendship on one's happiness and even lifespan. For instance, in a landmark study on the physiological effects of friendship among women, researchers at UCLA found that unlike men, when women experience stress, they go into "tend and befriend" mode. As one of the researchers put it, "It seems that when the hormone oxytocin is released as part of the stress response in a woman, it buffers the 'fight or flight' response and encourages her to tend to children and gather with other women instead. When she actually engages in this tending or befriending, studies suggest that more oxytocin is released, which further counters stress and produces a calming effect."

One of the researchers on the study, Laura Cousino Klein, Ph.D., says that this calming response does not occur in men because testosterone—which men produce in high levels when they're under stress—seems to reduce the effects of oxytocin. Estrogen, she adds, seems to enhance it. As Dr. Klein and her colleagues conclude via their Tend and Befriend notion, social ties reduce our risk of disease by lowering blood pressure, heart rate, and cholesterol. "There's no doubt," says Dr. Klein, "that friends are helping us live longer."

To take the pressure off having one perfect BFF and allow us to partake in these realistic friendships for the sake of our happiness and health, I'd like to propose a few new categories: BFRN (best friend right now), BFFHS (best friend from high school), BFTGITW (best friend to get into trouble with), BNF (best neighbor friend), BFFTO (best friend from the office), and, we can't forget, BFISBFW (best friend I shouldn't be friends with). Most importantly, let's just do away with the "F" that means "forever" and we'll be on the right track.

After a bit of Googling on the topic of forever friendships, I discovered a goldmine of information on Dr. Irene Levine's friendship blog. Levine's years of research included posing open-ended questions to more than 1,500 females between the ages of seven and 70. These questions lead to the publication of her book *Best Friends Forever: Surviving a Breakup with Your Best Friend*. By exploring the complexities of fractured friendships, Dr. Levine debunks some common myths, including one notion that she herself had swallowed. "From the time they are very young," Levine explains, "women want to have a best friend and be a best friend. But over time, the realization hits that they need different best friends for different reasons. It's unrealistic to expect any one person to meet all your needs." It's also unrealistic, as I see it, to expect the needs you have in your friendships to remain constant over time.

Another point Dr. Levine makes is that many assume friendships are solid until a betrayal or unforgivable act has occurred. But even if friendships merely dissolve, she says, it's not always a bad thing. Dr. Levine found that over 80 percent of the time, old friends simply fade away, often because two people aren't on each other's radars anymore. "As women evolve," she notes, "we graduate, we move, we marry, we mother, we get divorced, we become widowed, we change careers."

It should relieve more of the pressure of having one BFF that Dr. Levine's research revealed the average friendship lasts only about seven years. But Internet-based social networks, she adds, can be "a wonderful tool," enabling people to renew friendships broken apart only because of circumstance, and bringing people together based on common interests. Personally, I know that when friends from high school find me on Facebook, I feel as though I am legitimizing my past by continuing those friendships into adulthood. In the case of my high school friends, we all seem to remember the good parts of each other, leaving petty judgments and social standings in the past.

After considering the wisdom (and research) of Dr. Klein and Dr. Levine, I feel comforted in my never having had one perfect, supportive, always-game-for-getting-into-trouble friend for all four plus decades I've been on the planet. I can appreciate my longtime friendships and the comfort and humor they provide in shaping who I am, while still looking forward to my newer friendships and where they will take me.

Next time Natalie asks the BFF question, my new response will have to be something like, "That is a really good question. I've had so many great friends . . . I'd hate to pick just one."

Mimi Towle

Mimi Towle has enjoyed a diverse career in publishing. After a brief stint at Oracle, she spent some years working at a start-up magazine in the Tenderloin District of San Francisco, California, floated through a few corporate editorial departments, and is currently the executive editor at *Marin Magazine*, a lifestyle publication in Northern California. She authored a guidebook called *Bilingual Babycare* and recently she co-founded MakeItSimpleSister.com, which aims to simplify and enhance the experience of living for women of all ages. She adores her two daughters, dog, cat and husband . . . in that order (though the list changes daily).

Lessons from the Playground

Kimberly Danek Pinkson

Early relationships between girls plant the seeds for how women relate to one another in adult friendships and within communities. I met Pia, my first best friend, when we came to a stalemate crossing the bridge on our soon-to-be shared kindergarten campus. Neither one of us would move out of the other's way, so we stood there staring at each other, two stubborn five year olds on a wooden play structure. She told me her name was Elizabeth, because she loved the book *Elizabeth: The Birdwatcher*. Her Dad sternly said, "Pia?" and she ran away. I would later learn that she hated her name at the time. That moment became part of our shared lore, the "how we met" story that we have told over and over as the years passed.

Our families had many similarities: we both had European-born mothers, New York-born fathers, and younger siblings. We became best friends and our families grew closer through carpools, swapped baby-sitting nights, and shared holidays. We were living testament to the saying, "It takes a village," and our friendship taught me that those with whom we first connect as sisters can influence the type of women we become and the personal and professional paths we choose.

Of course, I would not realize the sweetness of our connection until years later. No, over the years we were too busy with ballet, gymnastics, soccer, toys, boys, slumber parties, and the sweetness of a childhood spent in the countryside of Northern California. We played pirates in the forest and ran away to her basement when we thought our parents were favoring our younger siblings. We would call each other on the phone just to be on the line at the same time, driving our parents crazy as we'd just laugh, and laugh, and laugh at nothing at all. The fact that we were doing it together was the important part. We dreamed of first kisses and devoured Judy Bloom books, which were much more exciting than talking about periods and breast development with our moms. Then, we watched as our boobs actually started to grow. (Hers grew a lot more than mine.) We got our periods. We went to different high schools and our friendship grew more distant, but we stayed connected, always checking in at the appropriate times.

Then, somewhere between the death of her mother and our college graduations, we began to realize the gift of female friendship and the value of our shared history. We began to reach across the miles much more regularly, she at college back in Boston, and me across the ocean at the University of Hawaii.

Our paths have yet to bring us back to the sweetness of living just down the street from one another, as we did growing up, but every time we visit or talk, we jump back into things as if we'd just said goodbye moments earlier. We've both lived all over the world and made many new friends, but it was in each other's hearts that we first learned about the kind of sisterhood not born from genetics.

As an oh-so serious UCLA undergrad, I was not at all interested in sorority life; I imagined it to be all beer-drinking fraternity dudes groping and vapid conversations about who had slept with who and under what conditions. But, there's a moment in every woman's life when she realizes she has indeed joined a sorority, like it or not, and that sorority is called womanhood. For some, it's the onset of menses that results in an "enter now" card that opens the door of womanhood. For others, pregnancy is a sort of hazing, and when you come out the other side, you've been accepted: you're now a member of the great sorority called motherhood.

My moment of realization came one snowy night about three months after my son was born. I was up nursing at around 2:00 a.m. The house was cold and quiet, save for the wind howling outside and the sound of the icy whiteness blowing against the window. Looking down at my son, I felt more love than I'd ever believed possible, but I was also exhausted, hormonal, and despite my literal connection to this little being, I felt terribly alone. Tears rolled down my cheeks.

Suddenly, I remembered a fellow Pilates teacher who'd said to me some months before, "When you get to that point where you feel like you just can't go on, think of all the other mothers out there, doing the exact same thing as you at that exact same moment." I began to imagine a mom feeding her baby in a Paris flat, the Arc de Triomphe holding court down the boulevard; an African mom nursing in her rammed earth hut, with several generations sharing the room; a mom nursing in a yurt in Tibet, with goats running all around. Maybe there was even a mom somewhere in my own community who was also up nursing. As the images continued to fill my mind—and heart—my loneliness was replaced by a sense of belonging. I realized that what I was doing was so much bigger than my family and it brought me a sense of purpose beyond what I'd ever imagined. I was sustaining life. Just as countless moms have done before me, and God willing, many more will do after me.

Whether one has a child or not, women are the nurturers, the caregivers, and the sustainers of life. This is not to say that men cannot and do not often exhibit the same characteristics, but while modern cultures have failed to recognize the power of typically feminine traits, many indigenous cultures have, and the power of the feminine anchored their belief systems. Tenets such as cooperation and living in balance with the natural world were key to their survival. Many creation myths, such as the Mesoamerican and Korean, look to a goddess as the ultimate deity for worship. Today, Western culture leans toward a more patriarchal belief system and much has been said and written about the negative effects of overusing typically masculine traits such as brute strength to negotiate and win. Of course, both masculine and feminine qualities are necessary. I pray that one day we will find balance between the two, but until then, we women know: life is largely in our hands.

As we sit in this era of testosterone-driven machismo, it seems more important than ever that we nurture our friendships within the sisterhood. It's an interesting time to be a woman. As women, we control 85 percent of the purchasing power in the United States; every dollar we spend is a vote cast in the world's largest economy, and that vote ripples out to affect our brothers, sisters, and children all over the globe. How we cast that vote is largely determined by the word of mouth we share with one another. As our ancestors shared around the cooking fire and the watering hole, so too do we share across school parking lots, coffee shops, offices, and online communities. So, the more purposeful the information we share, the more our actions influence others and have the power to create positive change. The more we trust one another, the more we can be open to collaboration and support.

If not for Pia and the lessons I learned early in my life from our enduring friendship, I might not so readily recognize the sweetness offered by the women in my life today. Nor would I so readily offer my hand and heart to other women newly entering my life. Because of Pia—and my mom, sister, and grandmothers to be sure—I know and value the richness of connecting with other women. Though I love my father, my son, my fiancé, and the many wonderful men who are a part of my life, there is an understanding among us women that cannot be named or replaced. We know one another's strengths and one another's weaknesses, and we nurture for the good and the bad.

"Be good to the woman," says a Lakota proverb, "for at both ends of your life, you will rest in her hands." While our culture struggles to find a balanced appreciation and recognition of the sexes, we band together because we know that life is in our hands. We must make choices that create and propel a healthy and sustainable world, and it is only through supporting one another that we find the courage and strength to do so. I worry about us, though. I fear that we are trying to do too much and be too many things rather than trusting our hearts and bodies to guide us to be the women we are meant to be.

My nine year old son came home from school today and said to me, with eyes wide and wondering, "Mom, did you know the army people are deciding if women should be allowed in the military again?" He shared an article he was reading that addressed the debate about whether or not women should be allowed in armed combat. I asked him his opinion. He answered quite clearly, without hesitation, "Well, all the women should get together and decide together, because the most important thing is for them to be able to choose as a team." Those words seem so fitting for so many of the battles we face as women today and I find it heartening that they came from a boy who represents the next generation of men, on behalf of me and my sisters.

Even in his youth, my son respects the right of women to choose and he understands the power of women coming together in unity. We may not be able to figure out all the world's problems, but by supporting one another in friendship and decision-making, our journey can be all the richer and more rewarding. Certainly, there is no relationship quite like female friendship. It influences you early on and runs strong through the currents of life.

Kimberly Pinkson

As the Founder of the international organization EcoMom® Alliance, Kimberly Pinkson is an expert in sustainable living and consumer behavior, producing campaigns that reach over one million people each year. Kimberly is an inspiring public speaker, holistic wellness expert, environmental health advocate, and mother. She is a popular media guest and has appeared on media outlets such as the TODAY Show, CBS Morning News, and 20/20. She has been a keynote speaker at events such as the World Women's Forum in Seoul, Korea. Kimberly loves cooking with her son, going on adventures in nature, dancing, and eating organic ice cream.

Ode to Women

Lenore Perry

An ode to the women who've loved me lifelong.
Well, some just a season, and some for a song.
Funny how right at the time we most need,
A woman is there who's spot-on for the deed.

Women, ah women, the short and the tall—
Some take a nosedive to break our hard fall.
Some hold our feet firmly up to the fire,
while others help manifest all we desire.

Women have tucked me down into my tears
with a hand and an ear and a look that quells fears.
Women have told me it's time to be strong
and wrench myself out of a love that went wrong.

Women have walked by my side, in my shoes!
pledging allegiance whatever I choose.
Women have told me to get off my bum.
Take action! Stop whining! And don't be so glum!

Women, ah women, they've been there for me
in ways no one ever could frankly foresee.
Friends and acquaintances, therapists too—
Good news for humans, that's what women do!

From early in life, I don't quite remember
support like this from our fair, softer gender.

Yes I had my sister, though our bond was strained
by the troubles at home and Mom's infinite pain.

I also had school friends, though most weren't so great
as my personal hatred skewed how I relate.
No doubt those encounters, through youth's uphill climb,
had a big hand in my growth over time.

And maybe the payoff of an awkward "back when"
is a rich, fertile network of women (and some men).
Old friends and new—it's a well-varied lot.
(The one constant factor is they're all pretty hot).

Mutuality too is an unwritten law.
It's my time plus two ears upon which they most draw.
There are days when my phone rings in rapid succession,
each with potential for a full-blown friend session.

Sometimes we're downloading and chatting and dishing—
Often we're analyzing the human condition.
Sometimes they really are seeking advice,
while sometimes they just need to laugh once or thrice.

Some workdays, I scuttle from one office to another
as resident therapist, sister and mother.
It's these days I know that if I weren't around
my office's "psych wing" would surely shut down.

Research has proven—it's built in our brains—
That good social bonding has limitless gains.
It elevates hormones that aid stress reduction
and even promotes good digestive function.

It augments our sense of peace and well being,
Reminds us our choices and, boy is that freeing.
It helps us to sleep more and feel anxious less.
It basically fixes the whole bloody mess!

Further, it encourages selfless behavior.
Progesterone clearly is the world's mighty savior.
The reason it's built into our DNA
is when women hang out, the planet's OK.

An ode to the women who've loved me lifelong
accepting me whether I'm tender or strong.
Encouraging me to be just as I am,
supporting and loving again and again . . .

Lenore Perry

Lenore Perry is a graphic designer and writer living in Los Angeles, California. She received her BA from the University Of Southern California in English Literature and Creative Writing, her MA in Spiritual Psychology from the University of Santa Monica, and her Certificate of Design Communication Arts from the University of California, Los Angeles. She is intrigued by the power of the intellect and heart, and the conjunction of those two in the pursuit of happiness, contribution, and personal fulfillment. She has had articles published in various online and print publications and has self-published a book about her life experience entitled *Look! I Woke Up!*

Friend Collector

Ana Hays

I knew breakfast with Jane was winding down when she excused herself to go to the restroom. Normally when I came to visit my parents in Peoria, Illinois, Jane and I would go out for drinks. This time, though, the responsibilities of motherhood prevailed. Instead of meeting at a local bar where I would've been happily sipping a Bud Light on ice, we'd met at a diner known for its choice of a "side of asparagus" with any breakfast selection. Thankfully, I'd had the foresight to stop at Starbucks for a latte on the way there; I'd had the feeling that espresso drinks weren't on the menu.

"Whatcha thinking about?" Jane asked as she plopped back into the seat of the booth across from me.

"Retirement."

"Who can afford that?"

"Seriously. The other day Ethan and I were talking about it and I asked him where he thought we might like to live when it's time to check into a retirement home."

"What'd he say?"

"That we'd think about it when he turns 80."

"When's that?"

"In 13 years!"

"Hmmmm."

"Since he's 17 years older than me, I imagine that he'll die first. So, that left me thinking about where I will want to live after he's gone."

"Why wouldn't you stay in California?"

"Because I want to be close to friends like you and Lindsay. You're two of my oldest and most loyal friends. Why wouldn't I want to be near you?"

"Because we live in Peoria."

"Right. But I'll have money to travel."

"No, it'd be better if we came and visited you. Besides, you can't move back here. That's insane. You have to live your life. You've got friends in California and in Chicago if you want to go back there. But not Peoria."

I watched as she dug around in her purse for her keys and slid out of the booth.

"Time for me to pick up Alizé. This isn't something you have to think about today."

We walked out to the parking lot and hugged, and I jumped into the black Mariner I'd rented at the airport. As I turned on the engine, the air conditioner blasted me in the face. A temperature of more than 90 degrees was one thing, but with 98 percent humidity, it was exhausting. How spoiled one gets in California.

Turning onto University Avenue, images of the faces of all my various girlfriends whizzed by like the oncoming cars heading south in the opposite direction. When Ethan and I had jumped into our relationship the previous year, he'd marveled at the number of my girlfriends.

"It's like you collect them," he'd said.

"I don't collect them," I replied, slightly incensed and wondering how I was going to balance time with my girlfriends with my new committed relationship. "If you were talking to my dad," I said, "he'd tell you that I've never lost touch with a girlfriend."

When I was ten, my parents moved my brother and me from Los Angeles to Stuttgart, Germany—our first major move. I left behind my best friend and neighbor, Nora. After her parents and she visited us in Germany, we began corresponding with each other and continued to do so for the next 20 years.

When we finally met in person again, she was studying for her bachelor's degree in literature at the University of California, Berkeley while working as a sous chef. Nora excitedly introduced me as her pen pal to her boyfriend and friends. They all marveled at the idea of 20 years of letter writing and how it had maintained our friendship.

I visited her several years later—she'd graduated and moved to Lake Tahoe to work at a four-star restaurant; I had relocated to Palo Alto from Chicago. She pulled out a box filled to the brim with letters from me and other friends and family members.

"If you want, you can dig out your letters and take them back home with you and read them," she offered.

The number of envelopes in the box astounded me—and I was saddened by the memory of my mother confessing that, while cleaning out my childhood closet, she had tossed Nora's letters into the garbage instead of the 20 letters from a college boyfriend that were tied together with a grosgrain ribbon.

I spent hours on the floor of Nora's living room in front of a roaring fire, pulling my letters from the box. I organized my 100 plus letters chronologically to take back with me to Palo Alto. Once home, I spent an entire weekend reading them. Some were short, depending on the timeframe of my life, while others, written during the years between seventh grade and high school graduation, were daily tomes invariably numbering 16 to 20 pages in length. Written in my handwriting *du jour*—I changed my style often—these missives recounted my teenage woes and the shocking reality of being a transplanted California girl, who was first introduced to the wonders of Europe and the idea of learning multiple languages, then plopped down into a place named Peoria.

When we arrived, it was July of 1973 and I had my first encounter with heat and humidity. The first school I attended rumbled with racial tension and the kids I encountered weren't too welcoming toward a tall and gangly girl they nicknamed "Tree." To them, I was just the girl who hailed from California, the state that could drop into the ocean at any moment, and had lived most recently in a country best remembered for its Nazis. Luckily for me, I befriended Lindsay and later, Jane, who were and still are good-hearted souls and loyal, time-tested girlfriends.

And thankfully, I also had my pen pal Nora to whom I told absolutely everything.

"I can't believe how angry I was," I shared with Nora over the phone one evening after reading the letters. "Man, was I pissed at my parents. And I'd completely forgotten about my harebrained scheme of running away to marry Richard, my African-American boyfriend. Did you remember that the kids threw bricks through our living room window and placed for sale signs in our front yard all because I was dating him? I must have been living in some sort of haze not to remember that. It seems my parents finally defeated my idea with threats of disinheritance and revoking my college tuition, because in one of the letters I wrote about how I broke up with him. And I was even angry with you. I spent pages upon pages chastising you for not immediately writing me back. How is it that you are still my friend?"

Nora was silent for a moment, then thoughtfully replied, "You know, I think I must have been your first therapist. Perhaps I was your outlet to write about all the things you didn't feel you could tell your other friends. Thinking about it now, if we hadn't been pen pals, who knows where you would be now."

I often ponder where I would be without my girlfriends—the women who have laughed with me during happy moments and consoled me when I've cried; coached me through bad bosses and job interviews that turned into great jobs; mourned with me the loss of our girlfriend when she died of cancer; packed up the personal belongings in my Palo Alto apartment and interviewed potential people to sublet when I decided to remain on Maui to become a writer rather than return with them to the Bay Area; cheered me on as I climbed the stairs to the front door of my birth mother's house on Lake Superior and watched me as I knocked and waited—then hugged me when the door remained closed; discussed recent weight gain and menopause, how to care for aging parents, and the best way to die; and who listened to 30 years of dating stories. They never doubted for a moment that someday I would find love, and they celebrated with me when it finally arrived with Ethan.

And then, there is the mourning and the loss of the friendships that have been altered by a move, illness, or marriage, and the time spent grieving the space that change leaves behind. But with patience and time, I find that new friends always appear seeking the same thing—a girlfriend to whom they can pour their heart out.

On the bookshelf in my office, I have created a shrine honoring my girlfriends. Picture frames contain snapshots of memorable moments: 50th, 65th, and 91st birthday celebrations, an annual visit with Tracy at her home in Chicago at Christmas, posing with Lindsay at our 30th high school reunion and a black and white snapshot of us dancing hand-in-hand at our seventh grade sock hop, the Shakti Circle gals at our various weddings, and the group's favorite photo displaying eight of us standing in a tide pool in the lava fields on Maui, arm-in-arm, flaunting our naked glory.

Perhaps I have collected friends along the road of my life, but I like to think of my friendships as a collection of interwoven stories about women who have come together to form bonds that last a lifetime. Sure, without them I would still be a version of myself, but together, we have grown into amazing women—friends who are loyal, loving, and caring. And in a life filled with the world's best girlfriends, who knows where I will retire?

Ana Hays

With a creative and business writing background, Ana Hays' writing has appeared in *Chicken Soup for the Adopted Soul*, *Walnut Creek Magazine*, *Sybase Magazine* and other publications. Ana also leads creative writing workshops at WomenCare, a non-profit organization in Santa Cruz, California dedicated to offering a safe haven for women who are making the cancer journey, and for SPARK, where she inspires students to follow their dreams of becoming published writers. She resides in Menlo Park, California and Angel Fire, New Mexico.

Section Five

Finding Yourself

A Breasted Development

Carol Pott

Though everyone has heard "it takes a village," our society is no longer structured to support people in that sense. As a single parent with a mortgage, life is always a delicate balancing act between finances and freedom. Sometimes, even when the whole village turns out to support you, there is still something lacking. For me, that gap turned out to be very personal.

In January of 2006, I was single, sexy, and successful while promoting my bestselling book, working at a job I loved, and juggling the schedules of my two young daughters. I had worked hard to get where I was. My girls were both doing great in school and were starting to feel more at home since our move to Marin in 2002. I'd never been healthier or in better shape. I was playing on two co-ed soccer teams and running hard on the trails near my home. My kids were happy and strong and I was dating and had an active social life. Sure, I felt guilty dropping the kids off at school way too early in the morning and picking them up way too late from aftercare, but my focus was on the basics and providing for them financially while advancing my career, not on spending quality time with them doing homework, participating in the parent association, volunteering in the classroom, or bringing cupcakes to bake sales. If anyone had told me I'd be doing this all alone, I might have thought twice. I certainly provided well more than the basic fundamentals of survival for my daughters—more than many parents even dream about—but I often felt I'd left behind the idea of being an active parent when I signed the divorce papers and faced building a life without financial support or the stability of a two-parent nuclear family.

In the course of the next two years, all of the promise it took many years to build would come crashing down.

In October of 2006, I was diagnosed with stage-3 breast cancer and my ability to keep up the fragile balance quickly toppled. After doing it all on my own for years, I was thrust into a world of structured dependence. Luckily, friends banded together and brought meals, organized weekly play dates for my children, volunteered to drive me to my weekly chemotherapy appointments, and helped with homework and household projects. People I barely knew came out of the woodwork to assist us and suddenly, I had a village. Oddly, the scourge of cancer also created the opportunity for me to volunteer in the classroom and for the first time, I experienced a supported existence. I was home every day when my girls came home from school, I had time to devote to music lessons, and I was there to kiss the boo-boos and make everything better. Even though I was sick, it was easy to recognize that priceless gift—I could finally be a participatory parent. Bald from the chemo, fighting nausea, and with half the skin on my chest burned away from radiation treatments, I would sit in the classroom with tears streaming down my face because it was such a gift to spend time with my kids . . . a bittersweet gift.

Just a couple months before I was diagnosed, I'd begun dating a man I'd known for over 20 years. Four treatments into my eight treatments of chemotherapy, he asked me to marry him. Though we'd both said we would never marry again, I felt a transcendent love for him and, in a place of absolute vulnerability, I said yes. We planned a winter wedding to take place just five months after I finished the last of 33 treatments of radiation.

I came out of cancer treatment completely depressed and without any of my earlier confidence. Even the "Hairless in Paris" tour of Europe my fiancé organized to celebrate the end of my active treatment couldn't raise my spirits. My body was forever changed: the chemo had thrown me into early menopause, I was fat from steroids, and the maintenance medication made me feel old and weak, quick to anger, and caused my hair to fall out in handfuls . . . not to mention the scars, physical and emotional, from the loss of my breast. Essentially, I was a mess.

Perhaps worried that I might remain a depressed, fat, and angry mess, my husband of six months left me. I was no longer the sexy super-mom with the fantastic career and sorted finances. Instead, I was an overweight, unemployed divorcee, with one breast and two kids.

It seemed things couldn't get worse, but they did. After over a year on disability, I scrambled to find a job in a depressed market, taking a significant drop in pay and accepting a junior position working in a depressing cube farm for a corporation miles from home promoting products I couldn't care less about. For the first time in over a decade, I just had "a job." Before writing my second book, I'd been doing sexy United Nations consulting gigs, flying all over the world from my home base in Paris, meeting important people, and feeling as if I was making a real difference with my work. I was well paid, loved what I did, and was good at it. Now, I was a single contributor in an undervalued department of a top-heavy corporation. The people I worked with were bored and complaining. Not so surprisingly, I didn't connect with any of them. I began to dread going to work. Each morning, as my hour-long commute neared its end and my arrival at the office neared, I'd feel my muscles contract and I would become increasingly tense. I was often sick and began having health troubles. A typical nine hour day began to tax me like I'd been doing hard labor. Once again, I was barely participating in my children's lives and very conscious of the guilt associated with extending their aftercare hours to meet the demands of my work schedule.

On top of everything, I had never felt so alone in my life. Now that I was a survivor and at least visibly healed, my supportive village had disappeared. Between that and the usual migration caused by divorce, I was dramatically solo. My three best girlfriends had all recently moved far enough away that even phone calls were a challenge. I was forced to face the fact that most of my close friends lived half the world away.

When my kids were away with their dads, I would sit alone marveling at the quick destruction of my life and feeling more and more disconnected from my self. I knew it made no sense to be depressed—after all, I had my health, my children were happy, and, despite the drop in pay, I was making a lot of money at my hated job—but that just made it worse. I couldn't see past my depression. Being the newly-dumped wife of a man from an old San Francisco family didn't exactly ingratiate me to the San Francisco and Marin social circles either, so I was not invited anywhere. I was rarely in the company of anyone other than my daughters or my family. I felt like the pariah single mom.

My loneliness and depression propelled me into social networking hoping that would be the panacea. Despite major reservations about my body image, I also decided to post an online dating profile. Like I had done many times in the past, I sought to find the key to happiness outside myself and put my energy into finding friends and a new relationship that would "solve" all my problems and make me happy.

At first, Facebook was fun and reconnecting with friends from all over the world made me feel social again. The online dating thing even created the illusion of interested men, though I never met any of them. Obviously, this interaction was all virtual. The reality was that I would spend hours alone, illuminated only by the computer monitor, feeling sorry for myself but never letting on. My posts from the time were all about my new job and surviving cancer and were aimed to create a picture of myself that would be palatable to my virtual friends. Of course, Facebook also kept me in touch with my girlfriends who were now far away, which made my interest in pursuing similar friendships here at home far less interesting. I created a virtual reality and a virtual me. Once again, I was sexy, single, and successful . . . at least online.

Not long after I posted my dating profile, I began seeing a man who seemed ideal on paper. He was a tall, handsome, emergency room physician, who moonlighted as a rescue diver, and sang sweet harmony while picking guitar in a cowboy band. I was so inexplicably attracted to him that my knees went weak just catching his eye across the room.

Everything seemed perfect initially, but it quickly became apparent that, as usual, things aren't as they seem. On top of everything, we maintained a pretense in our relationship that created more illusion: in his world, I was a single woman without children. He even joked about my turning off the phone and forgetting the kids the moment I walked in his door. I hate to admit it, but it felt blissful to play house with him, maintaining the pretense that I was kid free and, if even for just a few hours, to see myself as I wanted to be, as the successful woman I used to be. Warnings and alarms were ringing loudly in my head, but I closed my ears and held fast to my blinders while falling hard for the spitting image of my childhood romantic ideal.

In our profiles, we'd both claimed that we wanted a real relationship, but it was quickly apparent that, though he may have been ready for a serious partnership, he wasn't ready for a serious partnership with me. He eventually made it clear that he was neither interested in an exclusive relationship nor serious involvement with a woman who had children. After stumbling for several months and nearly breaking up a couple times, we started singing together, quickly propelling our relationship into a place neither of us were ready for and creating such romance and intimacy that much of the make-believe between us was actualized. We stepped it up: playing house as much as we could and splitting time between his place and mine—but always when my kids were away and mostly without any contact with our friends and family. We were obsessively attracted to each other and my worries about my incomplete body disappeared. In his eyes, I was childless, free, and whole. I poured everything into my relationship with him feeling sexy and complete—despite those incessant alarms.

Of course the relationship had to implode. I was hoping for happiness outside myself, putting all my hopes into a dreadfully imperfect relationship, and holding a completely inappropriate man responsible for my happiness when I was lonelier and more despondent than I had ever been. I kept making excuses for him and blaming myself for issues and conflicts that he had so obviously created to displace the relationship and undermine what little security there was. I finally had to decide to stop judging myself and get out of my own way. Once I did, the relationship quickly fell apart. When I wasn't trying to fix everything and provide solutions, it fizzled away amidst ridiculous accusations and months of lingering harassment and convincing nine-page love letters.

I fell into a deep depression after the final denouement. Part of it was the loss of the brilliant *trompe l'oeil* the relationship painted on everything around me gilding reality, but even worse was the realization that I'd spent nearly two years focused completely outside my own life, on someone who didn't hesitate to harshly cut me completely out of his. If only I'd listened to the bells and whistles. In my mind, I thought I could put all the energy I had toward building something unique and powerful with him, but in reality, I was relying on him to create my happiness and give me the courage to start my life over. I had, again, blindly allowed someone else to determine my life for me and had focused completely on his social life, his friends, his needs, and his interests, while allowing my own life and responsibilities to fall by the wayside. The utter stupidity I felt having fallen so hard for something so wrong was crushing. When I lost my job a few months later, realizing that I'd practically given it up to focus on a broken relationship, my self-judgment became even more acute. I felt like I'd left my brain behind inside a man's trousers. It was painfully obvious that I had to figure out how to create happiness within myself and for myself.

My sister, who was visiting from England, told me to pursue my passions and wondered, "Why do Americans work at jobs they hate?" We talked at length about reworking life to spend time with our families, pursuing creativity, creating work that expresses passions, and the importance and joy of being an active parent. My best girlfriend in Sweden gently encouraged me to pursue freelance work to ease my financial worries while I was looking for another job, then tried not to sound too worried when I explained that, amazingly, there were no jobs to apply for.

I don't remember ever being so concerned and frightened for my future. I spent many sleepless nights filled with worry and anxiety about making ends meet, losing my home to foreclosure, and finding work in the middle of the global economic downturn, but from afar, my girlfriends kept me on track and out of my head, so I could sort myself out and begin to create something fantastic for myself and my daughters.

A girlfriend from my daughters' school encouraged me to promote my freelance business and then miraculously hired me to help with some exciting projects she was working on, another woman I'd recently met asked me to work with her on a memoir, and a girlfriend from high school referred me to the contract recruiter at the design firm where she worked. I slowly began to crawl out of the deep hole I'd dug for myself, gain some confidence in my work, and see my freelance activity as a viable business.

I was still painfully lonely, spending far too much time viewing the world through Facebook-colored glasses and comparing my apparent failure to the "picture-perfect" lives of my "friends." The comparison was painful and I certainly wasn't going to make new friends by posting clever status updates and photos of myself looking successful. I had nearly forgotten how to make friends outside of the virtual world of social networks and Facebook, and was painfully unable to ask for what I needed from anyone, much less to ask women who seemed interesting if they wanted to be friends.

It took a lot of work to open up and make myself vulnerable to the women around me. In my life, I had not always felt that the women I encountered were supportive or worth investing my time in. I'd experienced petty jealousies that resulted in major disappointments both personally and professionally and catty remarks that were sent with such precision that they were bound to destroy. Still, I knew that my happiness required me to invest in myself and my community and the only way to do that safely as the pariah mom was to focus on the women right in my midst. After all, it was clear to me that, though it might be easier to befriend a man, the possibility of resulting drama certainly wasn't worth that investment.

It is amazing how the world works. No sooner had I determined my goal and focused on my intentions, when a series of doors opened and I found that there were many women out there just like me: vulnerable, lonely, and searching for connection in an over-connected world. Even women I'd always thought were surrounded by good friends revealed that they were longing for genuine connection and true friendship. I began to gather a group of people around me, slowly rebuilding my world, and beginning to see that I could be a good friend, a good mother, and a responsible member of my community, while still living my passion and being true to myself. I even founded a French go-go band with some friends, giving me the opportunity to sing and play with some very talented musicians and astonishingly accomplished people.

In 2008, when I felt I couldn't get any lower and reflected upon my sorry state, I would never have imagined looking at the world from where I stand now. I am genuinely happy and it is due to my friends and my own efforts to create happiness within myself and focus my attention on my own life. Sure, I am still the single pariah mom and parenting in society from that position is never easy. I am often lonely, too. But I have created a network of women and friends who are supportive, creative, and fun. We are all building community right where we live and changing the world one relationship at a time.

I love my work, my band, my family, and my friends. I am working harder than I have ever worked in my life, but I feel gratified knowing that it is me who makes me happy and that my focus is on sustaining my happiness, not on something outside myself, a pretense or virtual illusion, or a man who may walk out of my life and take my happiness with him. I own my own happiness.

The women in my life are strong social warriors. I am one of them. I am present in my life knowing that I am raising brave daughters who will face the world squarely. If nothing else, I hope that I am teaching them, not only by example, how to create their own happiness, how to foster genuine connection around them, and how to forge their art with passion.

Carol Pott

Carol Pott is a writer, the founder and editorial director at Editorial Girl®, and the lead singer for the French yé yé revival band Rue '66. In 1994, she witnessed the genocide in Rwanda yet returned with the United Nations to work in Africa for six years. She is the coeditor and author of *Genocide in Rwanda: A Collective Memory*, and the editor and contributing author of the bestselling *The Blue Pages: A Directory of Companies Rated by Their Politics and Practices*. Her work has been featured in the *Washington Post*, the *San Francisco Chronicle*, and the *New York Times*.

Untitled, sculpture by Dana King

Dana King

Award-winning broadcast journalist Dana King has worked in television news for 25 years. She has spent the last 15 with San Francisco, California TV station KPIX, anchoring the 6:00 and the 11:00 p.m. news. She arrived in San Francisco from New York after spending five years as a network correspondent for CBS News. King has traveled the world reporting on issues in Iraq, Afghanistan, Rwanda, Ghana, Honduras, Taiwan and more. King is also an accomplished sculptor. She spends countless hours in her studio creating art when not doing her "night job." Dana is represented by the Thelma Harris Art Gallery in Oakland, California.

Looking Through a New Lens

Lone Morch

I never wanted to photograph naked women. I didn't even like being around women much. But life talks to us constantly and has an uncanny way of getting us to where we need to be. My situation was no different. I was in my mid-thirties when I picked up a manual Nikon camera—to protest the rapid digitalization of my life and out of a desire to take real pictures. I was curious about the light and drama of black and white photography.

A series of seemingly random events followed. I transformed the bedroom I shared with my husband into a lush boudoir complete with cranberry red walls, a canopy bed, and a candelabrum. That the redecoration was more likely an outward expression of something I felt inside, I couldn't have told you at the time, but something was definitely stirring within me.

Deep into the fourth year of my marriage, the initial romance had worn off, my biological clock was ticking, and I felt oddly invisible as a sensual woman. Mostly, I found myself wearing overalls, trying to build our business, and attempting to clear the emotional drains in the gutter of our marriage. A less sexy, more jaded version of my passionate self met me in the mirror. What had started out like a magical carpet ride had become work. Tired of expounding upon our now clear differences, my husband preferred not to talk at all. "We have talked about that already. Can we talk about that later? I don't want to talk about it," was his standard reply. What was a woman to do? Clearly, I could no longer rely on his continuous desire and approval to make me feel sexy, attractive, and worthy, but what was my sexuality if not my husband's? How would it be expressed in my life? My sexuality was asking me to take its wellbeing into my own hands (no pun intended). These were good questions for me to ask myself, and their answers came in the most unusual way.

The approach of my husband's birthday gave me the idea to create a book of sexy photographs for him. A friend volunteered to play photographer and soon I found myself posing semi-awkwardly in front of her camera in my cranberry red bedroom. The boa around my neck egging on my inner superstar, I was soon a seductress, a sassy chic schoolteacher with glasses perched on my nose, a withdrawn mystic, and a wild woman. I was glamorous, romantic, sexy, silly, serious, and very cute. Even if my intent had been to remind my husband of the woman he'd fallen in love with, I was actually in the process of falling in love with myself again. Dormant facets of my womanliness came alive and in giving my naked self an expression, albeit a shy one, I felt more accepting of my body. Maybe it wasn't too shabby after all. Maybe I was sexy. My friend and I laughed, and soon I returned the favor. We agreed that every woman should do this for herself.

Lolo's Boudoir was born. My nickname Lolo referred to my more flamboyant alter-ego, while boudoir referred to lushly decorated bedrooms in seventeenth and eighteenth century France—women's private quarters in which they could entertain lovers, rejuvenate themselves, and do what ever else they pleased. I liked that idea. Much in need of my own space, I agreed with Virginia Woolf's ideas in *A Room of One's Own*. I began photographing friends in my bedroom and soon discovered that what I thought was merely about light and aperture was actually about something far more profound.

Something happens when you get naked in front of a camera. Your insecurities and bodily concerns reveal themselves, if not by words, then through sheer body language. In this vulnerable space, I could share intimacies with my subjects about our relationships to our bodies, sex, image, and beauty. We engaged in deep conversations about womanhood, balancing career, relationships, motherhood, and our love lives. We talked about neglecting ourselves or taking our femininity for granted, about the few opportunities that we allow ourselves

for playful, sensual expression, about the fun of dressing up and acting out different characters that live inside of us, and about lacking role
models to show us how to really be a woman. Just by daring to be seen
and exposing ourselves, all these crucial topics came up. It was rich. It
was juicy. I felt intrigued. Turns out, I wasn't alone in my insecurities
around all things female.

As a little girl, I loved to dress up like a lady in my mom's heels
and pearls. Proudly, I presented myself to my family, as if to say, "Look
at me, so pretty I am." My Dad laughed me off and said, "I think you
might suffer from *pyntesyge*" ("decoration disease" in Danish). To be
girly was made fun of in my family, and between my two brothers, girly
games weren't the first choice when we played together. Before I went
to school, I don't remember having many girlfriends. Once in school, I
was wary of the girls' cliques and afraid of their ability to turn on me
at any moment. But in my own world, things were different. With my
Daisy Doll (the precursor to Barbie), I enacted the life of an elegant,
independent lady. Daisy had a white closet filled with beautiful clothes,
a white leather couch, and all the boyfriends she wanted. The freedom
she had in my imaginary world stood in stark contrast to the confine-
ment I felt in the reality of my male-dominated family.

My father ran the house as if it was a military unit and to me it
seemed like he always had the upper hand. Heck, he didn't even like
when my mom wore lipstick. On the cusp of my teens, I recall two
defining moments: I cut the big red hair of my beautiful Daisy Doll
short like a punk rocker's and, in a moment of rage against my parents,
I tore their wedding picture down the middle and threw it outside my
locked bedroom door. My rebellion against male dominance and weak
women had begun. Determined not to live like them or by the rules of
others, I set out to carve a path of my own. I traveled, got an education,
and had my way with boys, all the while puffing myself up with masculine can-do vigor and a need to prove myself an equal. As I lived inde-
pendently, I preferred the company of men because I secretly resented
women for their weakness and sought to avoid their cattiness.

That I should find myself in a marriage that was slowly sucking the independence, freedom, and flamboyancy out of me was no surprise. Weak against my husband's apparently confident ways, I had become as sensitive as a temperature gauge. Would I be able to talk freely or would he not be in the mood? Could I seduce him and be sure he'd respond? Would he be hot, cold, or worse . . . lukewarm? The dynamic wasn't so different from that in my parents' house.

In Lolo's Boudoir, I found the girlfriend I'd never had. She came in many types, ages, and preferences. At times she was a shy woman, sweet woman, wild woman, or libido-starved woman. At other times, she was a lonely woman, a fake-breasted woman, or a voluptuous woman. She was a woman with an eating disorder and a cancer survivor. She was at one time a playful woman who confidently wore make up, garters, and hooker heels, and then another time a woman who couldn't or wouldn't. Sometimes she was a full-of-laughter woman and sometimes she was a sad woman. In the sacred space of my bedroom, we were just girls and we talked about everything. We shared our shame, fears, dreams, and giggles and found courage together. Because we were all the same in some way, I was learning to love women as a pathway to loving myself.

When women shared their photographs, they were implicitly telling their close girlfriends that they, too, were worthy, deserving, and courageous enough to gift themselves with such an experience. A community was growing around me, but even so, I resisted. I was a writer, I told myself. I was meant to save the world, not photograph naked women. Photographing women was a bizarre thing to be doing. But every time I tried to quit, I was offered a great gig, exhibit, or magazine feature and I ultimately accepted them, feeling as if there was something else pushing me forward.

A miscarriage finally took me over the edge in my marriage. Was I meant to have a child? I needed to be able to care for it, I thought to myself, simultaneously aware and in denial that I felt unable to count on my husband. I poured my grief and despondence into my new business. In the sacred space of my creation, a community of women woven together by intimate photography, I was held, and in turn I held my subjects through all aspects of their own womanhood. Lolo's Boudoir was a bridge to my independence.

Divorce was imminent. At Christmastime three years later, my husband and I sat at each end of our little bathtub, empty of words and empty of love. He moved out and I tried to move on. At first it seemed impossible to go to work. How could I see women who bared themselves, literally and figuratively, when my vision was so blurred with tears? My attempt to affect a jovial pretense quickly fell to the ground and finally, mercy found me in the form of honesty. I could do nothing but show up each day, just as I was, with my mask off. Sometimes my tears would fall, but I'd allowed so many other women to shed tears in that space that it was only fair I should be able to cry, too. I did, after all, preach about being real and genuine, and this was the real stuff. A second mask dropped when the longtime separation I'd felt from women began to mend. I did not need to be anything other than myself—shades of gray included–and through this, I gave others permission to be their most authentic selves. In hindsight, I am amazed at the poignant orchestration of my gradual unfolding. In the thick of it, you can't see that everything is, in fact, progressing perfectly.

Shortly thereafter, a young woman sat in the Victorian love seat in my boudoir and told me that the man she'd married a year before had betrayed her, and now they were divorcing. She looked at me and her dark eyes filled with shame. "I never felt beautiful," she said. "My family never told me I was nice, pretty, or sweet. My mom still tells me I'm too fat." She continued to tell me all her dislikes about her body and how she obsessed about her belly being too big.

"Oh my God," I said, "you're saying that when you dress in the morning, eat your lunch, have sex with a man, or consider buying clothes, your belly is right there with you, spliced between you and your ability to enjoy your experiences?"

We looked at each other as if we'd both seen something awful.

Could a body part actually get in the way of being present in your experiences? Absolutely! Similarly, pride, rejection, and fear had limited my ability to express myself freely. We sat for a while, letting our epiphany sink in. Then she said, "My husband called me ugly. From one day to the next, he stopped touching me. I didn't understand what I'd done and, of course, I soon began to feel ugly."

We both dabbed our eyes dry. In front of me sat a beautiful and broken woman, and in her, I saw myself. The truth was terribly simple. We'd all been there, her, my mom, her mom, the woman next door, and me. At the core of each woman, there are heartbreaks, wounds, losses, and sometimes even a profound terror of being female. The release from these things would be simple, too. By letting my despair breathe, this woman's pain could also breathe, and together we cried, laughed, and held each other in a tender, sacred space.

Life's initiations seldom come gift-wrapped with golden ribbons, but they do carry their own strange sense of logic. Finally, I was beginning to see that Lolo's Boudoir was my work; in helping women embrace their bodies, sexuality, and the many troubling facets of womanhood, I was also healing myself. By helping them reclaim their sexual, powerful selves, I was reclaiming the same for myself, slowly transmuting the shame of being girly, inferior, and hysterical that had been instilled in me during childhood. I was healing the same wounds that had flared up in the dance with my now ex-husband. By learning to love women, and honoring the sacred in each of them through their imperfect beauty, I was learning to see myself with gentler, more loving eyes.

Now nothing seems coincidental. There is no separation between my work, my passion, and my own journey. My journey has been as important as the experiences of the women I've worked with. We listen to one another with the knowledge that we can then express ourselves more freely as well. A sisterhood is blossoming around me as we weave a red thread of support, sacredness, and strength for each other in our commitment to our souls and our sensual lives. This sisterhood will stretch into my future, providing a springboard for my stepping more fully and freely out into the world with my mission. We evolve together.

Lone Morch

Award-winning author, photographer, and muse, Lone Morch (LoneMorch.com) is a passionate, wandering artist whose medium is intimate liberation—of you and the world around you. Founder of Lolo's Boudoir, she has recently created the program Free Your Sacred Journey to help more women reclaim their soul, sexuality, and sovereignty. She is the author of the memoir *Seeing Red: A Woman's Sacred Journey Toward Personal Power*. Her photography and writing has been featured in *InStyle*, the *San Francisco Chronicle*, the *SF Examiner*, *7x7 Magazine*, *La Bella Bride*, *Untapped*, Daily Candy, Splendora, the *Huffington Post*, anthologies, and more.

Boudoir, photograph by Lone Morch

Safe Sisterhood and the Good Girl

Kim Shannon

Women are social creatures. We tend to congregate and, like pack animals, find solace and support in one another. We gather much of our individual power from group support. This is where safe sisterhood is born and how women will build community and change the world.

Within any group, individuals play specific roles and women are no exception. We learn our roles young, and we implement, hone, and perfect them as we grow. The typical roles women play are: daughter, sister, friend, wife, mother, and businesswoman. I'm a daughter, sister, friend, mother, ex-wife and entrepreneur. But there is another foundational role that supports and defines us, a role that has a profound impact on how we execute and perform our other roles. This is the role of the good girl. I am a 44 year old good girl and as Lady Gaga says, "Baby, I was born this way."

Learning the ways to become a good girl began as soon as I came out of the womb. Good girls are indoctrinated into a belief system showing us what's considered good and bad and we're urged to fall in line and follow that path. Our moms followed the path, and so did our grandmas and our great-grandmas, so now it's our turn. It's considered good for us. It's appropriate. It's what is expected of us.

It's certainly what was expected of me. Being good, being seen as good, and coming across as good were of the utmost importance to my mom. It was the code of conduct she was raised with; it's what she knew and it's what she taught me.

As young girls, we are taught to be nice, kind, and honest. We are taught to have manners, values, and morals. We are told to share, be respectful, get good grades, and excel on the playing field. We are shown how to be popular, lady-like, and polite. We are also schooled in making others happy, performing to expectations, and following the rules. We are groomed to be people pleasers and to strive for perfection. Growing up a good girl can have both positive and negative effects.

Unfortunately, the mandates to be perfect and to please others come with some unpleasant and detrimental consequences. We learn to put other people's needs and happiness above our own, to be quiet and keep our mouths shut, to conceal our opinions, to doubt ourselves, and to feel self-conscious and uneasy about our looks. They can also cause us to be dismissive of our talents and abilities, worry way too much, become unable to handle criticism, and experience embarrassment when praised or given accolades. In extreme cases like mine, good girls disown their self-worth and become ashamed of their spirit. Good girls can grow up to feel that being good isn't good enough.

Not feeling good enough is one hell of a cross to bear, and yet for many good girls, it's a reality. I was the effervescent child who smiled easily and often. No one, especially my mom, intended my self-worth to take hit after hit, but I was a sensitive child, eager to please, and make others happy. My feelings of inadequacy began small and quickly snowballed out of control. When I didn't make someone laugh, feel better, be proud, or feel good, I felt bad. I was ashamed when I couldn't be the peacemaker, or live up to expectations. When I wasn't acknowledged for my sacrifices or for following the rules, I felt that meant I wasn't good. I was the good girl who wasn't good, and I kept proving it to myself over and over and over again at two, four, seven, ten, 12, 20, and 30 years old. It was a recurring theme.

All this internal drama, heartache, and negativity made me feel unsafe, unsure, and exposed, which in turn made the good girl in me fight tooth and nail to maintain composure. The good girl took on the role of the protector, and quite possibly the enabler, doing anything and everything to make sure my good girl image was intact and making sure I was thought of as good, nice, and perfect even if I didn't believe it myself . . . especially when I didn't believe it myself.

As many good girls do, before leaving my bedroom in the

morning, I put on my happy-face mask, tucked my emotions away, and prepared to greet the world. The mask protected me from being hurt, judged, or called out for my shortcomings and insecurities. But even though my mask made me feel safe, it was only a wearable lie. It kept me disconnected and alone. It kept me separate and served as a barrier to true connection. The good girl mask becomes the norm, and many of us don't even realize we do it or understand how it plays into and furthers our internal distrust and discontent.

There's a saying, "If mama ain't happy, ain't nobody happy." Ain't that the truth! From 1972–2007, the United States General Social Survey asked both men and women: "How happy are you, on a scale of 1 to 3?" The findings are extensive as the survey polled people from all ages, backgrounds, and income levels, but the two starkest discoveries showed that women aren't as happy as we were just 40 years ago, and that as we get older, we get sadder.

As I said, I'm now 44 years old and I'm determined not to be a sad, unhappy old woman. My unfolding into the woman I am today has been a roller-coaster ride of dramatic highs, lows, twists, and turns. I started "working on" and "self-helping" myself young, instinctively knowing I had a long way to go. Three years ago, I had to make a choice between the real, raw, authentic me, and the good girl mask I continued to wear to keep up appearances.

In 2009, I was at the tail end of two ill-fated relationships. One was my relationship with the man I thought would be my forever partner, and the other was my love affair with Pinot Grigio. Both were fueled by my addiction to being a good girl—I was an expert in projecting perfect appearances, holding my tongue, and putting myself last, and drinking was my sad attempt to drown my anger and numb the shame I felt for being out of control. Both needed to go in order for me to fully claim myself.

I couldn't have ended either relationship without the support and love of my sisters (biological and otherwise). They made me feel safe enough to be seen and accepted in my vulnerability. I couldn't have broken free from having to be a good girl without their we-got-your-back, rock-solid encouragement. My mom led the charge and with her support and by following her example, I found the courage to make change. When you feel alone and on your own, it's difficult to take positive steps forward, not only for yourself, but also for the world at large.

Even though we have made great strides as a gender, women are still discriminated against and suffering repression. We live in a man's world where the patriarchy endeavors to keep us divided. Our culture is conditioned to keep women off balance and out of touch—not only to our own individual power but blind to the unmatched potential of a community of women. Women are a force to be reckoned with! It is time now for women to not only know this, but to claim it collectively.

In order to survive, women have adopted a competitive stance instead of a collaborative one. We compare ourselves to one another and feel better when we put our competitor down. It's a gossip game, and the winner is thinner, prettier, and smarter. The winner is the one who exemplifies good girl grown up, and is envied as the good wife, good mother, good friend . . . good everything. She has adorable children, a cushier office, bigger house, nicer car, a hotter, funnier, smarter guy, and loads of those coveted Louboutins.

Luckily, women are savvy and smart and are questioning if staying separate and competitive is beneficial to us, especially when coming together and uniting in feminine connection feels so right. When we claim our power, we own our true nature as intuitive, collaborative, creative, and compassionate women. When we own our true nature, we embrace our innate tendencies to connect and teach, to truth-say and protect, courageously nurture, and wholeheartedly lead.

One of the first and most vital steps we must take to come into connection with ourselves individually and with other women is to remove the mask of the good girl once and for all. When we find the courage to take off our masks with one another, we free ourselves, and are able to recognize our power reflected in the eyes of others. In allowing ourselves to be vulnerable, we are able to access our true authenticity and acknowledge the genuine strength we share with other women. We see one another as allies rather than foes.

Women have an itch to create change and make a difference. We want more, and are dissatisfied with the status quo. We hear a call to reconvene the power of feminine connection, where strength lies not only in owning who we are individually but also in coming together collectively.

The power of feminine connection is a gift that once given and received changes a woman's reality. With this gift, I was able to break free from being a good girl, giving me the courage to embrace who I am as a great woman. I will spend the rest of my life making sure other women feel the safe support of their sisters.

We are ready for safe sisterhood.

Kim Shannon

Kim Shannon is an author, motivational speaker, intuitive coach, and good girl. Kim's forthcoming book, *The Good Girl Addiction*, will be released in Spring 2013, and her complementary coaching program, Good Girls Anonymous, helping women achieve the freedom, power, and fulfillment we all deserve, launches in Summer 2013. Kim co-owns The SHINE Factor with her mom, Mimi. Together, they help women worldwide find their power and let it shine. In 2011, they published the *SHINE Cards & Guidebook: 123 Aspects of What It Means to Be a Woman*.

One Good Reader

Chieko Murasugi

We meet once a week. Every Friday morning after my friend and I help the art teachers at our sons' school, we drive to our favorite café to discuss the books we are reading and the writing I completed that week. Through two school years we have cherished our routine.

Sunlight pours into our café through a sweep of glass that stretches heavenward from the sidewalk to the high ceiling. A giant neon painting of an anime girl watches over us, muse like, while above our heads, strands of glittering beads dangle and dance from a flowered chandelier. My friend and I order our favorite drinks and settle in at a small round table. During the next several hours even my ever-attentive husband knows: Don't text me, I'll text you.

It was over dinner with our husbands that she and I discovered that we both loved to write. "I'm halfway through my first novel," I told her, feeling sheepish at my ambition. I was not a trained writer or, like her, a graduate in literature and a lifelong prodigious reader of fiction. I had spent the last two decades painting pictures, and before that, doing research on the vision of humans and monkeys. At the time I met her, I had been writing fiction for two years, since I turned 50.

"May I read your novel?" she asked in her graceful British accent. I stiffened. I loathed exposing my work again. I had just left my writers' group after one of its members told me that my writing made her cringe, especially when I tried to be funny. Before I began my novel, the last pieces I had written besides diary entries and email notes were scientific papers penned in the passive voice. But I pushed on. For an entire year, I worked for hours every day on my novel, only to have it scorned by the implicit leader of my group. Even worse was the silence, the silence of the other writers who said nothing. I resolved not to show my work until after it was finished, or perhaps three, five, ten, or even 20 drafts into the process.

"You can read my stories," my friend said. "They're very short, one page at most."

A little while later, I did. I scanned the first line of her story and paused to savor the words. I read on, open mouthed to the end when I marveled at the cleverness, the wit, the wisdom, and the elegance of the writing. She was seven years my junior and wrote in her second language! I admire Conrad and Nabokov, for whom English was not their native tongue, but this was different; it seemed like sleight of hand when someone young and within touching distance pulled off a similar feat. "Your stories are gems," I told her. "Why don't you publish them?" She laughed. She replied that when she was 60 or so she would bundle up her stories into a collection. "Perhaps I'll write a novel, too," she said, "when I have something to say." "You already do," I told her, but she waved my words aside.

About a year later, she did publish a story. On a whim, she submitted a winning piece to a contest of horror stories, her first effort in that genre. I watched my 13 year old son read her 500 words about a woman who heats a large pot of broth while holding a stranger's baby in her arms. My son, who is undaunted by Stephen King and Edgar Allen Poe and watches the bloody combat scenes in *Gladiator* without flinching, looked up with grave eyes when he read what was to be thrown into the pot. "It's really creepy," he said.

Since I had read her work, I let her read mine. With trembling fingers I emailed her the first chapter of the second part of my novel. From that day, she has read and commented on every chapter I have written since: about 30 in all.

When my friend and I meet at our café, we usually begin by talking about books. One morning, she brought an autobiography of Winston Churchill, A.S. Byatt's *The Matisse Stories*, plus a couple of other novels she was reading that week. She was also listening to *The Hobbit* in her car. Astonished, I asked her how she kept track of so many books at one time. I was an inefficient serial reader, managing to finish only one or two books a month. She laughed. "I am so disorganized," she said. Because she has trouble locating any book she is reading, she has unfinished books scattered throughout her house. Whenever she is in a room—the kitchen, her bedroom, or her study—she picks up the book she finds there and opens it to its bookmark. Each book is a friend; she does not confuse one with another.

From her stack of books on the café table, she picks up A.S. Byatt's collection of stories. She is a great admirer of Byatt and introduced me to her work, and when the author came to San Francisco to lecture, my friend and I bought tickets to attend.

During the question period, after Byatt had demonstrated the depth and range of her knowledge and love of literature and history, she said something that struck me with the joy of recognition. Following decades of writing, reading, and analyzing literature, she yearned to know something about the material world, which drew her to study the life sciences. Like her, I too have learned to value the contrasting but complementary contributions of science and literature. Scientists, experiment by experiment, and in miniscule steps, build an understanding of physical phenomena—inanimate or living. Writers build, story by story, an understanding of human nature.

One day, my friend and I will tackle our signed copies of Byatt's *The Children's Book*. Meanwhile, I am following my friend's lead and reading in parallel: one book at the gym, another on the couch, another in bed, and an audio book in the car. Once again, she was right. I never muddle together the escapades of Raskolnikov with *Olive Kitteridge*, Humbert Humbert, or *The Tiger's Wife*.

Although my friend and I could talk about books until our café closes, my heart quickens when she opens her folder and removes the chapter of my novel that I had sent her the night before. She always begins the same way. "As you can see," she points to the barely marked page, "I have very little to say." I laugh, knowing better.

She employs the Socratic Method. At our initial meeting when I gave her the first chapter of the second part of my novel, she inquired about part one. "That's about the mother," I said, "and her past. Part two is the story of her daughter in the present." My friend looked puzzled and asked, "Are they two books?" I explained that the stories converge in the final chapter. She asked whether the reader must wait over twenty chapters before making the connection between the two. Yes, I admitted, and saw the problem.

One way to integrate the two parts of the novel was to interweave the two narratives, of mother and daughter, throughout the book. When I was writing alone, the technical challenge of applying this structure intimidated me. With my friend's guidance, I was able to implement the new form, but as is the case with writing, other weaknesses emerged.

During the next weeks my friend continued to query me. She seemed confounded by the comings and goings of my characters, and by the various changes in time and place. One Friday she arrived with a chart that summarized every chapter she had read. It was a spreadsheet.

When I returned home, I cut a sheet of graph paper into a three-foot square. Along the top, I numbered 21 columns, one for each chapter of my novel. I used the top half of the spreadsheet for the daughter's life, the bottom half for the mother's youth. Along the left side, I assigned a row to every character, with their birthdates noted in parentheses. Once I filled in the spreadsheet with names, locations, thoughts, and actions, I could see at a glance what happens in every scene, when and where the action takes place, who appears and what they do and think. With the elements of my novel thus delineated in time and space, what became equally visible were its flaws. Fortunately, I had filled out the spreadsheet in pencil.

The following Friday I rolled up my spreadsheet, the product of hours of work, and carried it to our café. My friend and I removed our books from the table and I unfurled the document as though it were an invitation to the king's ball. I stretched it across the table. Because the sides of the paper hung over the tabletop, we shifted the spreadsheet back and forth in several directions to read its contents edge to edge. With our heads almost touching, we studied the blueprint of my novel. It was incomplete, imperfect, and proclaimed how much work I still needed to do. But for the first time in years, I saw the promise of what my novel could be and my eyes filled with tears.

Next Friday is the last Friday of our boys' academic year. When their summer vacation starts, my friend and I take a break from our weekly routine. Come September we will begin again, but next year will be our last.

In a year's time, my friend may return to London and I will move to North Carolina. My one consolation, besides iChat, is the direct flight from Raleigh-Durham to Heathrow that crosses the Atlantic in a mere six hours. But it will not be the same. I will miss our Fridays.

Whether my friend is near or far, I cannot betray her; I cannot abandon my novel. One day, in a fit of frustration and despondency, I threatened to trash my pages and pages of miserable writing and call it quits. "Forget it!" I said to her, "I won't even bother trying to get it published." She stared at me, suppressing a smile. "What?! After I read all those chapters? Have you been wasting my time?" We laughed.

When I tell someone that I am writing a novel, often the person asks whether I have a publisher, an editor, a writing group, an agent, or a degree. I shake my head and face the inevitable look of skepticism. I explain that I have attended writers' workshops, fiction classes, and have studied a shelf full of books on the craft of writing. All those things, and even my ill-fated writers' group, have taught me how to be a better writer . . . but I owe the most to my friend.

Many years ago I attended a lecture at my daughter's middle school. The speaker had written several books on the social lives of children. What he described was hell; the mean girls, the cliques, the bullying, the exclusionary tactics, and the social hierarchies that can induce sufficient terror and loneliness to destroy a child's self-esteem, or at worst, life.

We anxious parents were desperate for an antidote. We asked how we can save our children from such horror and pain, and help them become well-adjusted adults. The speaker, who had counseled thousands of children and spoke with the conviction of experience, gave us a simple answer. "All a child needs to be happy," he said, "is one good friend."

For those who ask how I endure the loneliness of writing, the criticisms, and the self-doubts, my answer is equally simple. "I have all I need," I say. "I have one good reader." My dear friend and reader will first see this tribute when it is already in print. I hope in her modesty she does not wave aside my gratitude.

I could not have written this without her.

Chieko Murasugi

Chieko Murasugi was born in Tokyo and grew up in Toronto, where she received a B.F.A in Visual Arts and a Ph.D. in Experimental Psychology. She married her husband, a neuroscientist, and raised their two children in San Francisco, California. After living for 20 years in the city, she and her family recently moved to Chapel Hill, North Carolina, where she can write essays and stories without worrying about the Big One.

Section Six

Mischief Makers

Vexing the Ex

Judy Zimola

Mean Vick and I are on the lam. Skedaddled. Vamoosed. Amscrayed. January woke up pissy this morning, her skies as dense and grey as this stretch of I-80 running under the Jeep's tires. Sleet peppers the windshield as wipers spank their backbeat to my jangling thoughts. "Bad person, bad person," they thump. When the rain slackens and a little squeak enters the beat, they taunt me, rhythmically like kids on the schoolyard blacktop: "You're so screwed. You're so screwed."

Vick, on the other hand, is in her element. Feet on the dash, sucking Smarties, and looking out the window—she's a study in serenity. I'm frightened and inspired by her utter lack of remorse, but mostly I'm impressed. When it comes to dealing out retribution, Mean Vick is the most innovative person I've ever known—she is Jackson Pollock wielding a paintbrush full of "bite me." Early in our friendship, my blood turned to little BBs as I watched her methodically fill out and mail subscription requests to a couple dozen magazines in the name of her ex-boyfriend. "Should I really send *Knitter's Monthly*? Oh hell, why not." she snorted, dropping the last no-postage-required flyer into the mailbox.

Nothing less than her patented brand of goddamn would do for my situation: a love gone so far south it's playing maracas. Late one winter night, over black and tans at a bar in San Francisco's Mission District, she spelled out the plan. With every detail, it became clear that she had crafted not just another saucy little scheme, but a fully-realized opus: malfeasant, rhythmic, and layered with wit and vitriol. The victim (my boyfriend ex officio) would experience tics, trauma, and mental goiters the size of cantaloupes as a result of this act. It was a nasty, bitchy thing to do. God help me, I loved it! *Not only am I screwed, I'm a screwed sociopath.*

"Ooh, a coffee shop!" Vick is pointing out the window at a mom-and-pop diner. If she had a tail, it would be thumping against the console. "Let's get waffles!"

"Vick" I say, pulling into Red's Waffle Hut, "I feel kinda funny about, you know, what we did . . . to Steve."

She pretends not to hear. "I hope they make them crispy. I hate a limp waffle."

"We just left him there, Vick. He twitched. We saw it."

"Damnit, Judy, stop being such a drama queen," Vick demands. "Steve had it coming. No regrets, no looking back."

"Can you throw one more cliché at this?"

"There's lots of fish in the sea? It's better to have loved and lost? You want clichés, sister, I got a bag of them right here."

I really hate her sometimes.

Coffee that takes the enamel off my teeth and a plate of corned beef hash helps shift my perspective. It's still drizzling as we climb back in the Jeep, but that's good. The rain, mixed with the cold air's metallic smell, puts everything into sharp relief. Interstate 80's stark landscape has a kind of steel wool effect, scouring my muzzy core.

At half-past Winnemucca, rain turns to snow; giant flakes splat their icy guts across the windshield like polar June bugs. The Henry Mountains wrap the horizon as we near our destination, Elko's Cowboy Poetry Gathering. Vick leans against the passenger door as if to snuggle into their he-man contours. "I wonder if we'll see Jason White Feather."

Oh yes, Jason White Feather. Vick is a pushover for Crow Indian poets from Montana with cool hair and mystique; Mr. White Feather has been on her radar for weeks. Subsequently, White Feather updates are part of my daily news diet. JWF works at a school in admissions; JWF lives with his dad; a dreamy, four-color photo of JWF standing by a Montana stream, backlit, blue water flowing and black hair babbling, was just published in a poetry anthology. "He wears a ponytail, you know."

Do I ever know. "Yeah, you told me. So?"

"So, it'll make it easier for me to drag him around."

Slushy snow is still coming down as we pull into the parking lot of the EZ Sleep Motel in Elko. It's not a bad place for a fleabag, just misunderstood. There are your standard doubles with brown quilts (backache at no extra charge), bark cloth curtains over a window looking directly into the grille of a Dodge pickup truck, and a clanking radiator emitting dusty-smelling steam heat. The sight of the heavy, black rotary dial phone with a silver finger-stopper rips a serrated shiver straight between my shoulder blades. Sometime this weekend it's going to ring, and the bell will toll for me.

I need a drink.

Within the hour, we're in a bar redolent of brimming black ashtrays and Saturday boot polish. A couple glasses of well whiskey, a twisted best friend who's an ace conspirator, and Hank Williams on the jukebox makes this miscreant feel all woolly warm. Especially now that . . . "Say, Vick. What did you say Jason White Feather looks like again?"

"Like a Crow Indian with a ponytail." She shakes her head. "Moe-ron."

"Mmmm." I sip my drink and nod towards the end of the bar. "Like maybe, *that* Crow Indian? Moe-ron? I think I'll say hi."

"Oh God." Vick gulps. "It's him. Please don't. Wait. Do. But don't say anything about me. Shit. I have to go to the bathroom."

"Do you want me to talk to him or not?" I may be a moron, but I'll respect her boundaries.

"Sure. But be . . . surreptitious."

So, surreptitiously, I introduce myself to Jason White Feather while Vick takes a powder. I tell him I admire his work and offer to buy him a beer, which he graciously accepts. Mean Vick returns from the ladies' room, and I see that she's applied fresh lipstick.

"Hi," Miss Drag-Him-Around-By-His-Ponytail says, a little breathlessly. "Who's your friend?"

Sly dog. "Vick, meet Jason White Feather. He's a poet."

Vick acts smooth while suppressing hyperventilation, but clinging to the front of her shirt is a white, loosely-wadded, dampish goober. "Honey," I murmur, "there's a little something on your, um, your front there."

Confused, she looks down, then gingerly plucks the loogie of toilet paper from the front of her new festival blouse. Of the three of us regarding the small, soggy miasma, two of us think it's really damn funny. Mean Vick is mortified, JWF is composure squared. "Happens to me all the time", he utters in a voice that's 96 proof. "I'll buy the next round." Vick's not too appalled to order up a shot of Maker's Mark and branch water.

A smile skips across Jason White Feather's face, and with a boot-leather hand barely on the small of her back, he guides Mean Vick to the bar. Damn. She's right about those Crow Indian poets from Montana—all the ones I've met so far are very sexy. I'm really happy for Vick. When we get back home, she'll help me sweep up the shards of that broken romance. And thanks to her, my sendoff to Steve was wickedly stylish.

Watching old movies and drinking crappy red wine, Vick and I bided our time until Steve fell asleep. When his snoring sounded like a clapped-out garbage disposal, it was time to lock and load. I wouldn't allow myself to think about what we were doing—this simply had to be done. As we continued the grim task, Steve convulsed and threw his hand behind his head. Mean Vick barely paused before going back to it. I began to giggle helplessly.

"*Finish* it," Vick hissed.

Quashed snorts cleared my nasal passages, filling my eyes. "I will," I kacked. "*You* finish!"

Steve was overly fond of spouting things like, "If someone hits me, I hit 'em right back," and "That's your problem." Well, his problem will be hitting back with a bright red manicure once he wakes up. Wielding brushes laden with Revlon's classic Love That Red, Mean Vick and I stroked swaths of scarlet onto Steve's fingernails. We allowed just a moment to admire our work before walking brazenly out the front door and into the inky 'Frisco streets, getaway Jeep packed and ready. And on the bathroom sink, like a big, upraised middle finger, we left a bottle of fingernail polish remover—empty.

He had it coming.

I'll have to start over after this weekend, and that will suck. But right now, sipping whiskey with Vick, Jason, and Elko as our inamoratos, the ending is, in every way, poetry.

Judy Zimola

Driving long stretches of remote highway, messing around in the kitchen while sipping a nice pinot, or running along California's Bay Trail are a few of Judy Zimola's favorite things. She's a regular contributor to *Green Living Arizona* magazine, and has had several pieces run in *No Depression* and *Nebraska Life* magazines, as well as several anthologies. *It's All a Bunch of Fun Until Somebody Puts an Eye Out (and Sometimes That's Pretty Funny Too)* is the working title of her memoir. She knows that title is too long.

Mischief, photograph by Kristin Gerbert

Kristin Gerbert

Kristin Gerbert believes that each photographer's work should be unique and distinctive from the next. For years, Kristin modeled, acted, and performed with her band, and all of these endeavors taught her how to be photographed. She went to Vidal Sassoon Cosmetology School and spent years doing make up and hair for a variety of photographers on the West Coast, so she also got experience behind the lens, studying the elements that influence a picture. Her approach has always been to just photograph what inspires her, rather than to rely on formal training.

Jesse's Girl

Violet Blue

Ask any woman how she learned about sex, and I promise you'll get an answer that is as unique to each woman as her fingerprint. I can also promise you that somewhere in her answer, she'll tell you that one of the ways she learned about sex was one of the ways most women learn about sex—from another woman.

When I was young, cabals comprised of other girls my age held the keys to titillated enlightenment—or at least, in pairs and trios, we could be fearless enough to crack open the *Playboy* and *Hustler* magazines we'd found in someone's garage. We'd page through in silence for what seemed like hours, perusing the cartoonish photos depicting alien bodies of grownup women with their tan lines, giant breasts, and completely foreign-looking vulvas.

Those ladies and their sci-fi lady bits were freaky. Their heavily-styled and airbrushed pink folds whispered of a dystopian future of which we wanted no part. We each confirmed that no—none us looked like that now, and we were sure we never would. What a relief!

Of course, our bodies had different plans for us and eventually made good on their silent plot against us—right about the same time it stopped being okay for us to ogle *Penthouse* together.

That didn't mean we girls stopped talking about sex. To the contrary, in moments when we could sneak off behind closed doors or have sleepovers together, we dished on everything dirty we'd heard about since our last session.

Half of what we "learned" wasn't helpful or necessarily even true. But boy, was it exciting, scary, and totally interesting. We swapped stories about what we'd heard other girls did with boys and what someone told someone else about accidentally getting pregnant, and we'd share our own investigative research on the weirdest sex acts we'd heard about.

This did nothing to alleviate the growing distance we felt from our own sexual organs. In fact, for many girls, it got worse. By the way our vaginas had begun to behave between our legs—pain, smells, and general ickiness—it felt as though they were out to get us. It seemed like every day they looked different than the day before. It was almost like *Rosemary's Baby* down there.

Nope, this was definitely not a trustworthy body part.

I'll never forget the day that a member of our girl squad told us she'd seen a porn video for the first time. She confided in horror that the close-ups "looked like meat" and made her feel sick. We all screamed, "Ew, gross!" I remember thinking, *Oh God, please don't let me look like that!*

What may have started out as genuine alarm around and fascination about our sex parts didn't stop us from racing each other to get boyfriends to share those turncoat body parts with. As time went by, I became more comfortable with my pleasure centers and the way they looked and felt at any given time.

This was helped along by books of a certain era—namely, sex education books written by women. These particular women were of the Susie Bright and Carol Queen days—a generation of women from the 1970s and 1980s who fearlessly explored their own bodies and the frontiers of sexuality, and wrote down all their findings like lady pirates who had explored exotic, far away lands of orgasms and gender-bendery.

Once again, women made me understand sex better. Reading about far-out sex practices and women who tried exotic sex toys, same-sex adventures, stripping, or made their living as sex workers was a lifesaver as I began my sexual exploration with men.

When I finally did watch my first porn video (and felt shockingly turned on by it), I didn't think the vaginas were gross, even close up. I was versed enough in female sexuality, thanks to the female-authored, positive, sexual revolution, not to be freaked out by them. But I did walk away with a curious revelation. For me, a piece of my orgasmic puzzle was still missing.

Watching porn, it was clear that I wasn't experiencing pleasure the way other women seemed to be. I simply didn't understand how anyone could actually get horny from playing with a woman and turning her on. Perhaps I just didn't believe it could happen.

I could get turned on while playing with myself, of course. But once I put myself in the places of the women in porn videos, or between the sheets with my feminist writer heroes, things didn't add up; I didn't understand how going down on a woman could give a guy a hard-on, or give a woman the equivalent of a hard-on—whatever that might be called.

I figured that I would make peace with this confusion eventually— and I certainly hoped so, because I had a feeling that I wasn't going to have the kind of sex I wanted until I understood. Perhaps I was having a "grass is greener" moment. Did I hate my own body? Was my vagina actually out to get me, after all? The more I thought about it, the more I felt like I was going to jinx my ability to have an orgasm ever again.

I became obsessed with painting and drawing beautiful women. I knew I wasn't a lesbian, but I felt like in eroticizing the female body, there might be an answer for me as to what all the fuss was about. If Bright and Queen trod that path and came out masters of the vagina, then why wouldn't I? If I could understand the attraction to it, then maybe I could understand why someone else would be attracted to it, and then finally I'd be able to relax about getting my hands on some real pleasure.

One night, I took a break from painting and drawing to sit with a book at my favorite café on San Francisco's Haight Street. Jesse, one of the girls who worked there, was also an artist, and we were pals. She and I started talking about what I was working on. I didn't tell her why I was painting naked women, but she said she could relate. Then she asked me point-blank if she could come over after work so that I might draw her.

After I'd said okay, my blood went cold then hot, and it ran that cycle like a washing machine for about the next hour. My mind was on spin by the time Jesse came over to my Lower Haight Victorian. We sat where I'd set out paper, pencils, and drawing accessories and Jesse began to pull off her jeans, black t-shirt, and everything else, until a gorgeous naked girl was in front of me.

Still, it wasn't until she abruptly straddled my lap that I realized she was coming on to me.

By then, we were both laughing because we really didn't know how this thing we were doing was supposed to go. We kissed through the giggles. I was taken with how girls' faces are so amazingly soft; suddenly, I understood the other side—what guys feel when they kiss a girl. We smiled and slowed down, taking turns touching, exploring, asking questions, and then beginning to tell each other what we thought we might like.

Jesse was beautiful all over. According to her, I was too. I told her what to do to bring me to orgasm. *This is what it's going to be like from now on: my boyfriends are going to learn what I want and I'm going to do the same for them.*

When it was my turn to follow her instructions, I had the most curious reaction. I knew what I was doing to her felt fantastic for her and that turned me on. This is what my male lovers saw and felt when they were with me: the views, the sounds, the softness, the . . . everything. It was actually really sexy—not scary—and it was not happening outside of me. I was turned on and I understood why.

Sex with men was never the same after that. It was better than I ever expected.

My lessons about sex are like many women's. They're part of a lifetime arc of learning about my own sexuality and they have come from other women. Mine are different in that I've had a bit of hands-on learning with other women, which I don't think is a necessary experience. Though it was for me.

Violet Blue

Violet Blue (tinynibbles.com) is an award-winning author, columnist, blogger, and journalist, and is regarded as the foremost expert in the field of sex and technology. Violet is regularly featured at global conferences on the topics of sex, technology, and privacy, and her appearances range from Oprah to Google Tech Talks at Google, Inc.

#queensofrockingtheboat, collage by Tamara Holland

Tamara Holland

Tamara Holland is a recovering death penalty defense attorney, mom of adult kids, CrossFitter, and the boss-of-herself at Bean Up The Nose Art. She's also a writer of copy with her friends at Morning Coffee Productions, of blog posts on several sites, of spec screenplays, and of tens of thousands of tweets. You can find her on Twitter at @tamholland, or at the Bean Up The Nose Art website.

Ex Communication

Hyla Molander

Dana and I clink our tequila-filled shot glasses as our combined six children—ages two, three, five, six, eight, and 12—sprint across the hardwood floors of her home. Eight-year-old Tatiana shouts, "Get 'em!" and then, like a vulture in flight, her locks of matted Medusa-like hair pointing in every direction, she swoops down upon a squirming pile of elbows and stinky feet.

Voices squeal: "Get off . . . Mommy . . . Stoooppp . . . You farted on me!" Finally, the kids tumble aside one by one, and Jason, 12, reveals his sweaty, red face and says, "You wanna help me here?"

Poor Jason.

"Looks like you've got it handled, bud," Dana says, and I laugh, raising my glass. "Here's to being together." Dana tilts her head back, swigs the tequila, and then eagerly sucks the juice from her lime wedge. "Wish we could do it more often."

Dana is Jason's mom. I am Jason's stepmom. And yes, I really am drinking tequila with my husband's ex-wife. On a good night, Dana and I might even grab the guitar and microphone from Jason's Rock Band video game. We belt out "Eye of the Tiger" while the wee ones bang on the drums, jump on the bed, and dance in front of the TV.

To be clear, my own divorced parents never spoke kindly about each other, so when I entered the world of online dating as a 30-year-old widow with a newborn and a two year old, I did not include "rocking out with future husband's ex-wife" as a requirement in my profile. An ex-wife wasn't even in my realm of thought, much less something I was hoping for. No, when I made the decision to start dating again, my thoughts revolved mostly around the idea that I may now be damaged goods: a widow with two babies. *Why would any man want me?* But I had experienced deep love before and I was determined to find it again.

Managing to shave my legs and look presentable for dates was one thing, but the image of my late husband, Erik, sliding down the kitchen counter and lying motionless on our white-tiled floor kept repeatedly crawling into my mind. I threw myself into every possible type of therapy in hopes of being a good mother and eventually a good partner to someone else, but I could barely handle my own children, let alone a romantic relationship, someone else's kids, and a crazy ex-wife.

My ovaries screamed to find my girls a new daddy, but too many online dates with men who'd been married before quickly taught me to look for men without those attachments. Sure, I'd been married before too, but there was no chance that my late husband would be calling in the middle of the night to yell at me over child support.

After two years of dating different unattached men, however, I noticed that most of them would take a few evident steps back when they met my girls, who were two and three years old by that time. I started wondering if I would really ever know if a man was capable of being a loving daddy unless I could see him parenting his own children. That was when I finally opened up to dating men with kids; men who knew how to change diapers and might be able to fully grasp the impact of dating a widow with two little ones.

But men with kids meant men with wicked ex-wives. *Frightening.* One man I'd dated continued to sort through drama with his drug-addicted ex. Another convinced his teenagers to spy on their mom for him. Even the first time that I spoke on the phone with my future husband, Evan, I had good reason to be skeptical.

"So," I asked him, "How do you and your son's mom get along?"

Evan laughed, "There was tension like anyone would expect after the divorce, but now it's better than amicable. Much better. It's all about Jason. On occasion, I even watch her new baby, Jason's sister, when she needs help."

Wait up! "As in, you take care of a baby she conceived with some-one else?"

"Jason's sister, yes."

This was foreign to me. *If they got along so well, why weren't they still married?*

A week after Evan and I met in person, he invited me to the base-ball field, where he was coaching Jason's little league team. Already smitten from having watched how Evan and Jason rolled around in the grass with my Tatiana and Keira on a play date, I spent extra time pull-ing both of the girls' hair into pigtails and making them look just right. Both Tatiana and Keira's olive-toned skin glowed against their match-ing hot-pink sundresses as I held their hands and walked toward the concession stand.

Then, out of nowhere, something came toward me, and my infat-uation turned into panic. It was her . . . Dana, the ex-wife. *Where can I hide?* But Dana walked at me with certainty and her arms open wide. "Hyla, right?" she asked and leaned in.

What do I do? She's hugging me.

Everything Evan had told me about Dana made me feel more like damaged goods. She was a Stanford MBA who ran marathons, trav-eled the world, was an amazing mom, and always wanted to help other people. What Evan hadn't told me was that Dana also had gorgeous yellow-green eyes and a petite, athletic body exactly the shape—that perfect shape—that I was trying to shrink down to myself.

Seriously? You expect me to believe this is platonic?!

While I did my best not to appear as awkward as I felt, I noticed that Dana's one-year-old daughter, Sabrina, was already huddled beneath the bleachers with Tatiana and Keira; the three of them were instant friends. "Oh, look at that," Dana said. "How wonderful!" When Dana spent the next thirty minutes asking me all about my life, I feared that she might want to become my instant friend, too.

A few days after the baseball game, Evan said, "I hope it's all right. I talked to Dana. She said she thought you were great and asked if she could get your phone number. I think she wants to set up a play date with you and the girls." *But why?*

That night, I called my mom and told her about meeting Dana. My mom knew how enamored I was with Evan. She also knew that my widowed status made me feel insecure, so she wanted to protect me. I pulled the phone away from my ear as my mom cleared her throat. "What you're saying," she paused. "Is that you have agreed to have a play date with Evan's ex-wife?"

"Yessssss."

"Don't you think that is a bit strange?"

Uh, yeah, I thought, then said, "I'm trying to keep an open mind. Apparently Dana's parents are both married to other people now . . . and they occasionally vacation together."

This might have been normal to Dana, but it was not normal to me. In fact, it took years of soccer games, school plays, birthday parties, and swim meets before I could trust that the "wicked ex-wife" wasn't wicked at all. In reality, Dana was loving, supportive, and always willing to help out with Tatiana and Keira. She wanted Evan to be happy, so that Jason could be happy. Isn't that what we should all want for our children?

While we did not invite Dana and her husband, Adam, to our wedding, we did ask her to stay at the hospital with us as Evan and I waited for the birth of our new son. And, when our little Julian entered the world and felt his bundled body being passed between so many different, loving arms, he was introduced to his own version of normal.

Looking back, when I try to remember one specific incident that finally led Dana and me into becoming friends, I think of our daughters holding hands and spinning in circles; I think of that three-hour lunch Dana and I had, when tears seeped from her eyes remembering past struggles with the husband to whom I was now married; I hear splashing, a diving board bouncing, the chopping of watermelon, piñatas busting, children picking up candy, and our plates clinking against the table as we celebrate Mother's Day together.

Like many people, I would like to feel closer to much of my family, but through a mosaic of moments, Dana has become my cherished family member. She is there, without hesitation, for any one of us, and she is elated to help. The sense of security I feel from Dana is one of the many reasons Evan and I asked her and Adam to take care of our children, should anything ever happen to us.

"We'd be honored," Dana responded. And I knew she meant it.

As it turns out, from that first day we met, Dana never had any hidden agenda and, over time, I reached the place where I could openly confess my initial feelings of jealousy toward her. Now, we speak openly about any topic, including those that Evan would probably prefer his two wives leave alone.

What I've realized is that Dana has been cheering me on all along—as a mother, a wife, and a friend. The praise and love she consistently gives me have helped stop me from thinking of myself as less than desirable. Through Dana's eyes, I have learned to see myself as a strong, capable woman, and I know that part of my strength comes from knowing that she will be there for me any day I feel weak.

Divorce is tough. I'm certainly not claiming that it's easy to get to a place where you're doing tequila shots with your spouse's ex, nor am I suggesting that it's necessary to get as close as I have with Dana. What I do know, though, is that our children benefit when they see their parents playing well with others, and that each of us can experience more joy if we let go of resentments and treat each other with kindness.

Hyla Molander

Hyla Molander—speaker, social entrepreneur, photographer, widow, wife, and mother of four—is co-producer of Women Rock It events, founder of Widowed Web and Social Good Project, and the author of *Finding Light*. Her features and speaking engagements include the AllFacebook Expo, the keynote at Wal-Mart Corporate Headquarters,

Mama Monologues, *Writer's Digest*, *Marin Magazine*, the *Marin Independent Journal*, the National Association of Memoir Writers, HealthyPlace Mental Health Radio Show, the Southern California Writer's Conference, Litquake, and Camp Widow. Hyla is currently working on her forthcoming memoir, *Drop Dead Life: A Pregnant Widow's Heartfelt and Often Comic Journey through Death, Birth, and Rebirth.*

Section Seven

Race and Culture

Maggie

Yvonne Latty

With her crooked glasses strapped onto her head, my childhood best friend Maggie always made me smile. We made up games as we walked the three long blocks together to Resurrection School, the Catholic elementary school our immigrant parents scrimped and saved to put us through. We talked nonstop as we passed dilapidated buildings and guys hanging out on corners making comments at every teenage girl who passed them by. Trash and broken glass surrounded us. This was the landscape for Black and Latino children of bankrupt New York's inner city in the 1970s.

We looked at the clouds and said we could see the saints and Greek gods. I was positive that at some point the Virgin Mary would swoop down and rescue us from our fate. Even as a child, I had my words and they felt like magic as I weaved elaborate stories to Maggie's amusement. We ignored what was around us. Our landscape said we were doomed to a welfare check, but we looked at the clouds and told stories. We talked about our dreams and our favorite TV shows, and she always laughed at my jokes.

I loved school. During first and second grade I was a straight A student. I had everything a kid could want. I was great at "Red Light Green Light, 1, 2, 3," and Giant Step, and I could jump rope with serious rhythm. School felt easy. I loved to read and would devour the books I was given.

Maggie wasn't as strong a student, but she was always by my side. If I read, she would read. If I wanted to talk about *The Cat in the Hat*, she would listen. I was a happy kid, always smiling. My environment wasn't pretty, but I had my family, my dog Tootsie, and Maggie.

One day in third grade, after lunch recess, I was in line to go back to class when a couple of light-skinned Puerto Rican boys started asking me questions.

"Yvonne, you're Spanish, right?"

"Yeah, I'm Dominican."

"Then why is your last name Latty? Why are you so dark? You don't even look Spanish."

I began to panic. I really didn't know the answers to those questions.

"My father is from Jamaica. I know he is not Spanish, but my mom is."

"So then if your father is from Jamaica, he must be even darker than you, so you are a nigger. Ha, ha, ha, you're a nigger."

"No, I'm not. Stop it. I'm Dominican."

"So then speak Spanish, stupid."

I didn't know too much Spanish. My parents felt it was important for me to learn English. Plus, my Jamaican father didn't speak any Spanish and it was hard enough for him to communicate with my mom, who really struggled with English. My mother practiced speaking English with me, so I had an accent of sorts, but my Spanish was not strong. My first language was English as a second language, a blend of Spanish and English words my mom concocted that only her family could really understand. It wasn't what the bullies wanted to hear. For the first time in my life, as I looked at my classmates, I realized that I was different. Most of the kids on the line were light-skinned Latinos. I was not and they laughed at me because of it.

"*Yo quiero agua, perro, gato*, um um, *abuela, abuelo*."

"That's not enough. More!" they screamed.

"Leave me alone, you jerks."

"Yvonne, you were adopted. You can't speak Spanish or nothing. You don't look like your sister. She looks Spanish. You are a nigger, ha, ha, ha, ha."

At that point, the only two Black students in my class came over.

"Yvonne isn't Black, she's Spanish," they said.

"Oh no, Black."

"Spanish."

"Black."

"Spanish."

"Black."

I couldn't believe it. Not even the Blacks would claim me. I felt so low. I began to cry.

"Spanish."

"Black."

"Spanish."

"Black."

They wouldn't stop. For the next few weeks, I was teased by a lot of the kids. I kept asking my mother why she and my sister were light and my father and I were dark. Her answers did not satisfy me. She would say that my skin was beautiful. But I began to feel that being dark made me inferior and there was nothing I could do to change it. I felt trapped.

Maggie witnessed the taunts and bullying. She watched me cry. She was confused, but the one thing that remained a constant as I struggled, was her friendship. Each time I was teased, she would say, "Don't listen to them, Yvonne. Don't listen."

I heard her, but I couldn't help but hear the bullies' voices challenging my shaky self-identity over and over again. I was teased relentlessly. I didn't want to tell my parents or sister. I was ashamed. But Maggie kept saying to me, "Don't listen to them, Yvonne. Don't listen."

She still wanted to play with me. We played together, alone, because no one else would come near me. She didn't care what anyone said about me and acted like nothing had happened, like nothing had changed. I was still Yvonne, her best friend. Never once did she back away.

Although I dreaded going to school, wary that the teasing would come back and ashamed of my differences, Maggie never wavered. Not once throughout our elementary school years together did I not feel the protection of her friendship. It made me strong. It made me feel like maybe, just maybe, it was ok to be me. It made me know that people who mattered could see the real me and not just what was on the outside.

In eighth grade, still so bonded, so close, the school decided to spilt up best friends since we would soon be off to high school. Maggie and I were put in different classes. We still walked to school together. She was still my best friend. The issues were different at 13. Beauty was measured in my school by the color of your skin. So as one of the darker girls, I was considered ugly and the boys were all very clear about that. Maggie, even wearing bifocals and with her gapped teeth, was one of the lighter girls and was considered pretty. But still, she wanted to be my best friend even though my lowly rank was clear. She had boys interested in her. I had none because I was too dark. I remember her going up to boys I had crushes on to ask if they liked me. She'd march right up to them as though she was on a mission. She thought I was pretty and just didn't understand what they were talking about. She really wanted a boy to dance with me at our school dance, but she always got the same response . . . "no."

We wanted to go to the same high school together, but our parents had different plans. They wanted us to go where our older siblings went because of family tuition discounts. Our sisters were in different schools.

So, we parted in high school and our friendship slowly faded away.

I went to her father's funeral about 20 years ago and when we looked at each other there was still the connection. Her teeth were no longer gapped and she wasn't wearing those crooked bifocals. She looked beautiful. Even though my life had changed so much since we were kids, I saw her and immediately felt safe. And for an instant her grief melted away and we just smiled and hugged each other. It was a reunion of best friends. She seemed content with her life. She was in a serious relationship and had a great job. I was a young reporter.

But then her life took a bad turn. Her relationship ended and her heart was broken. She never recovered from the pain. I heard that she was suffering from a deep depression.

A few years later, my father passed away and my mother held a mass for him at our old parish. We had moved away a long time before, but in ways it still felt like home. As I sat with my mother in the front, I turned around to look at the churchgoers and I saw Maggie. She was sitting in a corner, alone. She looked very sad. It was as though the weight of the world was pressing on her. She was praying intensely. I tried to get her attention, but she did not look my way. She seemed completely overwhelmed by her grief. After the mass was over, I rushed out of my church pew to get to her, but she melted into the crowd and disappeared. I never saw her again.

With these words I reach out to her. I hope that somewhere in her sadness she knows what she did for me. She taught me the power of friendship between women; something that has strengthened my life, time and time again. I can be a good friend because Maggie was my best friend, and her friendship and love had a ripple effect in my life. She made me feel like I was not alone. She taught me that if someone cares about me, they would accept me and stand by me, no matter what. What a gift from one child to another.

What a powerful gift.

Yvonne Latty

Yvonne Latty is the Director of the Reporting New York and Reporting the Nation graduate programs at NYU's Arthur L. Carter Journalism Institute. Yvonne is the author of *In Conflict: Iraq War Veterans Speak Out on Duty, Loss and the Fight to Stay Alive* and *We Were There: Voices of African American Veterans, From World War II to the War in Iraq.* She worked for the *Philadelphia Daily News* and is the director/producer of the award-winning documentary *Sacred Poison.* Born and raised in New York City, she earned a BFA in Film/Television and later an MA in Journalism from New York University.

Women's Day

Diane Tober, Ph.D.

Be at the service of your mother, because paradise lies under the feet of mothers.—Words attributed to Hazrat-e Fatemeh

Dr. Tehrani started his speech with the familiar opening, "*Bismallah-e rahmaan-e rahim* (praise be to God, the beneficent and merciful) I am very thankful to have you all here, to celebrate Women's Day and the birth of Prophet Mohammed's daughter, Fatemeh, peace be upon her."

Gesturing in my direction, he continued, "I would especially like to welcome Dr. Tober, who has come to Iran from the United States to do research on family planning. We are very happy to have you here in our country and are pleased that you are here to celebrate this occasion with us." The group applauded and I felt my face turn red.

"As you know, Fatemeh was a devoted daughter to our Prophet Mohammed, wife to Imam Ali, and mother to Imam Hassan and Hossein, peace be upon them all. She was also a strong leader in her community. She is the model for the perfect Muslim woman ... "

I must have looked noticeably puzzled, as one of the office workers pulled me aside to explain what was going on. "Today is Women's Day," she whispered. "All the women come to the head of the department, and Dr. Tehrani distributes gifts to honor the work that women do. It is also Fatemeh's Birthday, the daughter of the Prophet Mohammed. Everyone celebrates Women's Day on Fatemeh's birthday because she is considered to be a perfect example of a good Muslim woman."

I wondered what this event meant, both in terms of what an ideal Muslim woman was supposed to be, as well as in regard to the real lives of Iranian Muslim women. Why was Fatemeh so important? I wished my friend Nargess was home so that I could ask her, but she was still on a *hajj* to Mecca. In the meantime, I waited to speak to Maryam on my next trip to Zeinabiyeh; surely she could enlighten me about Fatemah's significance.

By 8:00 a.m. a couple days later, I had left my two young sons in the care of our babysitter to head off in a taxi for Zeinabiyeh, where I was conducting my fieldwork in a health clinic. The babysitter had to travel three hours by bus to get to our home. Although she was married, she was solely responsible for supporting her husband and their six kids. He was "sick," she frequently told me about her husband. But I could tell by the look in her eyes that he was really addicted to drugs, probably opium. I often felt bad that she had to leave her children for so long in order to care for mine.

Zeinebiyeh is a poor section of urban Isfahan. Driving up, the taxi driver always warned me to be careful of thieves and drug addicts. At first, I struggled to have even the most basic of conversations with people, let alone to conduct interviews in Persian. Now I had been coming here for a little over a month, and the conversations with the women participating in my research were becoming more fluid. All the nurses sent their female patients to talk to me while they waited for the doctors to see them; my makeshift office was always filled with women waiting to be interviewed. Some women felt more comfortable talking to me in groups, others wanted to talk to me privately.

The first couple of hours always flew by until, at the stroke of 10:00, I was summoned to Maryam's office for teatime. Regardless of how many women were waiting in my office or how I tried to object, teatime was mandatory for anyone who wasn't a patient.

"After tea," Maryam said, "you and I will leave the clinic early. There is a very special mosque nearby. I think you will like it." We drank our tea and chatted for almost an hour, until it was time for the clinic to officially close. "Do you have a *chador* (head covering)?" Maryam asked. "To go to the mosque you must wear a *chador*."

Maryam's *chador* was made of a silky black fabric that flowed naturally when moved by the wind. I had begun to carry a *chador* with me in case an occasion arose when I would need it, but I hesitated after seeing hers: mine was navy blue with small white flowers. When I put it on, I felt awkward and obvious instead of secretive, anonymous, and hidden like most women do when wearing a *chador*.

It was noon when Maryam and I left the clinic for the special mosque that contained Zeinab's tomb. As we walked, I adjusted my backpack, which had been pulling the *chador* and *maqna'e* off the back of my head, and tried to find a comfortable way to move, carry my things, hold my *chador*, and not feel completely clumsy and conspicuous. I wondered how all the other women on the street seemed to effortlessly carry their bags, their children, and their groceries, with their *chadors* neatly in place.

As we approached the mosque, the call of *azân* emanated from the loudspeakers of the mosque. The building looked like it was falling apart or undergoing reconstruction. In fact, many of these "reconstructed" buildings were skeletal reminders of the Iran-Iraq War and its aftermath, which still weighs heavily on the hearts of people throughout Iran. We continued across the internal courtyard and approached the tall, sky-blue minaret. Behind me, people were washing their arms and feet in the fountain and preparing for their prayers. At the women's side of the mosque, Maryam and I lined our shoes up on the floor along with 20 or so other pairs. Throngs of Afghan children with messy hair, smudged eyeliner (a custom to protect again evil eye), and rose-colored lips were sitting on the steps outside.

As was the custom, Maryam put her forehead against the door, said a prayer, and kissed the door before entering. I followed suit. Once inside, I noticed the green marble floors and shiny brass bars in the center of the room surrounding a glass case containing Zeinab's coffin. Flowers and money had somehow been stuffed inside the glass case and women lined up with their heads pressed against its bars and prayed. Some women tied cloth or attached locks of hair or prayer beads to the bars hoping that their prayers would be answered. Maryam and I found a seat and she began to read from the Hadith of Ali.

"What's the Hadith of Ali?" I asked.

"The Hadith for all Muslims are the sayings and behaviors of the Prophet Mohammad. These are examples of his behavior and teachings that we follow to be good Muslims. Unlike Sunnis, Shi'as follow the Hadith for different Imams too, especially Ali. For us, Ali and Mohammad are practically the same. This book is from Ali. It has teachings and sayings that help me remember to be forgiving and to put others before myself. Ever since I was little, I've heard stories about Ali."

"Do you know any stories about Ali and his wife Fatemeh?" I asked.

"One of my favorites is about when Fatemeh was dying," Maryam started. "Protesters had broken down her door and it fell on her. Her last request was for a pomegranate. Ali left, and searched for a pomegranate, finding one at last. As he was going home to give it to his wife, he kept coming across poor and unfortunate people on the road asking for a portion of the pomegranate. He felt sorry for them and gave them some. By the time he arrived home, there was only one seed left for Fatemeh. She understood, though. Her husband had to share the pomegranate with the poor, and she, like Ali, always put others before herself. We have a saying that 'one seed from a pomegranate is a piece of paradise.' This reminds us that we should never be wasteful. Fatemeh had been a very generous wife, mother, and daughter, and believed it was a woman's responsibility to make sacrifices for the good of her family and her community—and to be involved in politics. When we think about Ali and Fatemeh, we try to be like them in our own lives—to be good Muslims."

We had been there over an hour, and Maryam was getting ready to leave. We gathered up our things to depart. As we walked out, I turned back to see the women praying at the bars of the tomb— perhaps for fertility or perhaps for the healing of a loved one's sickness.

I appreciated that they believed miracles could be granted there and I hoped their prayers would be answered.

My friend Nargess came back from Mecca to a clean house and, because socializing before and after a *hajj* was a standard part of the ritual, throngs of visitors with sweets (*shirini*) and congratulatory gestures. Nargess had likewise returned with piles of gifts from Mecca. She had yards of fabric from which her friends could fashion new *chadors,* as well as *tasbih* (prayer beads) and other items for male family members.

For me, she brought a lightweight denim dress. A month earlier, her sister had brought her one just like it and I had complimented her on it; she must have remembered. Knowing that she thought of me on her important journey made me feel closer to her.

I waited a bit before coming to visit her, knowing she would be busy with family and friends, but a couple days later, my boys and I arrived at her door, holding a huge box of sweets. She hugged the boys and we kissed each other's cheeks (a standard greeting in Iran among people of the same sex). There were so many sweets on the dining room table that there was not a spare corner left. Nargess cleared a spot for our gift as the kids ran off to play.

"Thank you for the sweets, Diane," she said.

"You're welcome. Welcome back. How was your trip?" I asked.

"I don't know if I can describe it," she said. "It was very powerful. Very moving. But everyone keeps asking me, and I can't find the words to fit the experience."

"It must have been overwhelming in some ways," I replied.

"Yes, you know, everyone is there for the same purpose—to pray and be closer to God. It is very emotional. When you are there, everyone is dressed in white, and we all go around the *Kabbeh* in the same direction. Everyone is the same—there is no Shi'a or Sunni. We are all just part of the same group with the same purpose. It is really very beautiful. You stop thinking about yourself as an individual, and have the sense of being part of something much larger."

"It sounds like it was a very intense experience."

"Yes, very. I am still trying to figure it out," Nargess continued. "It is complicated because on the one hand, I had this very special and spiritual time. But at the same time, I was very disturbed by how women are treated in the city. While worshipping in the mosque, everyone is equal, but out in the city, there is a huge difference between men and women."

"How so?" I inquired.

"It is not uncommon for men in Saudi Arabia to have four wives each. Arab men do that, but most Persian men don't. Women don't drive. They are completely covered from head to toe, with only a slit for their eyes. Sometimes, I was frightened by how the women looked: they were completely covered in black, their hands and faces were covered, and they were wearing black sunglasses. For many women, you couldn't even see their eyes. It looked frightening to me. This is not Islam. This is part of their culture, but it is not Islam."

She continued. "In Islam, the rights of women are very specific. Fatemeh, the Prophet's daughter and Khadija, the Prophet's first wife, were both very powerful women. Khadija was a very successful businesswoman, who owned her own property, which was very rare at that time. In fact, after Mohammad received the Qu'ran, I think his wife set an example for women, and I think partially because of her—but also because God knows the abilities of women—Islam was the first religion to specify that women have the right to own their own property. Before that, they didn't have that right. In fact, women were considered to be the property. Islam helped women to have the right to their own wealth, and more rights in marriage and even in divorce. Islam also limited the number of wives to four; before that, a man could have as many wives as he wanted. In Islam, in the Qu'ran, there are many powerful women. It is sad for me when I see other Muslim women unable to have the rights that their own religion provides for them. It is not right."

"Nargess, I'm really shocked you had that reaction. In the United States, people often think that Muslim women have very few rights, and that women in Iran are oppressed because of Islam and because they wear a veil. And here you are, a Muslim woman, going to another Muslim country and saying that the women there are oppressed because of culture, but also because of misinterpretations of Islam with regard to women. It seems strange because many American women see women in *hejâb* and think that is oppressive. But you are also a Muslim woman who wears *hejâb* and yet you find the Saudi style of *hejâb* oppressive. In a sense, when you travel to Saudi Arabia, your impressions are similar to those of an American woman coming here."

"Diane, in Iran women work, are politically active, drive, and go to the university . . . women do everything. We just keep our bodies covered. It is not a problem to wear *hejâb*. I like my *hejâb*; it makes me feel protected, more powerful, and respected . . . Iranian women would never tolerate a life like the Saudi women. And most Iranian men wouldn't even think about taking a second wife; it is very rare here. We are too outspoken."

Nargess had started me thinking about all of the assumptions I had before I first came to Iran: about veiling, about separation of male and female space, about what it means for women to have equal rights, and about what it means to be a Muslim woman in Iran, with Fatemeh as the symbol for strength, patience and self-sacrifice. Rather than seeing things in terms of positives versus negatives in women's lives, I began to think in terms of complexities: While many women found *hejâb* to be cumbersome and would rather go without, other women preferred to remain covered as it provided them with both more privacy and status as a Muslim woman; while many women enjoyed attending mixed parties, they also enjoyed having their private spaces in religious shrines, fitness centers, and spas, and special women-oriented celebrations. Within these feminine spaces in the Islamic Republic of Iran, sisterhood can be found everywhere.

I had missed our conversations and the way Nargess made me see things I wouldn't have seen otherwise. It was good to have her back.

Diane Tober

Diane Tober, Ph.D., is a Medical Anthropologist. She received her degree from the University of California, Berkeley. She conducted extensive research in Iran on gender and family among Afghan refugees and low-income Iranians in Isfahan. Women's issues are a key focus in her academic work as well as in her role as Executive Director at a non-profit agency. In 2010, she traveled to the Occupied Palestinian Territories to explore the challenges of a women's center funded by the Unique Zan Foundation. From 2011-2012, she was scholar in residence at the Beatrice Bain Research Group on Gender at Berkeley. Her forthcoming book is titled *A Path to Isfahan: Life in Iran with My Two Sons.*

Friendship Amidst the Ruins

Liesl Gerntholtz

I was ten years old when I first met Fatima. She was a Muslim girl on her first day at a white school in apartheid-era South Africa. I was a white, Catholic girl, who was asked by Sister Eucharia to show Fatima around the school and make sure that she settled in. At the time, I was largely unaware of how momentous the decision was to racially integrate the school, a choice made by the nuns who ran the small convent in Pretoria, at the heart of the apartheid regime.

Mixed schools were prohibited by law, and South African school children were educated in single-race schools, with white schools receiving more resources and providing better education than the schools that educated non-white children. I had no real sense of the consequences of that decision and took for granted the racist slogans that were regularly painted on the walls of schools. As I grew older, I began to understand the courage that it must have taken the nuns to racially integrate the school, and I also began to unpack how that decision, and my friendship with Fatima, profoundly influenced my life. That friendship helped shape the values that I continue to hold dear and that I hope I instill in my children.

I first became aware of the discrimination and prejudice suffered by the majority of South Africans when the barriers to my friendship with Fatima were presented. It was not possible for Fatima and me to do the things that I took for granted with my "white" friends: we couldn't go to the movies or a restaurant together, we weren't permitted to live in the same neighborhood, and we couldn't just hang out in the malls, even if our parents had allowed it. In a very small way, my friendship with Fatima gave me a window into a world of prejudice, discrimination, and violence. By the time I was 12 years old, I knew that I wanted to find some way to work for a better world.

Fatima and I have remained friends for almost 35 years now. We have five children between us, and both of us have lived through some difficult times when our partners were seriously ill. We've been out of touch for long periods, yet somehow, we find our way back to each other and pick up our conversations as though we were still schools girls who saw each other daily. The connection that we have is an indelible mark on my soul.

The power of friendship has influenced my life at a very personal level, but I have also seen the deep connections between women in my professional life. In my work as a human rights activist, first in South Africa, and now globally as the director of the women's rights division at Human Rights Watch, I have come across many examples of women's support and friendship, often during times of great crisis. It seems like a cliché that in the worst-case scenarios women come together to support each other, offer their care, and pick up the pieces. But, as I have seen for myself, amidst their tragedies and loss, women reach out to other women, comfort children, care for the sick, and bury the dead.

That ability was perhaps most starkly illustrated to me in Haiti after the January earthquake that devastated Port au Prince, Haiti's capital. Some 200,000 women, men, and children lost their lives that terrible afternoon, and 1.2 million people were displaced and living in spontaneous settlements, with little more than ragged pieces of cloth slung over sticks to protect them from the elements and whatever dangers lurked in the congested camps that had sprung up all over the city.

I had travelled to Haiti as part of a mission to investigate sexual and other violence against women in the aftermath of the earthquake. Sexual violence frequently increases during emergencies as people struggle to meet their basic needs for food, water, shelter, and hygiene, and tragically, media reports had suggested that Haiti would be no exception. The first thing that struck me, as we visited some of the largest camps in the city, was how vulnerable women and girls were. I wondered where women washed, changed their sanitary pads, and fed their babies, as these rudimentary shelters so obviously provided no privacy. As we parked our car at a large camp holding about 27,000 people, my question was answered: a young woman, naked from the waist down, was trying to wash herself, in full view of everyone. I was immediately conscious of many young men watching her and acutely aware of her vulnerability. I think, in the heat and dust that surrounded the city, she probably just wanted to feel clean.

As we walked through another camp talking to women, we were taken to a small tent. At that time, it was unusual to see a tent at all, as very few had been handed out by humanitarian aid workers. Indeed, many we interviewed expressed concerns and wondered how it would be possible to source and deliver the number of tents needed to shelter so many people amidst the damage of Port au Prince. In the oppressive heat and semi-darkness of the tent sat a young woman, Marie, holding what was clearly a newborn baby boy. I asked her where she had given birth and she told me, in broken English, that she had given birth about a week before, in the camp.

She pointed to an older woman, indicating that she wanted her to explain something to me. This woman, Mylande, told me that she had helped deliver the baby and that she had given the tent, one that she had received when she was displaced by a hurricane the previous year, to Marie. She also told me that she was helping Marie to care for the baby, joking that Marie was very young and needed support. I assumed that the two had known each other before the earthquake, and said it was wonderful they'd found each other in the chaotic aftermath of the earthquake. Mylande quickly corrected me, telling me that she had only met Marie just before she'd given birth. That simple statement overwhelmed me—Mylande had clearly lost her own home in the earthquake, and was living in unimaginably difficult circumstances, but she had still found the compassion to care for this young woman.

The primary concerns most often expressed to us by the residents of this camp were the lack of food and shelter. At the time, they had not received any food or information about when they would get food or what, if any, arrangements would be made to shelter them during the rainy season. Mylande herself expressed frustration about the lack of food and asked me if I had any information about when aid would arrive at the camp.

Despite the anxiety, fear, and sense of abandonment that Mylande had experienced, she had extended a hand of friendship and support to a stranger in profound need. She helped Marie give birth, found her somewhere reasonably safe to live, and continued to support her.

I am sure that Mylande and Marie's story is not unique—I imagine that there were many women in Port au Prince doing much the same: helping other women give birth, looking after children, supporting those who had lost loved ones, and simply offering the comfort of friendship in a very dark time. I know that many of them did so at the same time when they were struggling heroically, with very little assistance, to provide food and shelter for their own families.

The power of those friendships and connections and the ways that they will go on to shape the lives of all the women involved, reminded me a little of my own life. Amidst the horror of a profoundly abusive system in South Africa, I found a friendship that remains one of the touchstones of my life.

Liesl Gerntholtz

Liesl Gerntholtz, Director of the Women's Rights Division of Human Rights Watch, is an expert on women's rights globally, particularly in Africa. She has worked and written extensively on violence against women, gender and HIV/AIDS, sexual and reproductive rights, and economic and social rights. Her work at Human Rights Watch has included documenting access to abortion in Ireland, violence against women in Haiti in the aftermath of the earthquake, and gender-based violence and barriers to women's political participation in Libya.

Manti

Jen Siraganian

My grandmother's hands, wrinkled and stained
with sun spots, dig into a mountain of flour.
She breaks each egg deliberately into the well
with the same swiftness as when she tapped
my Armenian textbook after I misread a sentence
about smiling Socialist schoolchildren.

She rolls the sleeves of her dress up to her elbows,
massages the dough until elastic, and instructs me
to stretch from its center. I grip the moist edges,
pulling and pleading with awkward fingers. It hangs
over the table's corners like the embroidered tablecloth
she gave my parents for their fifteenth anniversary.

In broken English, she sends me back to the stool
to watch her knife slice the thin sheet into a grid.
After she drops a thumbnail of lamb, parsley,
and onion into each square's center, she dips
her fingers in a small bowl of water and folds
one half of each square over the other.

Pinching and sealing the corners, she sinks
the bulging envelopes into boiling broth.
We wait and wait until she waves me back
to the stove when they rise to the surface.

Jen Siranganian

Jen Siraganian is a poet, teacher of British literature and creative writing, and assistant coordinator of the Lit Crawl, the final night of Litquake, San Francisco's annual literary festival. She earned a BA from Brown and an MFA from the University of Arkansas, and has been nominated for a Ruth Lilly Fellowship and a Pushcart Prize.

Anatomy of a Story

Sarah Ladipo Manyika

In May of 2011, a young woman from the West African nation of Guinea working as a maid in a prominent New York hotel was reportedly sexually assaulted at her place of work. The suspect, a guest who had checked out by the time the crime was reported, was on his way from New York to Paris and was sitting comfortably in his first-class seat when, just minutes before takeoff, he was arrested and escorted off the plane. Turns out the man was Dominique Strauss-Kahn, then head of the International Monetary Fund (IMF) and a leading candidate in the next French presidential election. As news of the dramatic arrest spread, the Internet buzzed with chatter—many speculating on a political conspiracy while others promptly concluded that this was just another example of a rich and powerful man thinking he could get away with rape. As a writer, I was drawn in by the drama of this story; there were multiple metaphors and the symbolism was inherent in the event—IMF boss versus African maid, France versus a former colony. I am always intrigued by immigrant stories and this was one that instantly captured my imagination.

The headlines were all about him, but I was interested in her. I've never visited Guinea but I have lived in neighboring countries so I can picture the landscape changing between its wet and dry seasons. I can hear the call to prayer piercing the early morning quiet and the cacophony of car horns and bicycle bells in the cities. I can smell the sweet aromas of vegan food—roasted corn, groundnuts, rice, and fried plantains—and I can see quite vividly the colorful, billowing fabrics that people wear. This is, however, merely scene setting, which left me plenty of room to wonder and imagine what sort of life she might have led in Guinea and eventually in New York.

At the time the news story broke, I had just finished teaching two undergraduate classes in which two students, in response to the books that we were studying, confided in me that they had been victims of sexual assault. In one class, this confidential disclosure came in response to our reading of J. M. Coetzee's *Disgrace*, a novel that pivots around two instances of rape; in a second class, the disclosure came as the result of a heated class discussion on the facts surrounding the assault of CBS reporter Lara Logan at Tahir Square. The students who confided in me were of different ethnicities and social classes—proof, had I needed it, that such occurrences are not rare and can happen to any woman. But I didn't need proof. I had already heard too many of these terrible stories.

I also knew something of these experiences from my own encounter with a man, who was scheming for sex one winter afternoon when there was no one else in the office but me. He was not, as he led me to believe, calling me to his office to discuss my work. I was not raped (not even close, I would like to believe), but the incident left me frightened and silenced for years in a way that this cunning man must have counted on. I did not want to write my story, nor did I want to write the particulars of this real-life story between West African maid and IMF boss.

The latter, however, served as the catalyst that propelled me into writing a fictional story with a compulsion so strong that I longed to neglect everything else. I was supposed to be grading student papers, taking care of house and family, not to mention working on other, more legitimate writing projects. Yet this story that came to me on a whim, a story that would not necessarily go anywhere or even be published, consumed me. I wondered if I were crazy to be embarking on such a project at this time and sought the opinion of my friend, Xoliswa, a documentary filmmaker in Johannesburg whose work on women and children has always inspired me. She had once told me that when those of us who are artists do not do our art, it feels like a part of us withers and dies. Xoliswa is one of my most talkative friends, but when she heard my question, she told me to ignore the phone for as long as I needed to and write. "Just write," she repeated and proceeded for the next few days to leave brief, encouraging messages on my answering machine.

I started with a few notes, focusing first on what led to my character's sexual assault, then moving to the facts of the story as they might be presented to a jury. As I started to sketch things out, one thing kept bothering me about the news story serving as my inspiration: many of my male friends found it hard to imagine how an older man could force a woman to perform oral sex without the use of some weapon—a gun, for example, or a knife.

"Imagine," they said, "putting your most sensitive 'bit' into the mouth of someone who has every reason to hate you. Couldn't she bite?" Well, yes, of course she could bite, but what if she couldn't bring herself to bite? What if she was too terrified? What if she was gagging, or if he had his hands around her neck? Was it really that difficult to imagine?

One day in the park while we were minding our children, I asked my friend Katie about it, just to make sure I wasn't the only one who was flabbergasted that people would find this scene hard to imagine. After all, I easily imagined a number of scenarios in which such a thing could happen. For example, imagine a maid going into a rich man's room. Imagine that she's rummaging through his things, maybe even with the intention to steal, when suddenly the man emerges from the bathroom (or wherever) and catches her in the act. Imagine the guilt she might feel, the overwhelming fear of losing her job that a young woman in her position would experience. Imagine, for example, that she were an illegal or undocumented immigrant and how easily he might then force her to do the supposedly unthinkable act in exchange for his silence.

Katie listened to what was, in effect, the first draft of my story, and when I was done she turned to me and said, "Yes, but stealing is so cliché. What if the maid didn't snoop or steal? What if the guy was charming and the woman was lonely? Think of the loneliness of immigrant life—that's something you can write about, isn't it?" What Katie was doing in her usual, discerning way, was getting me to think more deeply about what I was trying to write. Her line of questioning caused me to see that, for all I was saying about wanting to invent the facts of my story, I was still clinging to the actual facts of the story. Katie also asked me what it was that I wanted to write about, which was a question that frightened me because at the beginning of any piece of writing my head is always a whirl of ideas.

Sometimes, my tangled thoughts will unravel before the writing begins, but usually, clarity only comes in the process of writing and during multiple rewrites. I am, as novelist Zadie Smith would say, a micromanager and not a macroplanner when it comes to writing, and this means that beginning any piece is tortuous. If I lose confidence in my writing or in myself at the start, it'll be the end of my story, and yet I knew that Katie's question was important. So, I held tightly to my passion for the story, remembered Katie's very important point about the loneliness of the immigrant, and sat down to write.

While still figuring out the circumstances under which my character would have been assaulted, I began to imagine the subsequent interactions between police, hospital workers, and lawyers. I had presumed that lawyers would have surrounded my character from the beginning, but my lawyer (and writer) friend Marti dispelled that assumption. Marti, like Katie, encouraged me to think further outside the box with my story. As a result, I began to consider a character that was a Muslim, or a non-observant Muslim, or even a born-again Christian. These new possibilities triggered even further possibilities. I could, for example, give my character a son rather than a daughter; maybe even a son who was my own son's age. I could create a character that didn't speak fluent English and needed a translator. I then began to imagine what might happen if the accuser was cleared of all charges (as was ultimately the case for Dominique Strauss-Khan) and whether this would make the man any less of a rapist in the eyes of my character. Little by little, the "facts" of my story fell into place. Looking back, I realize that these earlier drafts included subtle (and what I also thought at the time to be clever) references to the character of Melanie in Coetzee's *Disgrace*, but with each successive draft, I found myself dropping these references as if they were scaffolding that only needed to be there to support the story in its infancy.

What remained particularly difficult about this piece, however, was the question of voice. What right did I have to write such a story? I might be African and black, but I am not poor, have never worked as a maid, and have not been raped. As I was questioning my right to tell this story, I felt reassured by two conversations—one with Bibi, my spirited and untiring Abuja-based publisher, and the second with Melissa, my prolific writer friend from Los Angeles. These conversations led me to reformulate my question around the description of a character that I imagined to be silent—a silence born out of anger, fear, linguistic barriers, and the crushing realization that it was just her word against the word of someone much more powerful.

On one California morning (for me) and one Calcutta midnight (for her), I asked my friend Minal how one effectively captures this sort of silence. Minal, whose last project was to write a collection of unicorn poems, has always experimented with theme and genre. While she mainly listened to what I had to say and generously offered to read versions of my story, she also made the observation that, at the same time I was trying to write my fictional story, my personal thoughts on the matter were equally as interesting. Her comment gave me a boost of confidence that was reminiscent of my time at Hedgebrook, an oasis for women writers, where I first met Minal and other writers who continue to inspire me.

I took this confidence and experimented with the narrative voice in my story. I tried a first person voice, but found that third person afforded me the most distance in which to work with my character's silence. Still, third person was not totally sufficient, because at some point I wanted my character to speak directly to the reader. The story needed her voice, not to prove her innocence, but to convey the true weight of her feelings.

When I am feeling stuck with my writing, I often take a walk down the street to my neighborhood shop where I buy fruit or chocolate (usually both) and chat for some minutes with my friends who work there. One of these friends, whose name I don't know, is the inspiration for another of my stories; she's young, hip, and tattooed and walks arm-in-arm around the neighborhood with her 90-year-old friend. I saw her on one of my excursions while writing this story and asked if she had been following the news about the New York maid. She said no at first, but then remembered and told me that I should check out the latest *Newsweek* because there was an article about the case as well as a really good piece on climate change. It was climate change that she really cared about; she was tired of hearing about all these male jerks. That's when it hit me: when my character wanted to say something, she would just have to say it. She will bypass the translator and say what she had to in whatever English she could, or in her own language altogether.

Several days passed between the writing of drafts. I found myself still following the Dominique Strauss-Kahn affair and studying a video clip of maids being bussed in by their union to witness the arrival of the accused at a Manhattan courtroom. Many of these women were wearing their maids' uniforms and from the sounds of their accents, many were of African, Caribbean, or South American origin.

I felt uncomfortable watching the crowd, as I am always wary of a mob mentality. I also felt uncomfortable watching a group that was so small in comparison to the masses of media that surrounded them. They didn't seem to know what they were supposed to be doing until a moment or two before the accused stepped into the courtroom, and only then did they start chanting in unison, "Shame on you! Shame on you!" As I (somewhat inarticulately) narrated this story to my friend Anne, she nodded her head, knowing instinctively what I was trying to say. Anne has taught English as a second language for years and knows well the lives of immigrant women who struggle to make ends meet. She is kind and encouraging, and when I shared a draft of my story with her, she left a message on my phone saying, "Sarah, it's wonderful— wonderful." At that stage, my story was not in fact wonderful, but it was what Anne felt I needed to hear, and in this case, she was probably right.

Late, as I completed another draft in the month of June, a new headline caught my attention: the kerfuffle over V. S. Naipaul's dismissive comments about women's writing. He stated in an interview, apparently, that he could always tell a woman's writing because of its "sentimentality and its narrow vision of the world."

It struck me then that it is precisely because women are so often the subject of male scorn and assault that women's support of each other is vital. I found his comments so obviously nonsensical that I deemed them not worthy of my time, but I did pause for a moment to study the photograph that accompanied the article. It pictured Naipaul, sitting comfortably in a chair in front of some books. The books were obscured so I couldn't decipher which male writers occupied a place of honor on his shelf, but the picture of him was crystal clear. His beard was neatly trimmed and he looked dapper and English in his sports coat and peacock-green sweater. There was a flicker of a smile on his face as he gripped the left arm of his chair, and I wondered to myself what his story could possibly be. The papers called him a great writer, but I have never been so sure. I found myself pondering his statement that, "inevitably for a woman, she is not a complete master of a house, so that comes over in her writing too."

I reflected on this, thinking to myself that if he was alluding to the fact that women sometimes lack confidence in their abilities because they are told (by men such as himself) that they are peripheral, then yes, there might be an element of truth in what was otherwise a pile of pompous nonsense coming from the mouth of this curmudgeonly writer.

But what exactly does it mean to be the master of one's house? For me, being the master of one's house is mastering one's craft, which is an ongoing process that, for me, owes a lot to those friends who have consistently helped me to mine my ideas and broaden my perspectives. It is thanks to friends such as Bibi, Katie, Minal, Xoliswa, and Anne, with their lovely mix of sentimentality, honesty, and insight on the complexities of everyday life that I continue to grow as a writer. It is thanks not only to my real-life friends, but also to those friends who live on my bookshelves: Twinkle from Jhumpa Lahiri's *Interpreter of Maladies*; Glory from Marilynne Robinson's *Home*; Bolanle from Lola Shoneyin's, *The Secret Lives of Baba Segi's Four Wives*. The men on my shelves, including Naipaul, have been making room for such women for quite a while.

Sarah Manyika

Sarah Ladipo Manyika was raised in Nigeria and has lived in Kenya, France, and England. Her first novel, *In Dependence*, was published in the United States in 2011. She currently lives in California, where she teaches at San Francisco State University, and is working on her second novel.

Section Eight

Mother Earth

The Lions and Me

Deborah Santana

The first time I hugged a tree was twenty years ago. I was reading the books of Sun Bear, a Native-American medicine chief and sacred teacher of Chippewa descent, to become more educated about restoring balance to the earth. Sun Bear wrote that if people "wanted to survive the coming earth cleansing, if [we] wanted to be part of the new earth, [we] would have to reestablish [our] very personal ties with the natural world." I grew up in San Francisco in a neighborhood with cement sidewalks. My interaction with the natural world consisted of making mud pies with my sister in our backyard. Sun Bear and other indigenous leaders teach that the earth is sacred and we must honor its spiritual offerings to have harmony in life.

So, on a hot summer afternoon, I wrapped my arms part way around a rough-barked oak tree and heard the heartbeat of Mother Earth. I tried not to think about the bugs that might crawl up my arms or the dirt that was making a dusty pattern on my face. I was in a moment of awakening, doing something I was completely unfamiliar with . . . I was hugging a tree and developing a relationship with the natural world.

My head felt like it was spinning in the energy pulsing from the trunk. Standing still, with my arms extended, my heartbeat matched that of the birds in the branches, the horses on the distant hill, and the quietly moving insects on the ground. Our hearts were all beating to the drumbeat of Mother Earth, and I knew I was not separate from the trees, from the soil, from the poppies, roses, and doves in my garden, or the whales migrating from Alaska to Mexico. Hugging the tree awakened my connection with the origins of natural things and their relationship with me. Since that moment, when I walk on

Hoo-Koo-E-Koo trail on California's Mt. Tamalpais, or on Dol Dol Road in Nanyuki, Kenya, I notice the landscape with a tree hugger's sensibilities: the natural world tells me a story of a loving creator who guides me in my life.

Three months ago, I was in Lewa Downs, Kenya, on a safari. It was my second day there, and the expanse of the land was breathtaking. Not only did a cheetah cross our path right after our small plane landed on the dirt runway, but when I arrived at my tented cabin, small birds were flying in and out of the open windows, and fluttering their wings over my bed.

On our second afternoon, the camp was abuzz because there had been a lion kill the night before. We set out across the savannah in a windowless jeep—our driver, Saban, scanning the wiregrass to find the lions. Spotting a pride of lions is the crowning achievement of the best safari drivers. I was content sitting back in the seat, my body relaxing in the warm afternoon breeze as peacock-hued superb starlings flitted past. Elephants stood on a hill above us, and a herd of zebras glanced up from a watering hole. I couldn't believe how lucky I was to be in Kenya, on the continent where humankind originated.

We drove close to the evidence of a kill—a giraffe carcass being watched over by other giraffes whose long necks seemed to hang in mourning. I was struck by how the giraffes stayed close to the remains, not leaving the fallen member of the tower, and keeping the hundreds of vultures surrounding them at bay. We continued our drive, Saban masterfully maneuvering the jeep over rocky streams and rutted roads. I looked over the open right side of our jeep, and recognized a hide of some type lying about four feet away. It was the same color as the grasses and I pointed, saying, ever so slowly, "What is that?"

Saban had been looking over the left side of our vehicle. He quickly stepped on the brakes and the three other passengers and I lurched forward as the jeep stopped. One passenger leapt from the seat next to me to the rear, clutching her shirt and panting. I stood up and stared into the eyes of a very sleepy lion, full from the kill. I calmly raised my camera and took a photo. One by one, five lions stood and stretched, looked us over, and then lay back down to continue their digestion. For five minutes, no one spoke. The only sound was the click of camera shutters.

On the drive back to camp, everyone laughed at me for asking, "What is that?" But, I had not been able to tell the difference between the grasses and the fur, between the soft breathing of the lion and my own peaceful reverie. Although the other passengers had been frightened, I hadn't felt afraid. Twenty years ago, when I first hugged a tree and acknowledged my relationship with every aspect of life, I had been given a connection to all souls—not just people, but animals, plants, water, seeds, and sky. Out of respect for the natural world, I would never hug a lion, knowing its predatory nature, but, in a fleeting moment, the lion and I had communicated a harmless message to each other. It would all have been different had the pride not enjoyed a kill the night before. But they had, and I had been fortunate to feel the power of a 300-pound carnivorous mammal.

That evening, my three safari mates and I ate dinner together under brilliantly blinking stars on the dining room terrace. Our eyes glowed as we spoke about seeing the kings and queens of the rangelands in such close proximity. It had been such a thrill to be so close, and a sacred gift too. In a break in the conversation, I listened to the wind through the trees, and thought I heard a far-off roar.

Deborah Santana

Deborah Santana is an author, philanthropist, and supporter of peace and social justice. Her memoir, *Space Between The Stars: My Journey to an Open Heart*, was published in March 2005. Deborah is the founder of Do A Little, a nonprofit supporting women and girls in the areas of health, education, and happiness. She is executive producer of two short documentary films, *Road to Ingwavuma* and *Girls of Daraja*, both of which tell of her journeys to South Africa and Kenya.

Ancients, photograph by Caitlin McCaffrey

Caitlin McCaffrey

Caitlin McCaffrey is a photographer now based in Northern California. She has exhibited in solo shows at the Fresno Art Museum, the Sonoma County Museum of Art and has been included in group shows by the Oakland Museum and by the Pages Exhibition of Contemporary Art in Whitechapel, London. She worked as a photographer at the Metropolitan Museum of Art in New York City and has produced commissioned work for collectors, designers and architects. Her editorial work has appeared in magazines, journals and newspapers including *Esquire*, *Elle* and the *New York Times*.

Mother's Voices

Dominique Browning

I've spent the last nine months giving birth to a new organization, really an act of incredible team gestation, called Moms Clean Air Force. The labor took place on my kitchen table, but before I start hyperventilating, I'll leave off the birth metaphors. Let me just say, this work has been some of the most exhilarating I've ever done. I had forgotten how much we moms have to learn from one another. Only this time, we aren't talking about raising our babies, just making the world safer for them.

We are mobilizing to fight air pollution as a children's health issue—reminding moms that their voices are powerful and that there are some things money cannot buy, like clean air. We can only protect our right to clean air through being active citizens. We're using all the social media tools at our fingertips, but we're also sitting down and meeting with our senators, face to face, and writing old-fashioned notes reminding them that we are not just statistics. We are the people who vote for them, or don't.

I've been meeting with moms from all across the country who are Republicans, Democrats, Independents, and apoliticals (at least until now) and are fed up with the status quo. We are all sick of dollars first, babies second. I've met Alabama moms who don't want to make a choice between having a job and their children's health, Ohio moms who are alarmed by the research linking behavioral issues to air pollution, and Arizona moms who are making regular emergency room runs with their asthmatic children. I've met Pennsylvania moms who are outraged that the shale rush is fouling their skies and Michigan moms who want their teenagers to have job opportunities in clean energy, without having to leave their home state. The New Hampshire moms

I've met just want to eat tuna fish again and the Dallas moms are worried about that brown bubble of smog rising over their homes.

We are new moms with tiny babies. We are moms carting our kids to soccer games and school events and worrying about teenagers' curfews while chewing the nails off our fingertips when the hours get small. We are older moms whose children have grown up and moved away. We are grandmas enjoying our new grandchildren. Some of us are not moms at all, but we honor our own mothers who taught us about fair play and sharing. Moms or not, we all know we share the air. We may be past having hot flashes, but we're all having flashes of rage. How dare the polluters and politicians attempt to get away with compromising our lives and the lives of our children?

We are women who don't believe those who deny the science behind climate change. We have something else to deny. We deny that the situation is hopeless because as moms we've had to live our lives figuring out how to find hope in the darkest of times. And any mom will tell you that right now times are tough. We know what to do when we get overwhelmed: we take action! We can do something about climate change.

We respect science and doctors, and we listen when they warn us of danger. We know exactly who is going to be around to suffer the impacts of the extreme weather that will make today's floods, droughts, and heat waves look quaint: our children, the loves of our lives. We know that the crazy stuff we are seeing today is just the beginning of global warming, and it is already bad enough.

Is all of this terrifying? Overwhelming? You bet! Moms today feel like they have to be the EPA, FDA, and USDA all rolled into one. We're juggling jobs and babies while struggling to remember enough high school chemistry to understand the labels on beauty products so we know what to avoid. But we also know it is impossible to shop our way out of pollution problems. There isn't an air filter on the market that can protect us from what lies ahead. Money can buy the right to pollute, but money cannot buy clean air.

Sometimes, being a good mom means being a present and engaged citizen. That's what all these political moms from all across the country are teaching each other: there is strength, wisdom, and community when maternal voices join in a loud chorus. The only way to get strong regulations in place is to demand them. Moms hear the word regulations and we think, *Good! That means protection.* Republicans and Democrats have rallied around Administrator Lisa Jackson (the mom of a severely asthmatic son) because she has done a historic job of enhancing the Clean Air Act. Her work will have a long legacy. We're grateful for her vision and courage.

Do politicians really want to make their mothers angry? Most of us aren't marching in the streets or getting arrested—yet. But we're signing petitions, writing letters, meeting with our political representatives, and letting them know: listen to your mothers. We share the air. Stop polluting it. Mother love is the original sustainable, renewable energy. The supply is endless. We hope Washington gets a charge out of it. We do!

Dominique Browning

Dominique Browning is a co-founder and the Senior Director of Moms Clean Air Force, which fights air pollution as a children's health issue. She works under the aegis of Environmental Defense Fund. Dominique also blogs regularly at Slow Love Life and is the author of several books, the most recent a memoir titled *Slow Love: How I Lost My Job, Put on My Pajamas, and Found Happiness.* She writes regularly for the *New York Times, Whole Living, Good Housekeeping* and others. Dominique's career in journalism included editor roles at magazines as varied as *Newsweek* and *House & Garden*, where she was editor-in-chief for thirteen years.

Wrap-Around Porch

Tracy Chiles McGhee

The porch is now empty after much
womanifesting and storytelling
and sipping and fanning
and swatting and funning
and coming and going
through the screen door.
The mosquitoes have passed out,
so drunk, full of our blood moonshine.
Green-gold fireflies pulse again,
visible against the darkness.
The crickets, hushed by our belly-deep laughter,
rehearse a comeback song.
Then, slowly, night's moon,
full of herself, as a grand gesture,
releases her pull just enough
so that we may find embrace in our dreams
until we meet again,
here on this wrap-around porch.

Tracy Chiles McGhee

Tracy Chiles McGhee (TracyChilesMcghee.com) is a community activist and writer. Recognized as one of 2011's "Top 10 Women in Social Media" by *Liberated Muse*, her poetry, fiction, and non-fiction have appeared in several publications such as *Word Nation*, an anthology edited by Marita Golden, *BOMB Magazine*, and *Tidal Basin Review*. She is also the Founder and Executive Director of

WOMA (womanifesting.org), a non-profit focused on developing and supporting programs that foster self-empowerment, sisterhood, and service. Tracy is a graduate of San Francisco University High School, Georgetown University and Catholic University of America Law School. She enjoys passionate living and giving back.

Help a Sister Out!

Jessica Buchleitner

"Poverty . . . stole your golden shoes. It didn't steal your laughter . . . "
—Jewel, from the song "Hands."

Take a breath and imagine traveling thousands of miles from where you are to a remote area surrounded by mountains and deserts:

You awake to your baby stirring in the early morning hours as sunlight peeks into the room. You stare briefly at the cracks in the walls of the house and remember living with your husband in the days before he was found dead, his body discarded in a cemetery; the days before his perpetrators tried to convince you to become a suicide bomber by making sure you understood your own hopelessness and inability to provide for yourself.

You remember the times before they threatened to take your child away and you fled your country without money or resources, plagued with health problems. You know you cannot stay with your family. You are a threat to their lives. You don't want to become like the other widows, begging on your knees in the streets as your children starve, sleeping in makeshift tents in constant fear of kidnapping.

You have no guarantee of safety where you're hiding, but nowhere to run, either. You are branded because your husband worked to create a sustainable future for your country—a cause countless others battled against. You registered as a refugee, but the refugee office has since closed due to the bombings and can't help you. You are reaching, but no one extends a hand to you. Your brother-in-law comes to tell you that it is customary for you to marry him now that your husband is gone. You are in disbelief: he is one of those believed to be responsible for your husband's death. Because you refused, you are now also in hiding from him. You live in constant fear that you will be found and taken against your will. As you hear blasts in the distance you wonder: What will happen to your child? You stare at the first light of the breaking dawn and ponder what few options you have left . . .

Perhaps the most disturbing element of this vision is the fact that it is a true story, the reality of a 23 year old Afghan woman currently seeking refuge in Pakistan. The facts in this story were not fabricated or embellished but describe the life of one of our global sisters. Unfortunately, this is a reality that too many women in poverty share—struggling to survive with limited human rights and little to no access to the modern resources which could enable conquering such atrocities.

Current statistics paint an alarming portrait of the feminization of poverty worldwide. At least 80 percent of humanity lives on less than ten dollars a day. Of the two billion poorest people in this world, it is estimated that roughly 70 percent are women. More than one billion people in this world entered the twenty-first century unable to read a book or sign their own name. Women represent a large percentage of each of these groups.

Even in the ostensible affluence of the United States, men are the minority within existing poverty statistics. Over half of the 37 million Americans living in poverty are women. Even more worrisome, the gap in poverty rates between men and women in America is wider than in any other western country. Women are poorer than men in all racial and ethnic groups in America and they are also more likely to bear the cost of caring for children in single-parent homes, which only reinforces their financial burdens. Woven together, these statistics sketch a shocking picture of the societal position of women globally.

Years ago, I realized just how frustrated I was to hear stories of young women around the world being mistreated, abused, and abandoned. Participating in discussions with refugee women about the societal and cultural placement of women in their countries opened my eyes beyond my immediate world and forced me to consider all of the causes. In July 2009, I started The 50 Women Project to advocate for women globally. I felt that by gathering stories of survival and strength across different cultures, faiths, and ideas, I could create a sense of solidarity for women all over the world by sharing those stories. My hope is that the stories will allow women who are suffering to see survival as an option despite the obstacles of their circumstances. It is sometimes difficult for people under these devastating conditions to cultivate hope without any external support or sense of unity.

The stories of these refugee women became my bridge to advocating for women's rights in the developing world. A trend began to emerge from my research of their stories: Despite their disparate locations, all of these women lacked very basic rights. In poverty-stricken nations around the globe, women were denied education and thus could not sustain themselves or care for children in the unplanned absence of a husband. They were denied the right to work or were forced into low-wage, degrading, or dangerous jobs; and, as widows or single parents, their hope for survival seemed to be shrinking dramatically.

Becoming aware of these sad truths made it imperative that I dig deeper. I came to learn that refugee and displaced women truly are the most severely disadvantaged of all. On top of being forced into prostitution or labor-intensive, low-paying jobs just to survive, many of them are left to care for orphaned children in addition to their own. A Liberian refugee once told me that her mother was caring for 18 orphan children in an effort to keep them off the streets and out of the reaches of corrupt criminals. Estimates indicate that of the 2.2 billion children in the world, one billion of them (that's nearly every second child) exist in extreme poverty. We absolutely must ask ourselves what repercussions these realities will have on the future sustainability of this world.

There is a story I came to know through The 50 Woman Project that particularly demonstrates the profound unfairness a female in the developing world can experience for no reason other than her gender. A woman from Cameroon, Africa, told me of being born a disgrace to her family because she was not male. She described the pressing hardships of entering the world as a "failure" by no fault of her own and lamented the fact that it took her father months to stomach holding her as an infant. She explained that her gender prohibited her from being allowed an education. After trying to move to the United States, she was able to attend school and, through hard work and perseverance, received her nursing degree. Despite all of her achievements and the fact that she is now the most accomplished of all the children in her family, her father still rejects her simply because of her gender and can muster no pride for her. Although undoubtedly painful, she openly discusses her experiences with the hope that her global sisters will be inspired by all she has accomplished in the face of extreme adversity.

Women in this situation and situations like it should not be seen solely as victims, but as future agents of change. I have heard countless stories of women who show the drive and determination to better their lives and the lives of their sisters; they could and would excel if only they had access to resources we consider basic. The young Afghan woman described earlier is a perfect example of that fighting spirit which only needs to be nurtured. She wholeheartedly desires to attend school and become fluent in English. She is ready and willing to take advantage of any educational opportunity whatsoever, no matter how small. She hopes her daughter will go to school and have a brighter future, and will do whatever she needs to make that happen. Although her societal position is tenuous, she remains hopeful and even open minded about different cultures and ideas. Her pleas, though typed in broken English, show tremendous effort. She represents so many women in the developing world who have not given up and are waiting for one helping hand to be extended to them.

I am blessed to have so many culturally diverse female friendships in my life. It was these friendships that opened my eyes to the global community outside my own life and helped me to recognize my responsibility to that community. Through my friendships with women from all over the world, I have become witness to the atrocities they have survived and the emotional and physical scars these injustices have left with them. My responsibility is to ensure to the best of my ability that young women in my generation gain equal rights and access to the educational and societal opportunities they deserve. I truly believe that by working together, we can promote these fundamental and crucial concepts.

The women I've described from all over the world are your sisters as well as our friends. The estimated 20,000–60,000 women in Bosnia who were raped during the Bosnian war are your sisters and your friends. The women in Afghanistan who braved stones being thrown at them while protesting the 2009 marriage law that legalized rape are your sisters and your friends. The young girls in Bangladesh who are forcibly trafficked for sex are your sisters and your friends.

All impoverished nations have a vast, untapped, and undervalued resource that has the power to help them economically; a resource that has a strong spirit, an open mind and a problem-solving nature; a resource waiting and hoping for the equal human rights to free them. That resource is our global friends and sisters. I encourage you to find a way to help a sister out today.

Jessica Buchleitner

Jessica Buchleitner is an advocacy journalist working with the United Nations affiliated Women News Network, reporting on women's rights developments globally. She currently serves on a United Nations committee with the City of San Francisco. As an NGO delegate to the UN's 56th Session of the Commission on the Status of Women, she met with NGO advocates from around the world who are working toward advancing women's rights. She is currently finishing a book project entitled *50 Women*, which features the life stories of 50 women from 30 countries.

A Journey for Good

Joanie Wynn

My climb to the summit of Mt. Kilimanjaro was like childbirth—more difficult and more rewarding than I ever imagined. It required more concentration, stamina, and strength than I thought I possessed. I saw no choice but to push through the pain and keep climbing, though in those moments I questioned why I was doing it the first place.

I had been to Africa 12 years before, traveling for six weeks in Kenya, Zimbabwe, Tanzania, and South Africa with my husband to make a video on eco-lodges. This time, we were off to Tanzania to produce a documentary on a unique travel experience that combined adventure travel with hands-on volunteer work. A seven-day climb on Mt. Kilimanjaro followed by a four day volunteer project for a non-profit working with children orphaned by East Africa's AIDS epidemic.

The travelers were all women, representing diverse ethnicities and ages. There was Rollie, a 21 year old student from Denver who we affectionately nicknamed "Free Spirit" and Jolie, a 42 year old Detroit mom of three with the moniker "Mother." We were a band of disparate strangers with one essential element in common: we had each traveled across the world in search of an adventure that would stretch our limits physically, intellectually, and culturally.

My first challenge came before I even set foot on the African continent. I was leaving my six year old son Ryan behind for 17 days, the longest I had ever been away from him. He was in the capable and loving hands of my mom and I knew this trip was important for me both personally and professionally. Still, I could feel his vulnerability as I hugged him goodbye, both of us struggling to put on a brave front. It was excruciating. At the airport, I burst into tears and proceeded directly to the lounge to down a huge glass of wine, hoping it would numb my pain, steady my nerves, and steel my resolve.

The launching point for our seven day trek was Moshi, a town on the lower slopes of the mountain. We left early on a drizzling Sunday morning and drove several hours through tiny rural townships. Simple mud huts stood in stark contrast beside bright blue billboards for the local cellular provider. We passed fields of corn, carrots, and gigantic sunflowers. Chickens scratched amid the dust, dirt, and roadside trash. Villagers of all ages carried enormous bundles atop their heads. Brightly-dressed women, some with babies strapped to their backs, tended open fires and children ran barefoot toward our bus to see the *mzungus* (Swahili for white people).

At the ranger check-in station for Kilimanjaro National Park, a large sign detailed a long list of health precautions. Anyone showing symptoms of acute altitude sickness (dizziness, nausea, vomiting) must descend immediately and seek medical attention, it cautioned. I'd read the warnings sent by our guide company, but standing in front of that sign, the magnitude of what I was about to attempt began to sink in.

We were in good hands, though. Our guide was only 31 years old, but he possessed an air of quiet wisdom gained in more than ten years of experience on the mountain. His name was Good Luck Charles and we joked that we were glad to have good luck on our side.

The road to the trailhead had been washed out by heavy rains but our beat-up Land Cruiser delivered on its off-road promise, navigating through deep muddy ruts and exposed tree roots. Finally, we were ready to hike. We followed the Lemosho Route, one of the longest and most remote trails to the summit.

Day one began with a steady climb through dense rain forest. At places, the ground crawled with a living carpet of huge fire ants. "Careful, step over," Good Luck cautioned. We were more than happy to oblige, recalling those movie scenes in which some poor soul is attacked by swarms of angry ants and carried away screaming. We saw black and white Colobus monkeys swing in the upper branches of trees and came upon large mounds of fresh elephant dung, although the majestic creatures eluded us. Thick gray moss draped the trees and the air was dense, warm, and moist. Christine, a warm and intelligent woman in her late thirties, took a fall, covering the seat of her hiking pants in thick, wet, gray-brown mud. I held my breath to see if she would be all right or if the fall would upset her, but she picked herself up with a little laugh.

The conversation flowed easily as we began to get to know one another. The women were all strong and positive, not a whiner in the bunch. Before long, we peeled off layers and glistened with sweat. Under the shade of a large tree, we gobbled up a simple sack lunch. As we rested, our porters passed by, carrying our backpacks and camping gear, 40 to 50 pounds apiece. While we struggled not to trip over rocks or exposed tree roots, these men glided over the terrain, sacks of gear balanced precariously on their heads. They aptly called themselves *wagumu* (hardcore) and they earned our awe and respect. They also brought us our first Swahili lesson:

Mambo vipi?—"How's it going?"

Poa!—"Cool!"

Jo was the linguist in the group. Tall and lanky, she had a wide, beaming grin and an easy laugh. She listened intently and practiced the Swahili phrases over and over again to get them just right.

After four hours of hiking, we arrived at our first campsite where our tents sat under a thick canopy of trees. We donned headlamps and met for dinner at the mess tent. Togolai, our shy waiter, welcomed us with fresh water for hand washing in a large plastic bowl. Inside, we balanced on tiny triangular camp chairs to savor warm cucumber soup, bread, and chicken stew with vegetables. We laughed at each other and ourselves, sharing the travails of the day. Here, in this strange and new place, we found solace in the growing bond of the group. Though I had started the trip as an outsider there to document their journey, I already felt accepted as one of them.

At 3:00 a.m., my eyes snapped open to absolute darkness, the kind where you can't see your hand in front of your face. The tent was small, the roof just inches from my face. I started to panic, my mind racing: *What was I thinking? Why had I come here? How could I be so far away from Ryan? What if something happened to him?* I would never forgive myself. I began to fantasize about the next morning when I would apologize profusely as I requested that someone hike me back out and drive me back to Moshi so that I could get on the first plane back home.

Instead, as the sun came up, I tentatively approached Julie, pulling her aside. Julie was an attractive woman in her thirties who, as a consultant for the United Nations, had traveled extensively throughout Africa. She had a serene and reassuring presence and the previous nights she had burned sage to christen our campsite. I whispered my anxiety and asked if she might have anything to help calm my nerves. She slipped me a stash of herbal supplements and, as others began to move about the camp, I started to feel a bit better. Whether it was the sunrise or the herbs that gave me relief I will never know for sure, but I gathered my resolve and began the day's hike.

We left the rain forest and crossed into the giant heather moorland where there was little shade to protect us from the full strength of the African sun. After only two hours of steep climbing, we were all tired. Good Luck encouraged us onward. "Polé polé," he'd say, meaning "slowly." Polé polé is Kilimanjaro's essential mantra.

At midday we reached a small plateau. The porters, who carried four times as much as us and walked twice as fast, had set us a lovely lunch table. Enjoying the roasted chicken, boiled eggs, and oranges, I looked to the view and to the faces of my new friends. It was strange to think that less than 36 hours before, I had never set eyes on any of these women. I felt a connection to them that typically takes many years to develop and I experienced a profound sense of gratitude to be traveling in their good company.

That afternoon, as we crossed spectacular valleys and streams, the heat was relentless and I felt exhaustion setting in. Camp was "just over the next ridge," our guides said, but that ridge never seemed to arrive. It was like a desert mirage, always just out of reach.

Five, then six hours passed. I ran out of water and fell far behind the group. Regular hikes in the hills around my Muir Beach, California home had not prepared me for this. I knew I was getting dehydrated so I sucked hard on my chewing gum to help generate saliva and to extract any bit of moisture from it. Sam, a muscular guide with a serious demeanor, kept me going, "Just a bit further," he said, "Polé polé."

As I approached the camp, a group of porters stood atop the hill, celebrating my arrival with spirited singing, clapping, and dancing. I felt like collapsing, but I gave them a meek, grateful smile and tried to absorb some of the generous energy they were outpouring.

The destination that evening was Shira Ridge (elevation 12,628 feet), which rewarded me with stunning 360 degree views and the sight of Mount Meru, an extinct volcano in the distance. Night was clear and cold. The sky sparkled with more stars than I had ever seen. In the morning, thick clouds, seemingly thousands of feet below, extended to the horizon. I felt like Athena on Mount Olympus as the sky turned pink, then crimson as the sun rose.

Over the next few days, we ascended through semi-desert, then alpine desert. We scaled boulders up the Great Barranco Wall. We gained stamina and confidence as we conquered each day's challenge. At times we chatted and laughed, or practiced our Swahili with the guides. When we struggled, we quieted and focused . . . polé polé.

Throughout our climb, Good Luck acted as a watchful father, monitoring our health and offering solutions. Susan, a petite young woman in her late twenties was suffering from altitude sickness. She had bad stomach cramps and difficulty sleeping and, as the days wore on, she looked increasingly spent. We all worried about her and rallied around her, but she never once complained. Her mental toughness impressed me and inspired me when I tired.

We approached the final campsite at Barafu Hut (elevation 15,000 feet) under light snowfall. The temperature had dropped significantly and the air was noticeably thinner. We climbed into our tents with excitement and anticipation knowing that in just a few hours, the trek to the summit would begin.

We woke at midnight, donned headlamps, layered up with every piece of warm clothing we'd brought, and began a brutal, eight hour slog up steep and rocky terrain. We labored breathlessly one tiny step at a time. I looked up to see hundreds of tiny headlamps ascending thousands of feet above me. The sight was so discouraging that I looked back down again, vowing to concentrate solely on the two feet directly in front of me. I nodded, narcoleptic-like, into nanoseconds of sleep. Then I'd snap my eyes wide open, shake it off and say to myself, *wake up!*—all the while walking, walking, walking. No one spoke. We all needed every ounce of energy we possessed just to keep going.

When sunrise came, the sky glowed blood red and the astounding beauty refreshed me. At Stella Point, just below the summit, I saw the famed glaciers pulsing iridescent blue.

As one by one we reached Uhuru Peak, we hugged, cried, and celebrated. We snapped photos in front of the famous sign marking our arrival at the highest point in Africa. Jolie brought out photos of her three sons for an impromptu dedication ceremony. Good Luck beamed and cheered, "Congratulations! You have conquered the mountain!" Exhausted but invigorated, I looked intently at my surroundings, wanting to forever imprint my time on the rooftop of Africa in my mind.

Then, as the saying goes, what goes up must come down. It took me over three hours to descend. At times, it felt like skiing as I slid down the slope with my poles. When I arrived back at camp, I collapsed in my tent and immediately fell into a deep sleep. Sleep had not come that quickly or easily to me since childhood. My body had given all it had and did not resist the opportunity to restore itself.

About an hour later, we were roused to hike the remaining four hours down to our campsite for the night. There was no water at Barafu

Hut, so we had to hike out. As we walked into the dark, struggling over large boulders, I worried that my knees might give out. It seemed a bit inhumane, this 18 hour hiking day, but I knew it was necessary. At the final campsite, there was a tiny store that served cold beer and soda. We clinked bottles and toasted our success. As Good Luck had said, we had conquered the mountain or perhaps more importantly, we had not let the mountain conquer us.

After such an exhilarating week, we couldn't imagine an experience to top it, but we headed to Dar es Salaam for the volunteer portion of our adventure.

Dar es Salaam is the largest city in Tanzania and its bustling center feels like a circus on steroids. Street vendors hawk everything from sugarcane to cell phones. Driving is chaotic; cars, trucks, buses, pushcarts, pedestrians, and an occasional goat all vie for the right of way.

We stayed at a hotel right on the beach. It was nothing fancy but after seven days of camping, it felt like the Ritz. In the evenings, we ate spicy Indian food by candlelight under the stars. We sunk our feet into the cool sand and shared bottles of wine. We were giddy with a post-"Kili" fever, realizing that it was all downhill from there, literally as well as figuratively.

We traveled in a green and purple bus we fondly named "the mystery bus," partly because of its resemblance to the bus from *Scooby Doo* and partly because we were never sure when it would arrive. The bus came with a driver and two additional men for our protection. Dar es Salaam can be dangerous for tourists and the biggest guy positioned himself in front of the doors of the bus to prevent any unintentional passengers.

From our hotel, we drove about an hour to Mbagala, a small village on the outskirts of Dar es Salaam. The Bibi Jann School was started in 2001 by Fatuma Gwao, a retired teacher, who wanted to help Tanzania's almost one million AIDS orphans. Her dream, which began with a one room preschool, has grown to become the Bibi Jann Children's Care Trust. The program oversees the school with

130 students, teaches adult literacy, and supports grandmothers (*bibis*) who care for their orphaned grandchildren.

As we entered through the metal front gate, the school appeared bleak and colorless. Rusty, worn, and what looked to be mostly broken playground equipment filled a dirt courtyard, along with a forlorn stucco giraffe. It seemed so sad.

Inside, the children had prepared a welcome for us. A group of younger children stepped to the front of the classroom. A girl and boy began to sing. Their voices were so pure and clear that tears came unexpectedly to my eyes. Maybe I simply missed my own young son or maybe the purpose of our visit crystallized at that moment.

Soon, all the kids were singing, clapping, and stomping, acting out a complex set of tribal dances to the intricate rhythms of a small drum. In the audience, the younger kids crowded next to us, many of them climbing into our laps. Sitting on the floor, surrounded by children, Jolie beamed. A former teacher, she was clearly in her element.

After the show, the kids rushed out to the rickety playground and I saw how wrong my first impression had been. They were having a blast, spinning with abandon on the run down equipment. The giggles and squeals of delight assured me that there was nothing sad about the Bibi Jann School.

A tiny hand grasped mine. I looked down to see a girl of about four grinning up at me. We considered each other for a moment and then, seeing that I was nice, a dozen more children crowded around. They held my hands and touched my skin. They stared at my clothing and searched my face.

I showed them a photo of my son and the children took turns holding it. They looked from the photo, to me, and back again. We did the Swahili version of a high five, going to knuckle to knuckle to exclaim *Nepitano!* Just like that, we were friends.

We divided into groups and started our ambitious projects. We planned to build 30 desks, paint and decorate five classrooms, and install two new gas stoves and a freshwater filtration system.

We worked side by side with locals. Jeff, an energetic young kindergarten teacher, directed our classroom project. Christine worked alongside Rollie and Jolie to sand and prepare the walls for paint. At the end of each day, the three of them left covered in a thick layer of chalky white dust. On the third day, they got to the glory work of adding numbers, letters, and drawings to decorate the walls. One elderly villager wandered in and gave us his opinion, which George translated, "He says the bus is no good." It was good-natured ribbing and he picked up a pencil to help us "get it right."

Jo worked outside on the desks, taking direction from a local carpenter. He placed his hand over hers to demonstrate the right way to pound in a nail. At first, he was leery, doubting that any of these white women could put in an honest day's labor. But by the end of the second day, she'd won him over and he grinned as she practiced her Swahili with him.

I was impressed with the work ethic of each of these women. Even after the physical exhaustion of the climb, they brought dedication and diligence to their work. Jolie told me that during the first part of the trip she was working hard to accomplish something for herself. Now, she was working hard for the kids.

The days at the school were hot, dusty, and tiring. Each day, Fatuma welcomed us into her home for a traditional meal of rice, beans, and vegetables. We entered a cinder block room with a cement floor. Plastic chairs were set around the perimeter. Carefully, Fatuma's daughter served us the day's meal.

Sometimes, avocado or fresh oranges were added. One day, there were fish heads along with a broth. They were sharing the very best of whatever they had. We all recognized this as a very special opportunity that most tourists never experience and we graciously accepted their generosity.

The *bibis* ran a small storefront, selling their batik clothing and jewelry. We each stopped in to say hello and buy souvenirs. These women were living very hard lives full of struggle and loss. Still, the kindness in their eyes shone through and they smiled broadly as we purchased their beautiful wares.

On the last day, the children filed in and sat at the desks we'd made. The headmaster quizzed them on their letters and we beamed with delight as they recognized our hand painted drawings of fruits, vegetables, and yes, even the bus.

As we pulled away in the mystery bus, the children ran after us, smiling and waving goodbye. I looked out the window to wave back and attempted to memorize their sweet faces so that I could take them home with me.

Our remarkable adventure had humbled us and surprised us. We had struggled and worked alongside one another. We had marveled at the harshness and the beauty of Tanzania. We had been there for one another as compatriots and witnesses in a unique shared experience. Over the course of just two weeks, I had come to know and love this incredible group of women. Today we are scattered across the country and have returned to our busy lives, but we will always share this indelible moment in time, our journey of the heart.

Joanie Wynn

Joanie is an Emmy-nominated writer and producer for her documentary, *A Journey for Good: Tanzania*. Her volunteer travel experiences inspired her to establish Journeys for Good, a website dedicated to volunteerism opportunities around the world. She is also currently developing Journeys for Good as a public television series devoted to volunteer travel. Joanie owns and operates the Emmy-winning production company, Bayside Entertainment, with her husband, Steve Wynn. They produce creative content for Fortune 500 clients including Lucasfilm, Sony, and Electronic Arts. They also enjoy producing projects for start-ups, non-profits, and A Band of Wives.

A Moment in the Louvre, photograph by Monica Michelle

Monica Michelle

Monica Michelle lives on the San Francisco Bay Area peninsula with the best husband ever, two wonderful children, a cat who thinks she is a goddess, and two large dogs who firmly believe they are lap dogs. Monica runs a portrait photography studio in Menlo Park, California called White Rabbit Portrait Studio and a wedding, boudoir, and fine art studio called Monica Michelle's Photography. Monica is currently working on fine art photography series in Paris and a fairy tale photography series.